Object-Oriented Design with Ada

Object-Oriented Design with Ada

Maximizing Reusability for Real-Time Systems

Kjell Nielsen, Ph.D.

Senior Scientist
Hughes Aircraft Company

BANTAM BOOKS
NEW YORK • TORONTO • LONDON • SYDNEY • AUCKLAND

78085

Object-Oriented Design with Ada
A Bantam Book/May 1992

*Throughout the book, trade names and trademarks of some
companies and products have been used, and no such uses
are intended to convey endorsement of or other affiliations with the book.*

ISBN 0-553-08955-2
Library of Congress Catalog Card Number 92-70853

Published simultaneously in the United States and Canada

Bantam Books are published by Bantam Books, a division of Bantam Doubleday Dell Publishing Group, Inc. Its trademark, consisting of the words, "Bantam Books" and the portrayal of a rooster, is Registered in U.S. Patent and Trademark Office and in other countries, Marca Registrada. Bantam Books, 666 Fifth Avenue, New York, New York 10103.

PRINTED IN THE UNITED STATES OF AMERICA

0 9 8 7 6 5 4 3 2 1

To Vicki

Contents

4 Classes and Objects in Ada 35

Part 2 Object-Oriented Analysis and Design 61

5 Domain Analysis 63

6 Requirements Analysis and Object-Orientation 73

Appendix C Object-Oriented Analysis and Design for a Robot Control System   291

Appendix D Multiple Keyboard Input System (MKIS)   307

Acknowledgments

The author is grateful to Ken Shumate for his many valuable comments and suggestions.

A special acknowledgment goes to Alan Rose for his continuous support, encouragements, and gentle prodding.

Preface

The objective of this book is to describe how real-time systems can be developed using object-oriented approaches. The focus on real-time systems with multiple processes does not preclude the analysis and design of strictly sequential software solutions. A sequential solution is simply a subset of a multiprocessing system and represents a single-thread solution.

This book will not add to the debate of which is the better object-oriented programming language. C, C++, and Ada are emerging as the leading programming languages of the 1990s for real-time systems, and are sometimes used in the same application. The material included here is primarily intended for Ada developers. The design phase of an object-oriented methodology should be tailored to the implementation language(s) used for a specific project. It makes no sense to create artificial object-oriented entities just to say we have an "object-oriented" approach. Any object-orientation employed during the analysis phase can be language independent.

The basic premise for this book is that an object-oriented development approach will create superior software systems compared to the older, traditional methodologies. The primary benefits are a high degree of reusability, highly modular designs, and ease of maintenance.

The theme throughout this book is how we can build reusable distributed real-time systems, and how we can construct small, medium, and large systems in the same application domain from a core of common components. The approaches presented build upon existing software engineering technologies, i.e., we want to take advantage of the significant investments already made in training our software engineers. A major reeducation is not required to implement the object-oriented paradigms presented.

Reusability can be viewed from two different aspects: by the original developer of the software components, and by the redeveloper who wants to adopt previously developed software for a new system. Even though the concept of reusability has been around for many years, very few software organizations have established effective reuse depositories that can benefit developers within the same company or organization. We primarily take the view in this book of how to develop software for maximum reuse, rather than from the view of a redeveloper of already existing software. One of the later chapters deals with the creation of a library of reusable components, and the retrieval of existing software components.

Most object-oriented approaches ignore the concurrency aspects that are inherent in real-time systems, and concurrency is usually included as an afterthought. The focus of these approaches is *data abstraction* and the creation of objects that include a data type and the operations that act on objects of that type. The methods and paradigms presented here include the determination of the parallel design objects that represent the *process abstraction* of the concurrent system. These design objects are determined early on during the analysis phase, and the usual object-oriented paradigms such as data abstraction, encapsulation, information hiding, inheritance, etc. are used to create additional design objects in support of the concurrent objects.

Considerations are included for the construction of software in distributed architectures, including an interprocess communication mechanism. Special emphasis is placed on how we can transition from the requirements analysis phase to the design phase.

This book is intended for practicing software engineers who design and implement distributed, real-time systems in Ada. The book can also be used in an upper level undergraduate or graduate course in software engineering with students who already know Ada.

The first part of the book includes general object-oriented programming and design (OOP/OOD) concepts. Programming languages are classified with regard to their level of object-orientedness. Ada objects are described, and a package classification tailored for real-time systems is included.

The second part incorporates object-orientation during the various phases of the software development cycle. A domain analysis to identify potential real-world objects within the problem domain precedes the requirements analysis. This part includes the important transitioning phase from analysis to design.

The third part includes an object-oriented design approach that is tailored for reusability. The creation of reusable components is described with emphasis on producing tailored systems from a core of common software modules. The creation of a library of reusable components is described, with emphasis on ease of storage, documentation, and retrieval. This part provides a summary of the overall development process and includes an iconized illustration of the products created in each step.

The book concludes with appendices as case studies illustrating the object-oriented features presented throughout the text. The first appendix includes the analysis phase and top level design of an interprocess communication (IPC) mechanism, and a detailed design of remote procedure calls and external data representation (RPC/XDR) functions implemented in Ada. The next two appendices contain object-oriented developments for air traffic control and robot controller problem domains, respectively. The last appendix presents a mechanism for handling unprotected shared data in a concurrent environment under certain conditions.

P A R T 1

OBJECT-ORIENTATION

In this part we present the necessary definitions of object-oriented concepts and provide formal definitions of classes and objects. Specifications are listed for the most common requirements for object-oriented programming languages. A classification scheme is included to describe the degree of object-orientedness of a programming language. This part concludes with a classification of classes and objects tailored for Ada. This classification is based on a package taxonomy that forms the basis for the reusable design objects we will create for real-time systems.

1

Introduction

Object-oriented computing has been considered the most important software development tool since the advent of Structured Design. Object-oriented *programming* (OOP) has been advanced with programming languages like Simula [DAH70], Smalltalk-80 [GOL83], C++ [STR87, LIP89], and Eiffel [MEY88]. Object-oriented *design* (OOD) has been promoted with the approaches suggested by Abbott [ABB83] and Booch [BOO86, BOO91]. The major benefits claimed by proponents of OOD include a high level of modularity to support loose coupling, an encapsulation mechanism to support information hiding, data abstraction to support the creation of objects that refer to a single data type and associated operations, and a classification and inheritance mechanism that provide reusability and extendibility. (We will be using the word "object" in a loose sense in this chapter without a formal definition; that will be provided in the next chapter.)

As a consequence of recent efforts in expanding the object-oriented para-digms to the entire software development cycle, objects can be specified as part of the requirements analysis phase (OORA or OOA), even before the design phase begins [COA91, SCH88].

With an extension of an object-orientation to include the major phases of the software development cycle (i.e., requirements analysis, top level design, and detailed design), a mixture of objects will be created. Some of these objects will be pure abstractions that will exist on paper only, whereas others will actually be implemented as statements in a programming language. It is highly desirable to have a consistent approach for the various phases in the development cycle.

This should include a common nomenclature and a suitable set of tools to ease the development process. Incorporated with the tools should be a set of graphical representations to illustrate the various design decisions made, and heuristics for transitioning from one development phase to the next.

One of the important aspects of adopting a new software development approach is whether or not the method is readily teachable, and what level of investment is required for a successful organization-wide implementation of the new approach. A related aspect is what kind of returns can be expected after the new software approach is in place. There is a considerable amount of controversy, for example, about the "orthogonality" of OOA/OOD and traditional structured analysis and structured design (SA/SD). The OO faction maintains that OOA/OOD cannot be used in conjunction with SA/SD.

Many of the large, established software development organizations have successfully used some form of SA/SD over the last two decades, and it has not yet been shown that the tremendous gains espoused by the OOP/OOD/OOA pundits can readily be realized. It may be, for example, that the use of inheritance and polymorphism in C++ will add greatly to the complexity of the software produced and thus make maintenance more difficult and costly, compared to C or Ada.

Other problems associated with the use of OOP include the requirement for a sophisticated browser that can rapidly locate the hierarchy or path of an entity contained in a low level subclass. Compilation times may be significantly longer, and the use of dynamic binding may take extra execution time compared to the use of more traditional programming languages.

Problems associated with the use of OOA/OOD include the lack of a transitioning method from OOA to OOD, and that the concurrency inherent in real-time systems is not considered. Most of the existing CASE tools are immature and do not support the OOA/OOD paradigms. Undisciplined use of class hierarchies may render designs incomprehensible, and software certification is made more difficult by the inheritance relations.

A shortcoming of current object-oriented design approaches is that they are based entirely on data abstraction and do not address the problem of determining the concurrent elements of a real-time system. Nor do they address aspects of object-oriented software required for distributed architectures. They are thus not adequate as development approaches for large, distributed real-time systems.

What is needed is a development approach that incorporates the proven object-oriented paradigms like encapsulation and data abstraction with the established features of SA/SD. The chosen approach must directly support the design of real-time systems and include considerations for distributed architectures. The development strategy must result in software that contains a high degree of reusability to support an ever-toughening competitive marketplace. Software companies can no longer rely on cushioned cost-plus contracts, but must compete for the shrinking fixed-cost jobs. In this type of marketplace it becomes important that small, medium, and large software systems can be constructed from a core of common modules available for a given problem domain. The development approach should support the creation of a set of such flexible modules.

In the chapters that follow, we will describe design objects developed in the various phases of the software development life cycle. A layer of abstract classes is defined for each step of the methodology, and objects are created as instances of the particular class, if a class structure is appropriate. In some cases a formal class structure is not appropriate, especially if the implementation language does not support inheritance relations. Objects are then created directly without a class hierarchy.

Heuristics are used to implement the various steps of the methodology, and to allow a smooth transition from one development phase to the next. Graphical illustrations are used extensively as design tools for the representations of the major design decisions in each step.

The design approaches developed in this book are intended to be used for real-time systems, and a special emphasis is placed on the determination of concurrent elements. A process abstraction model is developed early in the development phase, and is represented as a network of cooperating nodes (processes). Each single-thread node is composed of a set of program objects in the form of a task, subprograms (operations), and data managers. A node represents a significant portion of the application functionality.

Before we can effectively describe object-oriented paradigms, we must establish the necessary vocabulary and identify the "lingo" used. This is done in the context of objects and classes. A brief discussion is given of the classification of object-oriented programming languages. Classes and objects in Ada are treated in some detail, since they form the primary building blocks for our real-time system implementations. A special Ada package classification is created to illustrate the kinds of objects we need to develop for our real-time systems.

2

Classes and Objects

The common characteristic of object-oriented programming and design is the extensive use of abstractions. An abstraction is a high level description or model of a detailed or complex concept. The complex details of an algorithm to perform coordinate conversions from (x,y) to lat/long, for example, are abstracted away by creating a procedure Convert_Coordinates and passing the appropriate parameters. The procedure represents functional (procedural) abstraction, and a single program call hides the details of the implementation of the conversion algorithm. Higher level forms for abstraction include a tasking model of concurrent elements (process abstraction) and the creation of data managers (data abstraction). These concepts will be treated in detail in Chapters 7 and 8, respectively.

Instances of abstract *classes* create the *objects* that are implemented in the particular programming language. The concept of classes and objects has its basis in the classical theory of mathematics [EIL45 and WHI10], and has been extended to current programming languages. Classes in Simula, for example, describe abstract program entities that permit instantiations of Simula objects (instances). Smalltalk uses the same concept of classes and objects with the addition of the ability to pass messages between the objects.

The terms *class* and *object* are used exhaustively to describe object-oriented concepts in OOA, OOD, and OOP. Numerous variations exist in the literature for their definitions, with many gradations in the levels of abstraction or abstruseness. We will first illustrate some of the rather abstract definitions, and then settle on what we will be using throughout the book. One common definition of classes and objects is the following:

> A *class is a collection of objects with similar attributes, and an object is a specific instance of its class.*

This is a circular definition, however, and is not very satisfying to the novice. We can strengthen the definition by insisting that a class is an abstraction and an object is a real-world object that belongs to the class. A class can thus be specified by the abstraction Aircraft, and an object within this class can be an F14 Fighter Jet, a 747 Jumbo Jet, or a Cessna 172.

In some object-oriented programming languages (e.g., Smalltalk [GOL83]), there is no clear distinction between classes and objects since a class is also considered an object. We will not use this notion here, and will make a distinction between classes and objects to make it easier to define and use the object-oriented concepts.

Problems associated with adequate descriptions of classes and objects can be attributed to the various contexts in which they are used. A Track Store, for example, can be an item identified on a Data Flow Diagram during the requirements analysis phase and represents an *abstract* "real-world" object as shown in Figure 2.1. It can also be a *design* object representation of the abstract object as is illustrated in Figure 2.2, where the Ada package Track_Store_Monitor encapsulates the data structure Tracks. This figure also depicts a third context of an object: the internal *programming* object Track_Store is an instance of the type Tracks, and represents a variable for which storage must be allocated. The Track Store may be (correctly) referred to as an "object" in all three contexts, and clearly illustrates the potential confusion of the use of this term.

We could specify "OOA" objects, "OOD" objects, and "OOP" objects as they apply to each development phase. This could become awfully tedious, however, and in many cases the context is obvious. If the contexts are ambiguous, we will amplify our notations and descriptions of objects and classes to remove the ambiguity. We now present a general specification of classes and objects. We will also describe object-oriented concepts that are closely related to classes and objects, such as inheritance, encapsulation, and polymorphism.

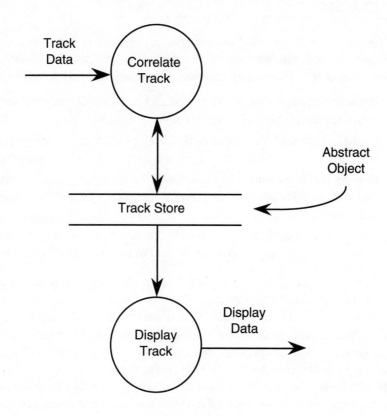

Figure 2.1 Requirements Analysis Object

```
package Track_Store_Monitor is
   type Tracks is private;
   procedure Add_Track (...);
   procedure Update_Track (...);
   procedure Drop_Track (...);
   ...
private
   ...
end Track-Store_Monitor;

...

Track-Store: Tracks;
```

> Design
> object

> Internal
> program
> object

Figure 2.2 Design and Program Objects

2.1 CLASSES

The concept of a *class* is used in specifying an abstraction that represents a collection of entities with similar attributes, where attributes describe the characteristics of an entity. The primary purpose for creating a set of classes is to:

1. Reduce the complexity of a large system by partitioning it into a set of smaller, manageable logical and/or physical entities.
2. Create independent entities that can be developed by teams of analysts and software engineers with a minimum of interaction between the teams.
3. Provide the framework for the creation of highly modular software components that can easily be modified and extended without a major redesign.
4. Create software components that can be reused within a given application or between applications to reduce the cost of the overall software effort.

A common application of classes for software design purposes is the identification of data structures and their associated processing functions (operations). This can be applied abstractly as early as during the requirements analysis phase, continued through the design phase with graphical and program design language (PDL) representations, and finally implemented with additional programming constructs during the coding phase.

The processing functions associated with the identified data structures are sometimes referred to as *methods* [GOL83]. A method is implemented in C++ as a function, and in Ada it can be either a function or a procedure (i.e., an Ada subprogram). We will refer to methods and processing functions as *operations* throughout this book, unless we are describing features of a specific programming language. In the latter case, we will use whatever name is specified in the programming language.

The class as an entity is included in C++ as a construct, and we could, for example, specify the following class for the creation of stacks :

```
class Stack {
private:
    long stackItems[50];
    int stackPtr;
public:
    void stackInit();
    long topOfStack();
    long pop();
    void push(long);
};
```

The class Stack is considered a type in C++, and this represents the specification part. The private portion of this specification includes elements that are not visible to users of this class. The only user interface available as operations is the list of *member functions* given in the public part. The private elements can only be used and manipulated internally by the member functions.

Ada does not have a class construct, but we can create the equivalent of a class using a package:

```
package Buffer_Module is
   type Buffer is private;
   procedure Enqueue
             (I : in   Integer; B : in out Buffer);
   procedure Dequeue
             (I : out  Integer; B : in out Buffer);
   function Empty (B : in Buffer) return Boolean;
   function Full  (B : in Buffer) return Boolean;
private
   . . .
end Buffer_Module;
```

A package in Ada is not a type, and Buffer_Module does not represent a class in the traditional OOP sense. Enqueue, Dequeue, Empty, and Full are the operations that manipulate objects of the private type Buffer, and the structure of Buffer_Module is referred to as an *abstract data type* (ADT). The concept of "member functions" as the user interface to a class is appropriate for C++, since functions are the only operations allowed. Ada, however, has both functions and procedures, and we will use Ada "operations" as equivalent to C++ "member functions." Booch [BOO91] makes the following distinction between methods and operations: all methods are operations, but operations include the methods that pertain to a class plus any other subprograms that may act on objects of the class. We will not make this distinction here since freestanding subprograms will be rare in an object-oriented design. If they occur, we will refer specifically to them as non-members of a given class.

The primary benefit of a class structure is with the implementation languages that support *inheritance*. Subclasses can then be constructed which will inherit data structures and operations of the superclass. In addition, the subclasses can modify inherited operations and add new ones. The inheritance concept is described further below.

The traditional class concept of OOP will later be modified (and deemphasized) with a specific tailoring for Ada. We will also include class concepts for the earlier software development phases of domain analysis, requirements analysis, and design, and will thus consider classes in a much wider scope than merely OOP.

2.2 OBJECTS

An *object* within a given class is considered an *instance* of the class. The class provides an abstract template for the real-world objects that belong to the class. A further definition of an object includes the following [BOO86 and BOO91]:

1. An object is an entity that can be abstracted, classified, or categorized by its type, i.e., an object is a member of a class, or can be considered an instance of the class.

2. The class of an object has associated with it a set of operations that are allowed on the objects belonging to that class.

3. An object has certain states, e.g., a task can be running, ready, or blocked, and data can be initialized or uninitialized.

4. An object is denoted by a specific name. The name provides a unique identity for the object, and allows us to distinguish it from other objects.

5. An object can be observed either by its specification or by its implementation. This implies a form of encapsulation associated with information hiding. The specification will provide the interface to the object, and the implementation the details of the operations that will affect the behavior of the object.

An illustration of a design object (using the graphical notation suggested in [BOO87]) is shown in Figure 2.3 for the module we have called Track_Monitor. The outer rectangle represents the encapsulated boundary of the program entity. Everything shown on the left boundary with one half inside the large rectangle and the rest outside depicts entities that are visible to the user of this module. The ovals are type specifications, and the small rectangles are operations necessary to access the hidden object Track_Store. The small rectangle with the notch on the right side is an exception that may be raised inside the module and is expected to be handled by the user of the module. This type of design object is referred to as an *object manager*, since the single object (Track_Store in the example) is declared internally within the module and is managed locally.

A different kind of design object is shown in Figure 2.4, where the type Track_File is visible. The user of this module will declare one or more track file objects and then use the visible operations to manipulate the objects. This kind of module structure is referred to as an abstract data type (ADT), since it operates on objects (instances of the type) that are declared externally to the module. This is the same structure as was shown above for the Buffer_Module package.

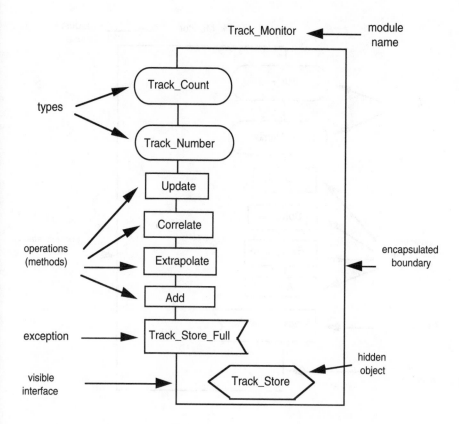

Figure 2.3 Encapsulated Object

We have seen two important concepts of objects here: (1) design objects in the form of a module as an object manager and as an abstract data type; and (2) internal programming objects as implementations of data structures (e.g., Track_Store). We will later encounter more abstract objects when we examine the domain analysis and requirements analysis phases of the software development cycle.

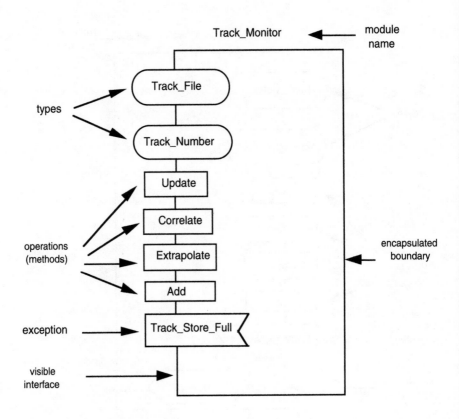

Figure 2.4 Abstract Data Type

2.3 INHERITANCE

The concept of inheritance is used to describe the creation of subclasses from one or more superclasses. Each subclass inherits the structure and behavior of its superclass, including the operations specified. If a subclass is allowed to inherit from more than one superclass, the particular programming language supports *multiple* inheritance.

The inheritance relation is shown graphically in Figure 2.5, where the superclass is Flying Machine and the subclasses are Rotary Wing, Airplane, Glider, and Lighter than Air. The subclass Airplane has lower level subclasses of Land and Sea. The Land subclass contains the lower level subclasses of Single Engine and Multi Engine.

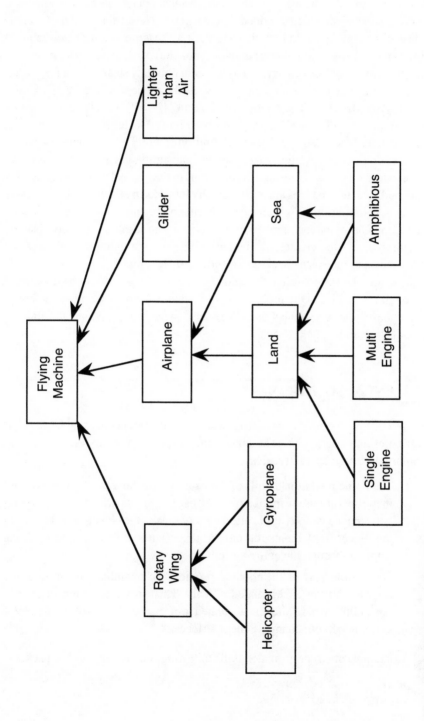

Figure 2.5 Inheritance Relations

The applicable attributes (characteristics) and operations of superclasses are inherited by each subclass as a subset. Additional operations that are unique to a given subclass can then be added as extensions. The attributes of an Airplane class, for example, could include weight, fuel consumption, usable amount of fuel, and cruising speed. The operations could be to calculate range in nautical miles, estimated time of arrival, and fuel remaining. The arrows in Figure 2.5 point from a subclass to a superclass to denote the concept of "is a," e.g., a Glider is a Flying Machine. The relation of "kind of" [BOO91] is also expressed by the arrow, e.g., a Rotary Wing is a kind of Flying Machine.

The inheritance feature allows a redefinition of (child) classes based on parent classes. This provides a tool for organizing and building reusable classes based on existing modules. If any of the operations in the higher level class structures are modified, the changes are automatically inherited by the lower level classes (after recompilation). Without the inheritance feature, every class must be developed as an independent entity in a bottom-up fashion. Any consistency required across the classes will be based on a programming discipline rather than type and interface checking performed by a compiler.

The net effect of inheritance should be a reduction of code to be developed through reusability. One problem to anticipate is a more complicated debugging phase, unless a sophisticated browser is available to navigate through the various hierarchical class levels.

2.4 ENCAPSULATION

A well designed object encapsulates a single real-world entity that has a set of attributes and operations. The proper encapsulation of a module has several important design characteristics:

1. The implementation details of the data structure and the algorithms used in the operations are hidden from the user. This provides a loose coupling between the various application modules using the object, and changes to the object implementation can be made without design modifications rippling through the entire system.

2. The visible part of the module provides an unambiguous and unique interface to the encapsulated object. This provides a high degree of reusability where the encapsulated objects can be used in different systems without changing the interfaces.

An example of an encapsulation is the following Ada Buffer_Module package:

```
package Buffer_Module is
   type Buffer is private;
```

```
procedure Enqueue
          (I : in   Integer; B : in out Buffer);
procedure Dequeue
          (I : out Integer; B : in out Buffer);
function Empty (B : in Buffer) return Boolean;
function Full  (B : in Buffer) return Boolean;
private
   . . .
end Buffer_Module;
```

The only visible operations are Enqueue, Dequeue, Empty, and Full. The buffer object itself and how it is manipulated is completely hidden from the user of the package. The details are implemented within the (hidden) package body. The buffer could be circular or of fixed length, and its implementation could be modified without affecting the software that is using it. Data integrity of the buffered data could be implemented with an Ada task and a selective wait statement, or a user defined locking mechanism.

2.5 MESSAGE PASSING

Communication between software modules is, typically, implemented with some form of message passing. It can also be accomplished with shared data, but that is not of interest here. The concept of an object sending a "message" to another object is usually implemented with a combination of parameter passing and returning value results. In Ada, for example, parameters are passed via procedure calls and returns, and values are returned as results of function invocations. To put an item in a buffer declared locally, the "message" could be

```
. . .
Buffer_Item : Integer;
New_Buffer  : Buffer;
. . .
Enqueue (Buffer_Item, New_Buffer);  -- message
. . .
```

and the "message" to get the value of a square root could be

```
. . .
Y := Sqrt (X);  -- message
```

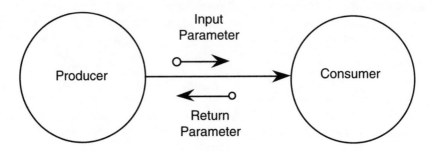

Figure 2.6 Direction of Message Passing

The direction of message passing can be indicated with a directed graph as shown in Figure 2.6. Data passed as parameters can flow in both directions, as shown with the small arrows with open circles. A closed circle can be used to show the passing of a flag rather than a data element.

So far we have only mentioned message passing in connection with the calling of subprograms that are assumed to execute sequentially. Since we are primarily concerned with real-time systems, however, we also need to consider message passing in a multiprocessing environment. We will modify Booch's [BOO91] classification of message passing, which covers both sequential and multiprocessing environments:

1. **Simple.** This applies to a sequential system and implies simple subprogram calls. Data can flow in both directions.

2. **Synchronous.** When two processes (e.g., two Ada tasks or two Unix processes) need to communicate, they must be synchronized. This is usually implemented with a blocking mechanism such as the Ada rendezvous. Both tasks are willing to wait "forever" for the rendezvous to take place. The parameter passing can take place just as for procedure calls.

3. **Conditional.** If the called process is not immediately available for synchronization, the caller executes an optional sequence of instructions rather than wait. This can also be implemented within a called process, e.g., Ada's "selective wait" with an "else" clause.

4. **Timeout.** The caller is willing to wait for synchronization for a specified time only. At the expiration of the timeout, the caller executes an optional sequence of statements. This can also be implemented within the called process.

5. **Asynchronous.** The caller does not wait for synchronization with another process. The data to be passed is simply deposited by the producer, and the consumer process will receive the data via an intermediary. The intermediary mechanism can, for example, be implemented as a mailbox, or by including a buffer process between the producer and consumer.

The particular message passing mechanism used will be determined by the desired coupling between a producer/consumer pair. This will be described further in Chapter 7 when we discuss process abstraction.

2.6 GENERICITY

The concept of genericity refers to a *parameterized* class, or *generic* class. The generic class is created as a template with formal parameters, and instances of the class are created by providing the corresponding actual parameters. This concept is illustrated by modifying the Buffer_Module package to include two generic parameters. The first parameter generalizes the size of the buffer, and the second the type of element that can be stored in the buffer:

```
generic
  type Index_Type is range <>;
  type Element is private;
package Buffer_Module is
  type Buffer is private;
  procedure Enqueue (I : in Element; B : in out Buffer);
  procedure Dequeue (I : out Element; B : in out Buffer);
  function Empty (B : in Buffer) return Boolean;
  function Full  (B : in Buffer) return Boolean;
private
    . . .
end Buffer_Module;
```

An instance of the package Buffer_Module can be created by specifying the two actual parameters and declaring an instance (User_Buffer) of the generic package:

```
. . .
type User_Index is range 1 .. User_Size + 1;
type User_Element is
  record
    Char : Character;
    Lost : Natural;   -- no. of chars lost
  end User_Element;

package User_Buffer is new Buffer_Module
                     (Index_Type => User_Index,
                      Element    => User_Element);
```

The generic package represents a higher level of abstraction than the ADT or object manager described earlier. It supports reusability directly since a multitude of instantiations can be made by simply varying the type or value of the actual parameters.

2.7 POLYMORPHISM

Polymorphism refers to the characteristic that an object can exist as an instance of different classes at run-time. This is more extensive than the overloading mechanism employed in Ada. The latter allows the same operation, e.g., a multiplier ("*"), to operate on objects of different types. The types, however, are static, and references are determined at compilation time. In a programming language that implements polymorphism, operations have both static and dynamic types associated with them, and the dynamic type reference may change during execution.

A class hierarchy to illustrate the concept of polymorphism is shown in Figure 2.7, where a Polygon is the superclass and Rectangle, Parallelogram, and Triangle are the subclasses. A C++ code skeleton for the superclass Polygon and subclass Rectangle can be sketched out as follows:

```
class Polygon { // superclass
protected:
  void Display ();
public:
  short Perimeter ();
  points Translate ();
  virtual short Area (void);
  virtual boolean pointInside ();
};


class Rectangle: public Polygon { // subclass
private:
  short Top;
  short Bottom;
  short Left;
  short Right;
public:
  virtual short Area (void);
  virtual boolean pointInside ();
  void setRectangle ();
};
```

An implementation of a member function to calculate the area of a rectangle can be specified as follows:

```
class Rectangle::Area (void) {
  return ((Bottom - Top) * (Right - Left));
};
```

Different implementations of Area will be specified for a parallelogram and a triangle. Three separate instances of the same member function can thus refer to three different classes.

Polymorphism can also be illustrated with an array of elements that refer to objects of different types (classes) as suggested in [MEY88, p. 225]. The array is shown in Figure 2.8 and includes pointers to different point types that are all derived from a superclass. In a programming language that does not support polymorphism, the corresponding structure would have to be implemented with a record whose components would refer to the different point types. The latter would be static references, whereas the polymorphic references could be dynamic.

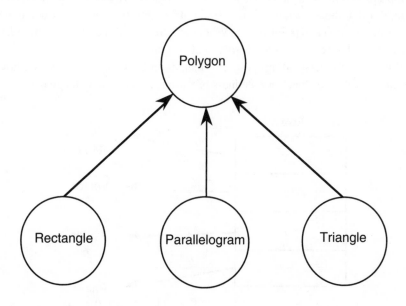

Figure 2.7 Class Inheritance

2.8 BINDING

The concept of *binding* used in connection with a programming language pertains to the binding of a message (e.g., procedure call) and the code to be executed on behalf of the message. In a programming language with static binding, all references are determined at compilation time. Dynamic, or late, binding, however, means that the code to be executed in response to a message will not be determined until run-time. This is often used to implement screen windowing and pull-down menus where the "buttons" are associated with a set of messages that will activate a corresponding function.

Inheritance, polymorphism, and binding are closely related, and the execution of a call to an operation is associated with a polymorphic reference that depends on the type of the reference. During execution of the C++ program shown above, the appropriate reference to an Area member function will be made by the run-time system. The class association may be determined at compilation time or at execution time. The use of the *virtual* keyword tells the compiler that the association is deferred until execution time, as shown in our example for Area and pointInside. Whenever the virtual specifier is omitted, it is assumed that references are resolved at compilation time.

With a basic understanding of object-oriented concepts, we will next look at how we can classify the object-orientedness of various programming languages.

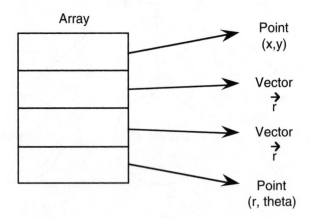

Figure 2.8 Polymorphic References

3

Object-Orientation and Programming Languages

We have already seen that the term "object-oriented" is used in many different contexts with many different meanings. In this chapter, we will relate object-orientation to programming languages and their constructs, with special emphasis on C++ and Ada.

The programming languages that are considered "object-oriented" (e.g., Simula, Smalltalk, Prolog, List, and Eiffel) are not widely used for real-time systems. The primary programming languages currently used for real-time systems are C and Ada. Ada was designed specifically for the implementation of real-time systems. Although Ada may not satisfy all the major properties of an object-oriented programming language (e.g., inheritance and dynamic binding), it does support an object-oriented design approach, and is usually referred to as an "object-based" language [WEG87].

C is less "object-oriented" than Ada, and cannot even be considered "object-based." Numerous object-oriented extensions have recently been added to C, however, and the resulting language is C++. This language includes a classification, inheritance, polymorphism, and dynamic binding, and is considered a bona fide object-oriented programming language. For the kind of real-time systems we are considering here we could implement these systems with a combination of Ada, C, and C++. Ada would be the primary language for all of the applications modules, and C (or C++) may be used as interfaces to existing software packages such as the X Window System or the communications protocol TCP/IP (Transmission Control Protocol/Internet Protocol).

3.1 OBJECT-ORIENTEDNESS

Wegner [WEG87] has created a taxonomy of levels of object-orientedness for programming languages, which we will adopt here. The primary classifications include object-based, class-based, and fully object-oriented:

1. A programming language is *object-based* if its syntax and semantics support the creation of *objects*, where the properties of objects are as described in Section 2.2.

2. A *class-based* programming language is object-based and, in addition, supports the creation of classes, where the attributes of classes were described in Section 2.1.

3. A fully *object-oriented* programming language is a class-based language that also supports inheritance, i.e., a subclass may be derived from one (single inheritance) or more (multiple inheritance) superclasses.

This taxonomy of object-orientedness provides a strict definition for those programming languages that are considered fully object-oriented. It is not sufficient for an object-oriented programming language to support only the creation of objects; it must also include constructs for classes with inheritance as a class property.

The taxonomy for object-orientedness can be illustrated graphically as shown in Figure 3.1. Ada, for example, supports the creation of objects as abstract data types using packages, and is thus object-based. An Ada package, however, is not a type definition (a type is considered a class), and Ada is neither class-based nor object-oriented. C++, on the other hand, supports the construction of classes with inheritance, and is fully object-oriented.

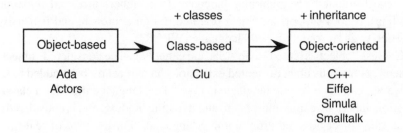

Figure 3.1 Taxonomy of Object-Orientedness

3.2 PROGRAMMING LANGUAGE REQUIREMENTS

Whether or not a programming language is object-oriented in the strict sense described above, is of little value to us if it doesn't support the creation of software modules for our specific application domain. If we need to implement real-time systems in a multi-processor architecture, for example, object-orientation is simply a nice feature of a programming language. More desirable properties would include a mechanism for modeling process abstraction and inter-module communication.

The primary application domain considered in this book includes real-time systems that are implemented on distributed architectures, and the programming language(s) we utilize must support the features required for these systems. This is reflected in the following programming language requirements:

1. **Object-orientation.** The language should be at least object-based and support the creation of abstract data types. This benefits the construction of reusable software modules with clearly defined interfaces. A fully object-oriented language with a class structure and inheritance is preferred, if it also has the other requirements we demand.

2. **Strong typing.** This is a highly desirable property which greatly supports the software development effort. Programming errors related to parameter types and module interfaces are detected during the design phases (when we use compilable PDL), and will usually reduce the testing effort.

3. **Encapsulation.** It is highly desirable that the language support information hiding with separate specification and implementation parts. This can provide a loosely coupled design that is easily tailored for different hardware architectures.

4. **Inheritance.** This is considered one of the required features of a truly object-oriented language, and is directly related to a class construct. Subclasses can then be constructed from superclasses. The new classes can define additional operations, and inherit the operations of the superclass(es). This can provide extremely flexible designs with high reusability. (But the class hierarchy may be extremely complex.) Inheritance is not a required feature of a real-time programming language.

5. **Genericity.** Parameterized classes and operations also supports a high degree of reusability. The generic elements are prestored templates that are instantiated with the proper parameters for particular instances of modules to be compiled, and later linked and executed. This is also not a required feature, but highly desirable from a reusability standpoint.

6. **Concurrency.** It is highly desirable that the language supports the creation of operating system independent processes. This simplifies the

formulation of concurrent elements and the software modeling of multi-thread processing. The implementation of the language features (i.e., the run-time support) should include capabilities for process management such as activation, scheduling, queueing, prioritization, preemption, and termination. It should also include features for process synchronization and communication. Software systems designed with these features can readily be implemented on distributed architectures.

7. **Message passing.** It is highly desirable that the language support some form of message passing between the modules. This provides for loosely coupled modules and flexible designs. It should also be possible to pass signals between modules, without actually passing any data elements.

8. **Shared data.** It is desirable that modules be able to communicate via shared memory. This may be required in those systems where message passing is deemed to be too inefficient.

9. **Interrupt handling.** It is highly preferable that interrupt handlers be written in the same programming language as the application modules rather than having to resort to assembly language. This reduces the complexity of the interrupt handlers, and integrates the asynchronous handlers with the rest of the concurrent modules.

10. **Binding.** A highly desirable feature of a programming language is dynamic binding. This is particularly useful in the implementation of graphics systems. A procedure or function (or a pointer) may be passed as a parameter at execution time to, for example, designate a menu selection made by a console operator.

11. **Polymorphism.** It is highly beneficial that program elements be allowed to refer to an object name that may belong to different classes that are related to a superclass. This means that operations can be used to manipulate objects of different types at execution time without reprogramming these methods.

None of the currently available programming languages satisfy all of the requirements specified above. In general, the object-oriented languages do not have concurrency features, and the real-time languages are not object-oriented. C++, for example, is classified as object-oriented, but does not have concurrency features built into the language constructs. To build concurrent elements with C++ requires an interface to an executive that can handle the required tasking functions.

The language that comes closest to supporting our real-time requirements is Ada. It is only object-based, however, since it does not support a class structure and inheritance. We will now take a closer look at Ada to determine how well it supports the requirements listed above with regard to object-orientation and real-time features.

3.3 ADA FOR REAL-TIME SYSTEMS

As a prelude to an analysis of the general requirements that Ada supports, assume that we have decided that Ada is the most suitable programming language for our real-time application domain. Another assumption is that object-oriented design is the preferred approach among the various existing design methodologies. An analysis of the object-oriented and real-time features of Ada will help us determine an overall design strategy that will provide a flexible design with a high degree of reusability.

3.3.1 Object-Orientation

Ada is an object-based language with support for data abstraction. The *package* construct is used to create abstract data types (ADTs). A stack for a small range of integer values, for example, can be written as:

```
package Stack_ADT is
   type Stacks is private;
   subtype Elements is Natural range 0 .. 100;
   procedure Push (Stack : in out Stacks;
                   Item  : in      Elements);
   procedure Pop (Stack : in out Stacks;
                  Item  : out     Elements);
   function Top_Of (Stack : in Stacks) return Elements;
   Empty_Stack : exception; -- raised in Pop and Top_Of
private
   -- code for type Stacks
end Stack_ADT;
```

The package specification includes the private type Stacks, and subtype Elements. The only operations allowed on objects of type Stacks are the procedures Push and Pop, and the function Top-Of (aside from the predefined operations for assignment and comparison of equality). The exception Empty_Stack is returned to the caller if an attempt is made to pop or read an element off an empty stack. The implementations of the operations are contained in the package body, and are not visible to the user of the package. This is especially evident in Ada with separate compilations of package specifications and bodies.

A program that requires the creation and manipulation of a data structure for a stack imports the package Stack_ADT and declares a local stack object:

```
with Stack_ADT;
procedure Using_Stack is
   Local_Stack    : Stack_ADT.Stacks;   -- stack object
   Local_Element : Stack_ADT.Elements;
   . . .
begin
   . . .
   Stack_ADT.Push (Local_Stack, Local_Element);
   . . .
end Using_Stack;
```

3.3.2 Strong Typing

Ada is a strongly typed language, and the compiler performs consistency and type checking throughout an Ada program. We will see in a later chapter how this is of great benefit to us when we create the PDL for the top level and detailed design.

3.3.3 Encapsulation

The Ada package structure supports encapsulation and information hiding. Visible entities are declared in the package specification, and implementation details are hidden in the package body. In the Stack example shown above, objects of the private type Stacks are declared in a program unit using the package Stack_ADT, and only the operations Push, Pop, and Top_Of are allowed on the objects. How the stack is implemented is hidden in the package body. The operations may represent ordinary subprogram units, or they may be calling task entries in a task declared in the package body. These details are hidden from the user of the package.

3.3.4 Inheritance and Genericity

Inheritance is normally associated with a class structure, and since Ada does not have classes (packages are not types), the strict definition of inheritance is not supported. There are two other forms of inheritance implicit in Ada, however. One is associated with types, the other with generic instantiations.

Ada subtypes will share the data structures defined by its base type, and all the operations defined for objects of the type. If we declare a subtype

```
subtype Small_Matrix is Matrix (1..3, 1..3);
```

Small_Matrix inherits the data structure defined for the base type Matrix and the operations defined for objects of the base type.

Ada derived types will inherit the data structure defined by the parent type, the operations specified for objects declared of the parent type, and additional operations can be defined for the derived type. In the following package the type Credit_Card is the parent type:

```
package Credit_Card_Manager is
   type Credit_Card is private;
   procedure X (...Credit_Card);
   procedure Y (...Credit_Card);
   ...
private
   type Credit_Card is ...;
end Credit_Card_Manager;
```

We can now declare derived types:

```
type Personal_Card is new Credit_Card;
type Business_Card is new Credit_Card;
```

and we have extended the operations for the type Credit_Card to include unique operations on objects declared of type Personal_Card and Business_Card.

Ada's variant record construct also represents a type inheritance. The value of the discriminant specifies a given instance of the type, and the operations defined for the record specification are inherited for any object of the type. Here is an example of a variant record:

```
type Radar_Class is (Primary, Secondary, Multi);
type Radars (Kind : Radar_Class) is
   record
      Location : Lat_Long;
      case Kind is
         when Primary =>
            Primary_Plots : Primary_Data;
         when Secondary =>
            Secondary_Plots : Secondary_Data;
         when Multi =>
            Radar_Data : Multi_Radar;
      end case;
   end record;
```

Objects can now be created by supplying the value of the discriminant:

```
Primary_Radar : Radars (Primary);
```

All of the operations defined for the type Radars are inherited by the object Primary_Radar.

Generic Ada packages can be created as parameterized classes:

```
generic
   Size : in Natural := 20;
   type Item is private;
```

```ada
      with procedure Consumer (C : in Item);

   package Generic_Relay is
      procedure Enqueue (I : in Item);
   end Generic_Relay;

   package body Generic_Relay is
      task Buffer is
         entry Enqueue (I : in  Item);
         entry Dequeue (I : out Item);
      end Buffer;

      task Transporter is
         -- Calls
            -- Buffer.Dequeue
            -- Consumer
      end Transporter;

      task body Transporter is
         X : Item;
      begin
         loop
            Buffer.Dequeue (X);
            Consumer (X);
         end loop;
      end Transporter;

      task body Buffer is separate;

      procedure Enqueue (I : in Item) is
      begin
         Buffer.Enqueue (I);
      end Enqueue;

   end Generic_Relay;
```

This is an example of a relay placed between a producer/consumer process pair to reduce the coupling between them as illustrated in Figure 3.2. To instantiate this generic package, we must specify the three generic parameters for the size of the internal buffer, the type of items to be stored in the buffer, and the name of the consumer to whom the items should be passed:

```ada
   package Radar_Relay is new Generic_Relay
         (Size    => 64,
          Item    => Radar_Data,
          Consumer => Radar_Handler.Radar_Input);
```

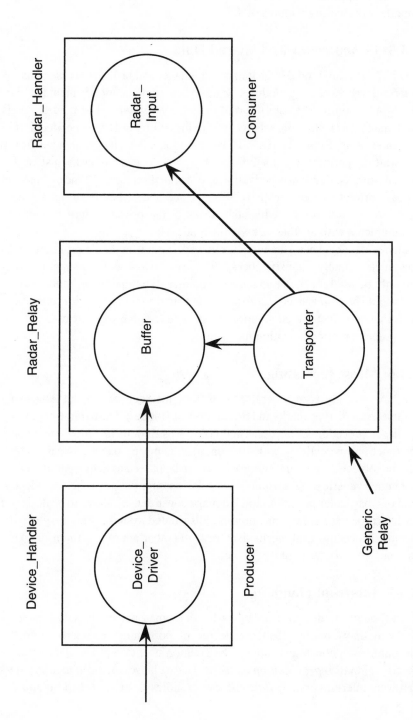

Figure 3.2 Instantiation of a Generic Relay

The package Radar_Relay inherits all the operations and attributes associated with the template class Generic_Relay. This example illustrates one of the important reusability features of Ada.

3.3.5 Concurrency and Shared Data

Ada has a tasking model built into the language, and tasks can be declared as independently executing modules. Inter-task communication is included via a synchronization mechanism referred to as a *rendezvous*. The rendezvous is implemented as a blocking scheme, where the calling task is suspended during the rendezvous. Similarly, if a task is waiting for callers, it is suspended during the waiting period. Parameters can be passed between tasks just as for procedure calls. Basic task activation and termination is part of the elaboration process prior to execution [SHU88b]. Once a task has been activated, it executes asynchronously with other tasks in the program until it needs to communicate with another task via the rendezvous.

Shared data between Ada tasks is allowed, but it is up to the programmer to guarantee mutually exclusive access. The *pragma Shared ( )* is supported, but can only be used for scalar and access (pointer) types and is of limited value.

It should be emphasized that Ada does not support remote rendezvous across processors. A distributed solution must include some form of user defined interprocessor communication mechanism.

3.3.6 Message Passing

We have already seen several examples of message passing in Ada using parameters with type marks and in, *out*, or *in out* modes. The parameter passing applies to procedures, functions, and tasks. Restrictions include *in* mode only for function invocations, and subprograms cannot be passed as parameters. Internal objects, types, and subprograms can be passed as actual parameters to instantiate generic program units. A special message passing scheme, independent of a particular programming language construct, will have to be designed for interprocessor communication in a distributed system. This may use the Remote Procedure Call mechanism, or some other approach if non-blocking communication is required.

3.3.7 Interrupt Handling

Even though the design of interrupt handlers may not be directly related to OOD, it may greatly affect the degree of portability associated with the program. Ada constructs support the creation of interrupt handlers with the specification of *representation clauses*. These clauses are used to associate a hardware interrupt or hardware buffer with addresses in our Ada program. An interrupt can be vectored to our interrupt handler, and we can send to or get data from hardware buffers:

```
task Transmit_Msg is
  entry Channel_Interrupt;
  for Channel_Interrupt use at Channel_Address;
  entry Transmit (Msg : in Msg_Format);
end Transmit_Msg;

task body Transmit_Msg is
  Hdw_Buffer : Character;
  for Hdw_Buffer use at Hdw_Buffer_Address;
begin
  loop
    accept Transmit (Msg : in Msg_Format) do
      for I in Msg'Range loop
        Hdw_Buffer := Msg (I);
        accept Channel_Interrupt;
      end loop;
    end Transmit;
  end loop;
end Transmit_Msg;
```

This example illustrates the interrupt mechanism that can be used for a character oriented output device. An interrupt occurs after a character has been placed in the Hdw_Buffer at Hdw_Buffer_Address. The interrupt occurring at Channel_Address will be vectored to the entry Channel_Interrupt, and signals that the device is ready to receive another character.

The ability to write interrupt handlers and device drivers in the high level implementation language can greatly improve the potential for reusability as a program is ported from one system to another. The only modifications to be made may be the values of the interrupt and the hardware buffer (Channel_Address and Hdw_Buffer_Address).

3.3.8 Binding and Polymorphism

Ada only supports static binding, and a case statement structure will have to be used to simulate dynamic binding of operators. Since Ada does not have a class construct, polymorphism is not supported. Overloading of operators is simply a renaming mechanism where an operator with the same name is associated with different types. Attributes of the operators are only inherited from a single type and are, thus, not polymorphic.

Summary

Even though Ada does not strictly support all the features required of a truly object-oriented language, it has a number of features that can be utilized to create loosely coupled design objects that promote reusability. These features are described further in the chapters that follow.

4

Classes and Objects in Ada

Our primary objective for using an object-oriented development approach is to create robust software modules for real-time systems that are easy to port to other hardware architectures and that provide a high degree of reusability. Our design strategy must take concurrency into account very early in the development phase, and this is something that is not normally considered in OOD approaches. Another important issue that is not covered by any of the object-oriented approaches is how to design for distributed systems.

Most of the commonly used software development approaches are based on a top-down strategy where larger abstractions are decomposed into smaller subsets. The decomposition is continued until software modules of a certain approximate size have been identified, e.g., 50 to 100 source lines of code (SLOC) for the given implementation language.

An object-oriented development approach doesn't fit exactly into the strict top-down model, since one of the objectives is a high degree of reusability based on software components that are used as building blocks for a new system. The building block approach is a bottom-up strategy similar to the construction of a computer system using CPU and memory chips that have already been built. A top-down view of a system is desirable for determining a balanced set of processes in a concurrent application, and the resulting development approach is a combination of top-down and bottom-up paradigms.

As an aid to creating software components in a real-time system, we describe a classification scheme for Ada packages that can be used in the construction of tailorable software modules.

4.1 ADA PACKAGE CLASSIFICATION

We have already seen that Ada is not an OOP language in the strictest sense, but that it is object-based. We will expand on that notion and raise our level of abstraction from OOP to OOD and create a set of *design* objects that fit nicely with Ada's package structure.

The Ada package construct is the primary mechanism for creating modules in Ada. Packages are passive software elements that are elaborated only each time an Ada program is being prepared for execution. These packages may contain executable statements for initialization, but their primary function is to *encapsulate* active program units such as tasks and subprograms, constants, type definitions, and localized non-portable system features. Packages are used to promote information hiding by providing two separate programming constructs: (1) the package specification, where everything is visible to the users of the package; and (2) the package body, where we can hide implementation details from the users.

The Ada package construct is also important in considering distributed issues, because it forms a basic building block from which we can create virtual nodes that can be allocated to specific processors. (Creation of virtual nodes is described in Chapter 11.)

Other package classification schemes have been suggested beside the one we will recommend below. The "Ada Rationale" [ICH86, Section 9.2] offers the following guidelines for the creation of package classes:

1. **Named collection of declarations.** This would correspond to our Definitions category.

2. **Groups of related subprograms.** This fits with our Services category.

3. **Encapsulated data types.** This is equivalent to our Type Manager category.

To these, Booch [BOO87 and BOO87a] adds:

1. Abstract State Machines.
2. Structures.
3. Tools.
4. Subsets.

These classifications are quite useful, but they are not complete for a generalized classification that supports real-time systems. We need to be able to categorize packages containing tasks that do the main work of the system. In addition, tasks whose primary function is to allow other tasks to communicate should often be in separate packages. Such packages do not fit clearly within the scheme above. To place them in the category of "groups of related subprograms" seems to ignore an essential characteristic of real-time systems, i.e., the concurrent elements.

The taxonomy developed here does not represent a set of classes in the classical OOP sense, but symbolizes abstractions of design objects that are required for the implementation of a real-time system. The use of abstract data types and generics will significantly reduce the amount of software development efforts required for future, similar systems and will support a high degree of reusability. Major portions of the application domain can be encapsulated in a set of packages that can form the core modules from which small, medium, and large systems can be built within a given problem domain.

The package taxonomy is illustrated in Figure 4.1, and represents a classification of all the different packages necessary for a large real-time Ada program. The categories include Application, Communication, and Helper packages. Helper packages are further subdivided into Definitions, Services, and Data Managers. Data Managers are further divided into Type Managers (ADTs) and Object Managers. A Type Manager can be of an Open or a Closed type and depends on whether or not a *private* type is used. Each of the categories described as part of the taxonomy is illustrated below with a coding example that shows both the package and how the package is used. (The material presented here is adapted from information published in [SHU88a].)

Use of the Ada package categories shown in Figure 4.1 is recommended to realize a high degree of reusability. These categories are described as follows:

1. **Application.** An application-oriented package contains the subprograms and tasks that perform the processing required to satisfy the functionality specified in the software requirements document. These packages are created top-down, and implementation details are deferred using the Ada *separate* clause.

2. **Communication.** The purpose of a communication-oriented package is to provide for data transfers between the program units embedded within the application packages. Communication packages are typically generic units containing tasks that provide buffering, relaying, and transportation of data between producers and consumers. They affect the caller/called relationships of the tasks that are encapsulated within the application packages, and the degree of coupling between a producer/consumer pair. Many of the needed communications packages will be available as library units. Additional communications packages required will be created bottom-up before the application packages are designed. In a distributed system, communication packages will be created to support the chosen IPC mechanism.

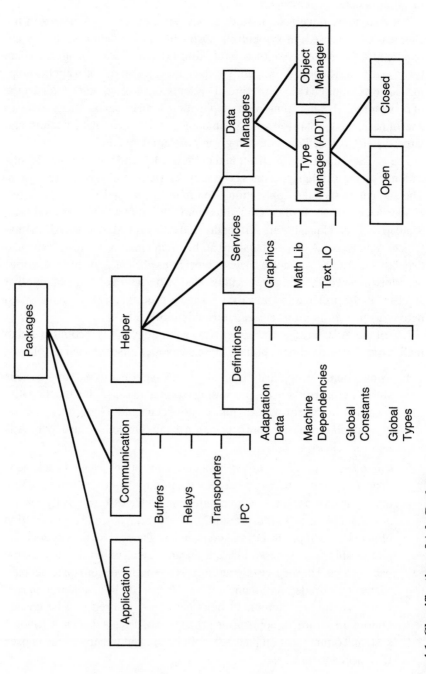

Figure 4.1 Classification of Ada Packages

3. **Helper.** A helper package provides a set of services to "help" an application package accomplish its function. The Helper category includes previously developed software such as graphics packages and mathematical routines, in addition to packages that provide needed information, such as a package of constants and type definitions. An important use of a helper package is to provide a set of data managers that hide implementation details. This provides direct support for the object-oriented paradigm, and encapsulates abstract data types and internal objects as major data structures. The helper category can be divided into the following subcategories:

a. *Definitions.* A definition package is developed to isolate non-portable machine dependencies, to provide a collection of adaptation data, and to offer global constants and types required by the application packages.

b. *Services.* A service package may already be available as a library package such as Text_IO for input/output functions, or a mathematics library for general mathematical functions, e.g., Sqrt, Sin and Cos. Other service packages may have to be developed to support the application packages, e.g., a set of graphics routines, or operations on a track file (where the track file type is specified in a Definitions package).

c. *Data manager.* A data manager is developed to provide the required data type abstractions and the operations allowed on objects of the given type. Such a manager can be further subdivided into abstract data types (ADTs), also referred to as type managers, and object managers, also referred to as resources:

- Type managers. Users of an ADT allocate their own data stores based on an exported type. There will typically be several of these data stores in a single program. ADTs may employ "open" (visible) types or use the *private* type construct to create "closed" (hidden) data types. In either event, the ADT exports operations on objects of the type, and the objects are passed as parameters between the user and the ADT.

- Object managers. An object manager provides a single hidden data store that is shared by the users of the resource. The users of the internal data store do not pass the object that is shared as a parameter in the operations, since the object is declared as a local variable inside the manager.

From an object-oriented view, the helper subcategories presented above are in order of increasing desirability. A definition package provides a tight coupling between the modules that import it. A service package only contains a set of operations and not the associated types. A data manager supports the data abstraction and encapsulation paradigms and represents the type of design object we are seeking. In some cases it may be beneficial to combine types from a definition package and the corresponding operations in a services package into data managers. This will reduce the coupling between the modules and enhance reusability.

The package classification shown in Figure 4.1 provides a set of abstract design objects that directly supports the design and implementation of real-time systems. The concurrent program elements, including device drivers and interrupt handlers, are encapsulated within the application packages. The communication packages provide inter-package data transfers and proper coupling between producer/consumer processes, including distributed systems. Major data structures are encapsulated as either type managers or object managers and support the important paradigm of information hiding.

4.2 EXAMPLES OF ADA PACKAGE OBJECTS

In this section we illustrate the package categories described above with a set of examples from a simplified air traffic control application domain as shown in the context diagram in Figure 4.2. The Air Traffic Control System (ATCS) displays aircraft tracks on a controller work station based on radar data obtained from one or more radars. ATCS accepts radar inputs that provide estimates about the location of aircraft being tracked and operator inputs to initiate new tracks, update the location of a specified track, or drop a track. The system periodically extrapolates all aircraft locations, assuming a constant heading and speed and no wind corrections. There are three methods of updating an aircraft location in ATCS:

1. An operator can initiate or change a track manually.

2. Radar inputs are correlated with established tracks.

3. Track locations are extrapolated at periodic intervals.

4.2.1 Application Package

Here is an application package that communicates with and takes data from a user interface. It also takes information from an input buffer and correlates it with existing information in the track file. A periodic extrapolation function is hidden inside the package body. The interaction with the user interface, the removal and processing of items from the buffer, and the extrapolation all take place concurrently. Here is a listing of the package specification and body:

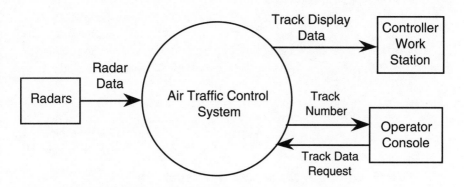

Figure 4.2 ATCS Context Diagram

```
with Track_Defs;   use Track_Defs;
package Track_File_Monitor is
   procedure Add_Track (X, Y      : in  Coordinates;
                        Track_ID : out Track_Number);
   Track_Store_Full : exception; -- raised by Add_Track

   procedure Get_Track (X, Y      : out Coordinates;
                        Track_ID : out Track_Number);
   procedure Update_Track
                  (X, Y      : in Coordinates;
                   Track_ID : in Track_Number);
   procedure Drop_Track (Track_ID : in Track_Number);
end Track_File_Monitor;


package body Track_File_Monitor is
   task Monitor is
     entry Add_Track
                  (X, Y      :      in  Coordinates;
                   Track_ID :      out Track_Number);
     entry Get_Track
                  (X, Y      :      out Coordinates;
                   Track_ID :      out Track_Number);
     entry Update_Track (X, Y      : in Coordinates;
                         Track_ID : in Track_Number);
     entry Drop_Track (Track_ID :    in Track_Number);
     entry Correlate (X, Y : in Coordinates);
     entry Extrapolate;
   end Monitor;

   task body Monitor is separate;
```

```
procedure Add_Track
                (X, Y      : in   Coordinates;
                 Track_ID : out Track_Number) is
begin
   Monitor.Add_Track (X, Y, Track_ID);
end Add_Track;

procedure Get_Track
                (X, Y      : out Coordinates;
                 Track_ID : out Track_Number) is
begin
   Monitor.Get_Track (X, Y, Track_ID);
end Get_Track;

procedure Update_Track
                (X, Y      : in   Coordinates;
                 Track_ID : in   Track_Number) is
begin
   Monitor.Update_Track (X, Y, Track_ID);
end Update_Track;

procedure Drop_Track (Track_ID : in Track_Number) is
begin
   Monitor.Drop_Track (Track_ID);
end Drop_Track;
end Track_File_Monitor;
```

The *entrance procedures* Add_Track, Get_Track, Update_Track, and Drop_Track provide the interface to the package, and the implementations are hidden in the package body. This demonstrates the use of the object-oriented encapsulation paradigm and supports a loose coupling between the modules using this package. This type of design object has excellent potential for reusability since operations can be added to the interface without affecting the rest of the system (except for recompilation).

4.2.2 Communication Package

A communication package may provide four general mechanisms for data transfers between processes (or Ada tasks):

1. **Buffer.** A package with operations that are called to enqueue items into a storage area and to dequeue the same items.
2. **Relay.** A package with operations that are called to store information, but then calls another package to provide the information from storage.

3. **Transporter.** A package with an operation that calls to obtain information from a storage area and also calls to deliver the information.

4. **Interprocess communication (IPC).** A package with operations that hide the details of a communication mechanism implemented for distributed systems.

Additional information on these three intermediate storage mechanisms and the IPC can be found in [NIE88, NIE90]. There are many different ways to implement a typical communication package. Here is an example of a simple buffer:

```
with Track_Defs;   use Track_Defs;
package Radar_Data_Buffer is
   procedure Enqueue (X, Y : in  Coordinates);
   procedure Dequeue (X, Y : out Coordinates);
end Radar_Data_Buffer;

package body Radar_Data_Buffer is
   task Buffer is
      entry Enqueue (X, Y : in  Coordinates);
      entry Dequeue (X, Y : out Coordinates);
   end Buffer;

   task body Buffer is separate;

   procedure Enqueue (X, Y : in Coordinates) is
   begin
      Buffer.Enqueue (X, Y);
   end Enqueue;

   procedure Dequeue (X, Y : out Coordinates) is
   begin
      Buffer.Dequeue (X, Y);
   end Dequeue;
end Radar_Data_Buffer;
```

The Radar_Data_Buffer enqueues sets of coordinates received from the radar and stores them in an internal buffer. When the buffer is full, old information is overwritten. The Radar_Data_Buffer dequeues a set of coordinates upon request, blocking a caller when the buffer is empty. The blocking mechanism is inherent in the implementation of the buffer as an Ada task, and is hidden from the users of this communication package.

4.2.3 Helper Package

The helper packages are subdivided into definitions, services, and data managers as described below.

4.2.3.1 Definitions

Here is an example of the Definitions form of helper package:

```
with Calendar;
package Track_Defs is
   -- Adaptation data

   Update_Periodic          : constant Duration := 1.0;
   Display_Periodic         : constant Duration := 5.0;
   Maximum_Number_Of_Tracks : constant := 200;
   Proximity                : constant := 1000;
                                -- correlation parameter
   Speed                    : constant := 200;


   -- Type definitions

   type Coordinates  is range -100_000 .. 100_000;
                                -- needed for proximity
   type Track_Count is range 0 .. Maximum_Number_Of_Tracks;
   subtype Track_Number is Track_Count
                   range 1 .. Track_Count'Last;
   type Track_Record is
      record
         X, Y     : Coordinates;
         Timetag  : Calendar.Time;
      end record;
   type Track_File is array (Track_Number) of Track_Record;
end Track_Defs;
```

This package includes some global types that will be used by several of the application packages, and a set of adaptation parameters. The maximum number of tracks in the system is embedded in the definition of the type Track_Count. If we wish to refer to the number later, it is always available as the attribute Track_Count'Last. We defined new types for Coordinates and Track_Count in order to take advantage of Ada's strong type checking. Track_Number is a subtype of Track_Count since objects of the two types must be compatible and they will both refer to the tracks in the system.

A similar package can be constructed to isolate a set of machine dependent entities, e.g., interrupt and hardware buffer addresses.

4.2.3.2 Services

Services packages will often provide operations on objects that have their type defined in a definitions package. This applies especially when we reuse a graphics or mathematical package that is not designed as a data manager. The object to be manipulated (e.g., a track file) is declared in an application package. The application package then uses the operations provided by the services package. The relationship between the packages is illustrated graphically in Figure 4.3. Here is an example, using the type Track_File defined in the section above on definitions:

```
with Track_Defs; use Track_Defs;
package Track_Services is
   procedure Add (Tracks    : in out  Track_File;
                  X, Y      : in      Coordinates;
                  Track_ID : out      Track_Number);

   procedure Get (Tracks    : in out Track_File;
                  X, Y      : out     Coordinates;
                  Track_ID : out      Track_Number)

   procedure Update (Tracks    : in out Track_File;
                     X, Y      : in     Coordinates;
                     Track_ID : in      Track_Number);

   procedure Drop (Tracks    : in out Track_File;
                   Track_ID : in       Track_Number);

   procedure Correlate (Tracks : in out Track_File;
                        X, Y    : in     Coordinates);

   procedure Extrapolate (Tracks : in out Track_File);
end Track_Services;
```

Note that the type definition for Track_File is imported from the global definition package Track_Defs. It is not defined within the services package.

Here is an example of how we can use the Track_Services from within the Monitor task declared inside the package body of the Track_File_Monitor application package:

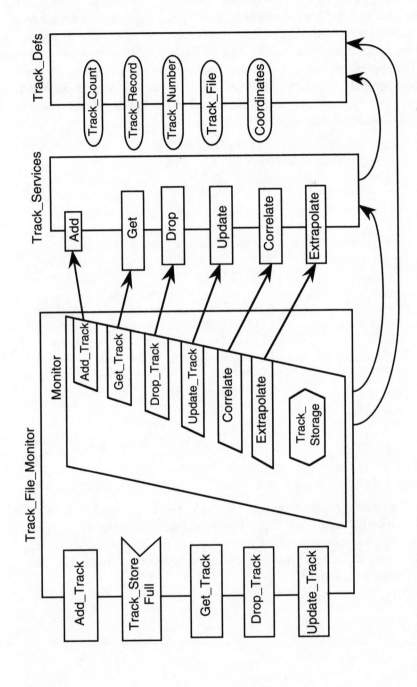

Figure 4.3 Using a Service Package

```ada
with Track_Services; use Track_Services;
separate (Track_File_Monitor)
  task body Monitor is

    Track_Storage : Track_File; -- the actual object
    Last_Track    : Track_Count := 0;

  begin
    loop
      begin
        select
          accept Add_Track
                  (X, Y     : in  Coordinates;
                   Track_ID : out Track_Number) do
            if Last_Track < Track_Count'Last then
              Last_Track := Last_Track + 1;
              Track_ID   := Last_Track;
              Track_Services.Add (Track_Storage,
                                 X, Y, Last_Track);
            else
              raise Track_Store_Full;
            end if;
          end Add;
        or
          accept Get_Track
                  (X, Y     :    out Coordinates;
                   Track_ID : out Track_Number) do
            Track_Services.Get (Track_Storage,
                               X, Y, Track_ID);
          end Get_Track;
        or
          accept Update_Track
                  (X, Y     : in Coordinates;
                   Track_ID : in Track_Number) do
            Track_Services.Update (Track_Storage,
                                  X, Y, Track_ID);
          end Update;
        or
          accept Drop_Track
                  (Track_ID : in Track_Number) do
            Track_Services.Drop (Track_Storage,
                                          Track_ID);
          end Drop_Track;
        or
          accept Correlate (X, Y : in Coordinates) do
            Track_Services.Correlate
```

```
                                  (Track_Storage, X, Y);
            end Correlate;
         or
            accept Extrapolate do
               Track_Services.Extrapolate
                                  (Track_Storage);
            end Extrapolate;
            end select;
         exception
            when Track_Store_Full =>
               null;
         end;
      end loop;
   end Monitor;
```

Notice the relationship between the packages (see Figure 4.3). The definitions package provides the type definition. It is *with*ed by the services package to provide the type specification required by the operations. The application package *with*s Track_Defs to obtain the type to create an object, and the Track_Services package to obtain access to its exported operations.

An important point to note here is that with the use of a service package that operates on an object provided as a parameter, the application package declares and owns the data structure that is the object of the system. This is not necessarily the preferred object-orientation to obtain maximum reuse of such a design. This will be explored further in the sections that follow.

4.2.3.3 Data Managers

The preferred design approach is to consolidate the type definition into the package providing the services. Such a combination is called a *data manager*, and provides a better object-orientation than the use of a services package. The Track_Defs package will no longer contain the definitions associated with the Track_File. We will now demonstrate the different design decisions to be implemented for an open ADT, a closed ADT, and an object manager.

Open ADT

With an *open* ADT the structure of the exported type is visible to the user of the package.

```
with Calendar;
with Track_Defs; use Track_Defs;
package Track_Manager_Open is
```

```
type Track_Count is
               range 0 .. Maximum_Number_Of_Tracks;
subtype Track_Number is Track_Count
               range 1 .. Track_Count'Last;

type Track_Record is
  record
    X, Y     : Coordinates;
    Timetag  : Calendar.Time;
  end record;

type Track_File is array (Track_Number)
                                of Track_Record;

procedure Add (Tracks    : in out Track_File;
               X, Y      : in     Coordinates;
               Track_ID  : out    Track_Number);
Track_Store_Full : exception; -- raised in Add

procedure Get (Tracks    : in out Track_File;
               X, Y      : out    Coordinates;
               Track_ID  : out    Track_Number);

procedure Update (Tracks    : in out Track_File;
                  X, Y      : in     Coordinates;
                  Track_ID  : in     Track_Number);

procedure Drop (Tracks    : in out Track_File;
                Track_ID  : in     Track_Number);

procedure Correlate (Tracks : in out Track_File;
                     X, Y   : in     Coordinates);

procedure Extrapolate (Tracks : in out Track_File);

end Track_Manager_Open;
```

Notice that the only difference between the Track_Manager_Open and the previous Track_Services is the location of the type definitions needed to define the track file, as shown in Figure 4.4. Here is an example of the use of the package providing the open ADT, where the actual object is still declared in the application—just like in the use of the Services and Track_Defs packages:

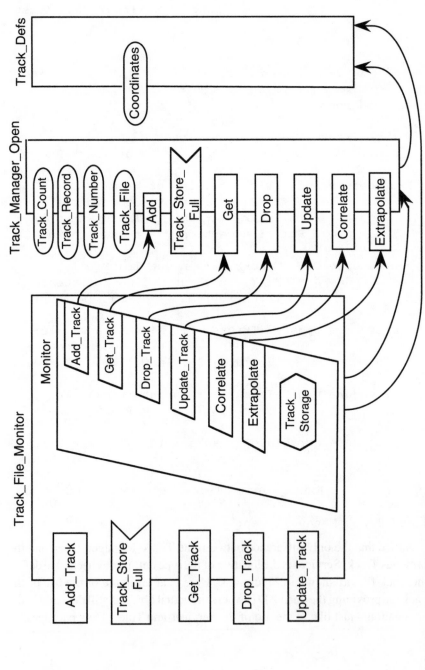

Figure 4.4 Using an Open ADT

```
with Track_Manager_Open; use Track_Manager_Open;
separate (Track_File_Monitor)
  task body Monitor is

    Track_Storage : Track_File; -- the actual object

  begin
    loop
      begin
        select
          accept Add_Track
                    (X, Y     : in  Coordinates;
                     Track_ID : out Track_Number) do
            Track_Manager_Open.Add (Track_Storage,
                               X, Y, Track_ID);
          end Add;
        or
          accept Get_Track
                    (X, Y     : out Coordinates;
                     Track_ID : out Track_Number) do
            Track_Manager_Open.Get (Track_Storage,
                                 X, Y, Track_ID);
          end Get_Track;
        or
        accept Update_Track
                    (X, Y     : in Coordinates;
                     Track_ID : in Track_Number) do
            Track_Manager_Open.Update
                    (Track_Storage, X, Y, Track_ID);
          end Update;
        or
          accept Drop_Track
                    (Track_ID : in Track_Number) do
            Track_Manager_Open.Drop
                        (Track_Storage,Track_ID);
          end Drop_Track;
        or
          accept Correlate (X, Y : in Coordinates) do
            Track_Manager_Open.Correlate
                            (Track_Storage, X, Y);
          end Correlate;
        or
          accept Extrapolate do
            Track_Manager_Open.Extrapolate
                                (Track_Storage);
          end Extrapolate;
```

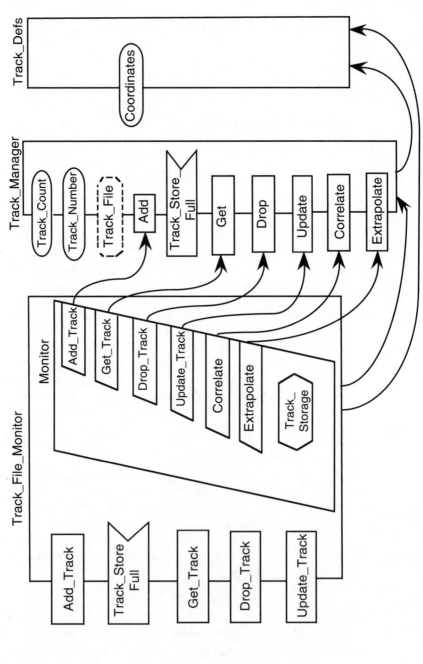

Figure 4.5 Using a Closed ADT

```
      end select;
   exception
      when Track_Store_Full =>
         null;
   end;
  end loop;
 end Monitor;
```

The accept bodies for Get_Track, Update_Track, Drop_Track, Correlate, and Extrapolate are similar to the previous version. Whereas they originally used the operations provided by Track_Services, they now use the operations provided by Track_Manager_Open. The accept body for Add_Track, however, includes some significant changes. In the old version it accessed the data structure directly. In this approach, we remove the dependency on the data structure by using Track_Manager_Open and shift the responsibility for dealing with track numbers to the data manager. The exception Track_Store_Full is now raised in the data manager and passed back to the caller of Add_Track.

Closed ADT

A better design is obtained by employing a level of information hiding for the track file structure, in addition to the encapsulation mechanism used for the open data manager. This is done by making the type definition *private*. The relationship between the packages is shown in Figure 4.5. We now have a *closed* ADT rather than the previous *open* ADT:

```
with Calendar;
with Track_Defs; use Track_Defs;
package Track_Manager is

   type Track_File is private;

   type Track_Count is range
                   0 .. Maximum_Number_Of_Tracks;
   subtype Track_Number is Track_Count
                   range 1 .. Track_Count'Last;

   procedure Add (Tracks    : in out Track_File;
                  X, Y      : in     Coordinates;
                  Track_ID  : out    Track_Number);
   Track_Store_Full : exception; -- raised in Add

   procedure Get (Tracks    : in out Track_File;
                  X, Y      : out    Coordinates;
                  Track_ID  : out    Track_Number);
```

```
procedure Update (Tracks   : in out Track_File;
                  X, Y      : in     Coordinates;
                  Track_ID  : in     Track_Number);

procedure Drop (Tracks    : in out Track_File;
                Track_ID  : in     Track_Number);

procedure Correlate (Tracks : in out Track_File;
                     X, Y    : in     Coordinates);

procedure Extrapolate (Tracks : in out Track_File);
private
   type Track_Record is
      record
         X, Y    : Coordinates;
         Timetag: Calendar.Time;
      end record;

   type Track_File is array
                   (Track_Number) of Track_Record;
end Track_Manager;
```

The significant difference between the Track_Manager and the previous
Track_Manager_Open is the location of the type definitions needed to define
the track file. Here the definition of the track file is hidden, and Monitor cannot
have any dependencies on the data structure. The only operations allowed on
objects of type Track_File are the ones given in the package specification. With
the open ADT a user is allowed to create additional operations since the data
structure is visible.

Object Manager

If there will only be a single copy of the track file in the whole system, and none
of the application packages need to see the data structure, an even stronger
encapsulation can be accomplished by using an *object manager*. The track file type
is now moved into the package body, making the information hiding even stronger
than for the private type. The relationship between the packages is shown in Figure
4.6. The object itself (the track file) must be declared inside the package body and
will, thus, not be passed as a parameter to the operations manipulating the object.

```
with Calendar;
with Track_Defs; use Track_Defs;
package Track_Object_Manager is

   type Track_Count
              is range 0 .. Maximum_Number_Of_Tracks;
```

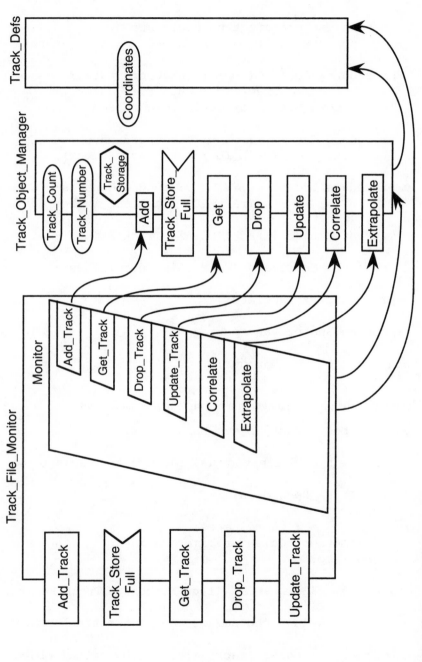

Figure 4.6 Using an Object Manager

```
    subtype Track_Number is Track_Count
                        range 1 .. Track_Count'Last;

-- notice: no private type declaration
-- and no passing of the track file as a parameter

    procedure Add (X, Y     : in  Coordinates;
                   Track_ID : out Track_Number);
    Track_Store_Full : exception; -- raised in Add

    procedure Get (X, Y     : out Coordinates;
                   Track_ID : out Track_Number);

    procedure Update (X, Y     : in Coordinates;
                      Track_ID : in Track_Number);

    procedure Drop (Track_ID : in Track_Number);

    procedure Correlate (X, Y : in Coordinates);

    procedure Extrapolate;

-- notice: no private part

end Track_Object_Manager;
```

The body of the object manager can be implemented as follows:

```
package body Track_Object_Manager is

-- now the type definition is hidden in the package body

    type Track_Record is
      record
        X, Y    : Coordinates;
        Timetag : Calendar.Time;
      end record;

  type Track_File is array (Track_Number) of Track_Record;

-- and now we use the definition of the track object

      Track_Storage : Track_File; -- the actual object
      Last_Track    : Track_Count := 0;
```

```
-- the remainder of the package body is the same as the
-- closed abstract data type
   ...
end Track_Object_Manager;
```

Here is an example of how we use the package providing the object manager:

```
with Track_Object_Manager; use Track_Object_Manager;
separate (Track_File_Monitor)
  task body Monitor is

  begin
    loop
      begin
        select
          accept Add_Track
                  (X, Y      : in  Coordinates;
                   Track_ID : out Track_Number) do
            Track_Object_Manager.Add (X, Y, Track_ID);
          end Add;
        or
          accept Get_Track
                  (X, Y      : out Coordinates;
                   Track_ID : out Track_Number) do
            Track_Object_Manager.Get (X, Y, Track_ID);
          end Get_Track;
        or
          accept Update_Track
                  (X, Y      : in Coordinates;
                   Track_ID : in Track_Number) do
            Track_Object_Manager.Update
                           (X, Y, Track_ID);
          end Update;
        or
          accept Drop_Track
                  (Track_ID : in Track_Number) do
            Track_Object_Manager.Drop (Track_ID);
          end Drop_Track;
        or
          accept Correlate (X, Y : in Coordinates) do
            Track_Object_Manager.Correlate (X, Y);
          end Correlate;
        or
          accept Extrapolate do
            Track_Object_Manager.Extrapolate;
```

```
            end Extrapolate;
          end select;
          exception  -- needed to keep from exiting loop
            when Track_Store_Full =>
              null;
          end;
        end loop;
      end Monitor;
```

Notice that the only difference between Track_Object_Manager and the previous Track_Manager is the location of the type definitions needed to define the track file.

The package taxonomy presented here supports the object-orientation needed for real-time systems. It incorporates earlier distinctions between the various uses of packages [ICH86, BOO87, BOO87a] and adds, particularly for concurrent systems, the important categories of "application" and "communication." The latter two are usually ignored in most other object-oriented design approaches.

4.2.3.4 Degree of Encapsulation

An important characteristic of the package taxonomy is that it illustrates the increasing encapsulation of a type and associated object. There are four levels of encapsulation, based on four decisions that a designer may make about how the data and data definitions are to be controlled.

1. **Services.** The services package provides operations on objects, but does not encapsulate a type. The type definition is shared among the application packages and the service package. This type definition is made globally visible by residing in the separate Track_Defs package. (The Track_Defs package has no operations.) Objects are created in the application packages using the type specification in the Track_Defs package. This is illustrated graphically in Figure 4.3, where the type Track_File is seen on the boundary of Track_Defs. There may be multiple (user-defined) objects in a program, and the objects (the single Track_Storage object in our case) are passed as parameters to the operations in the services package.

2. **Open ADT.** Moving the type definition to the visible part of the services package creates an open ADT. The user of the open ADT is free to manipulate the components (x, y, and Timetag) of the data structure (type) Track_Record. The package specification includes the operations on objects of the type, and a user can declare additional operations, if desired. The open ADT has several shared characteristics with the combination of definitions and services packages. Objects are created by application

packages, and there may be multiple (user-defined) objects in a program, with each object passed as a parameter to the operations. An example of an open ADT is shown in Figure 4.4. The type Track_Record has been moved into the package Track_Manager_Open and is specified with the operations. The internal object Track_Storage is declared in the application package Track_File_Monitor (inside the task Monitor).

3. **Closed ADT.** Moving the type definition to the private part of the open ADT package creates a closed ADT. There may still be multiple objects passed as parameters to the operations provided by the closed ADT. The closed ADT is a highly desirable form of helper package. It makes programs easy to develop, test, and modify. It is the preferred design choice when multiple objects must exist and there are no good reasons for an open ADT or services package. The example of the closed ADT is shown in Figure 4.5, where the private type Track_File is indicated with a stipled oval. The internal object Track_Storage is still declared inside the application package.

4. **Object manager.** Moving the type definition to the package body creates an object manager. Now there is a single object, which is only visible inside the body of the Track_Object_Manager package, as shown in Figure 4.6. There is now no object passed as a parameter since the single object is declared entirely within the object manager. This is the preferred approach when only one object of the specific type is required.

Summary

A taxonomy of Ada packages is presented in this chapter. These packages represent design objects that support our objective of creating software systems that are portable and reusable.

To achieve the highest degree of reusability in a design, a closed ADT or object manager provides the best encapsulation of an object. If only a single encapsulated object will exist within a program, the paradigm of choice is the object manager. This combines the highest degree of information hiding and encapsulation with the narrowest (loosely coupled) interface between program modules.

P A R T 2

OBJECT-ORIENTED ANALYSIS AND DESIGN

The importance of having a specific development strategy in place before a major software project is started has been emphasized by numerous authors for about two decades, going back as far as Dijkstra's papers on Structured Programming [DIJ68, DIJ72]. We may not always be able to follow the chosen strategy perfectly step by step; some of the steps may be performed iteratively. The importance of why we need a design process and why we may end up "faking" it when we discover the process not to be perfect, has been most eloquently stated by Parnas and Clements in their paper "A Rational Design Process: How and Why to Fake It" [PAR86].

The "rational" development process presented in this part includes all the steps required from (even before) the start of the requirements analysis and culminating with preliminary design. The recommended approach is a blend of proven structured analysis and design modified for real-time systems [NIE88] and object-oriented concepts. This approach does not represent a radically divergent path from existing methods, and does not require a major investment in educational efforts. It builds upon proven methods and adds object-orientation that directly supports reusability and the creation of common software components. The development strategy represents a *software-first* technique that is specifically adapted for distributed real-time systems.

Our recommended approach is to perform a domain analysis as a prelude to the requirements analysis. This will directly support the strive for reusability by identifying real-world objects, in-house expertise in the problem domain, and software modules already available within the organization. The requirements analysis phase follows the domain analysis and employs a combination of functional decomposition and data modeling. The functional decomposition is used to create the process abstraction that will represent the concurrent elements of our real-time system. The data modeling portion is used to uncover the major data abstractions.

This part includes a chapter on the preferred design of modules and interfaces, and how we should create objects in a distributed system. A special emphasis is placed on creating layers of objects. This supports the paradigm of loose coupling and reusability since complete layers can be modified or replaced with only minimal effect on the rest of the system.

5

Domain Analysis

One of the primary benefits of using an object-oriented development approach is that it promotes a high degree of reusability. The major objective of any company developing software products is profitability, and one of the principal factors in achieving profitability in a competitive marketplace is reusability. We do not want to have to redesign a system for every new contract awarded to us. When we refer to *reusability*, we mean reusability-in-the-large. We are not simply looking for a listing of an isolated software module. The primary focus is to identify reusable software modules, associated documentation, and systems and software experts for the specific functionality.

The logical starting point for any major software development project is for the company to carefully analyze the requirements of the proposed marketplace, and to evaluate its existing expertise and available resources against those requirements. Such a starting point is a domain analysis that will clearly identify a common set of requirements that will form a baseline for a software product line. Very few system applications are truly unique, and a domain analysis will be beneficial in most cases.

5.1 BACKGROUND

In the previous chapters we dealt with classes and objects as they apply to programming and design. It can be highly beneficial to carry object-orientation further and apply it to the initial phases of the software development process, i.e., the requirements analysis phase. The objects identified during this stage of the development are referred to as *real-world* objects and are different from the design objects we have encountered in earlier chapters. Abstract real-world objects have a set of attributes and operations associated with them that can form the basis for the creation of design objects.

Most real-world objects are associated with major data structures that can be identified during a data modeling analysis. One problem with this approach, however, is that it ignores the concurrency issue of real-time systems. When an object-oriented analysis (OOA) approach is based on data modeling, the creation of concurrent processes is performed as an afterthought. This makes it very difficult to determine the relationships and coupling between the processes. This is particularly awkward in Ada, for example, which has an asymmetric rendezvous, and where the proper caller/called relations are extremely important.

A solution to this problem is to precede the requirements analysis phase with a domain analysis, and to include a proper transitioning phase between the requirements analysis and design phases. By domain analysis we are referring to the process of identifying real-world classes and objects that are common to related applications within a specific problem domain. Examples of such problem domains include air traffic control, robot control, military command and control, and satellite tracking systems.

The domain analysis precedes the other, more traditional development phases, as shown in Figure 5.1, and sets the stage for gaining invaluable insight about the system to be developed. The primary inputs to this analysis are available system specifications and the expectations of future customer requirements. A System Specification document is the initial source for the identification of real-world classes and objects. For an air traffic control domain, for example, system requirements will be specified for radar data processing, flight data processing, data display, human-machine interface, data recording and playback, and meterological data processing [FIE85, NOL90]. Real-world objects with their associated attributes and operations can then be specified for each system requirement. A class can be identified, for example, for Tracks with objects (instances) as External Tracks (in a world coordinate system) and System Tracks (with local (x,y) coordinates). Attributes of Tracks could include track identifier, position, speed, altitude, and heading. Typical operations could be to add, update, drop, extrapolate, and correlate tracks. The classes and objects identified in this phase are used to determine the potential for reusability in terms of existing software and associated documentation, and in-house expertise.

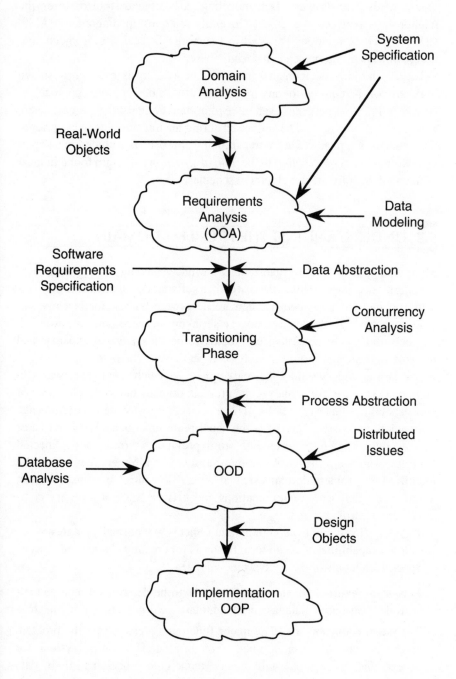

Figure 5.1 Software Development Approach

The real-world objects and their interfaces are explored further during the requirements analysis phase. Data modeling can be used as a tool to express the relationships between the objects in entity-relationship diagrams [BAI89, CHE76]. These relations are used to transform the real-world objects into design objects in the subsequent design phase.

The transitioning mechanism from requirements analysis to design, as shown in Figure 5.1, is required for any real-time software development approach to be successful. This becomes even more important for real-time systems where concurrency issues should be addressed during the transitioning phase prior to the actual design phase. Such a transitioning approach is included in this part by adding *process abstraction* to the *data abstraction* paradigm found in most of the modern software development schemes.

5.2 UNDERSTANDING THE PROBLEM DOMAIN

More and more software organizations are understanding the importance of creating product lines to reduce the cost of their software development efforts. This is true not only for developers of commercial software, but also for developers of military systems. As the defense budget is shrinking, fewer contracts are awarded, and only those companies that can capitalize on their existing expertise and reusable software can survive in such a competitive environment.

The key to understanding the marketplace in which a company wants to participate is to carefully analyze the problem domain and to develop a set of core capabilities that can be tailored for a wide variety of system requirements.

The domain analysis precedes the usual requirements analysis and takes into account known requirements from previous, current, and expected contract awards or projects. A common subset of requirements can usually be identified for problem domains such as air traffic control systems, robotics, avionics, air defense, communications and networking, and military command and control systems.

The identification of the common requirements will normally create a set of functional capabilities that can form the basis for creating classes and objects. Specific elements of the analysis include:

1. **System features.** Basic system features to be determined include real-time, distributed, database oriented, message driven, time critical, etc.

2. **System requirements.** The major functional areas within the problem domain should be determined. For an air traffic control system, for example, these areas will include radar data processing, flight data processing, monitor and control, human-computer interface, data recording, playback, and simulation.

3. **System architecture.** This will include a determination of the range of systems to be developed, e.g., small, medium, and large with regard to the required functionality. The expected hardware architectures and associated operating systems should be specified. Examples include VAX/ VMS, Sun/Unix, Ethernet or other LAN connections, MC 680X0 with VMEbus, or Intel 80x86 Multibus II configurations.

4. **Real-world classes and objects.** This represents an abstraction of the major functional areas, and is used as an aid to understanding the complexity of large real-time systems. The classes and objects should be associated with a level of stability (i.e., resistant to change) for a range of systems. The attributes should be evaluated for their potential volatility, i.e., how they will change from system to system within the problem domain.

The general domain analysis process is illustrated in Figure 5.2. The combination of existing requirements, anticipated future requirements, and in-house expertise serves as the basis for the identification of a common set of functions. The functions are described in documents that can be used as marketing material and a system functional specification. The common functions are subsequently expanded into the key abstractions and operations from which classes and objects can be derived.

The domain analysis will lay the foundation for the planning and effort required in establishing the amount of software to be developed, and the functionality of potential software available for reuse.

5.3 CAPTURING EXISTING EXPERTISE AND SOFTWARE

Unless an organization is developing a brand new product and intends to start the software development from scratch, there is most likely a significant amount of in-house expertise available from previous projects. Before any software development gets started, an attempt should be made to match this expertise to the common requirements determined during the domain analysis. It is quite likely that a significant amount of software exists that can be reused in one form or another for an upcoming project. And from this point forward, the primary emphasis within the organization should be to develop a set of reusable components that can be tailored for small, medium, and large systems within the specific problem domain.

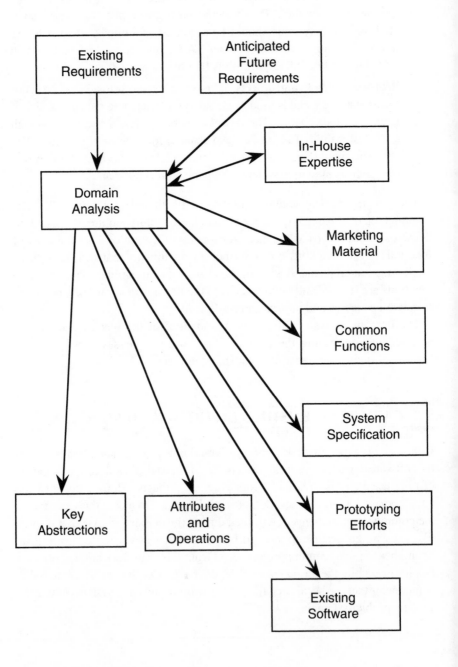

Figure 5.2 Domain Analysis Relationships

The actual development of the core functions may involve a combination of transitioning existing software to the programming language of choice, and developing all new software required in the chosen language. A company may, for example, have a collection of Fortran and C modules which have been used in previous projects, and has determined to develop all new software in Ada. The Fortran and C modules may be transitioned into Ada via a partial redesign and/or translation, or the modules may be imported directly into an Ada program "as is" via the pragma Interface.

5.4 CREATING REAL-WORLD OBJECTS

As a preview to the definition of formal classes and objects, the key abstractions and operations are identified in terms of real-world objects. For an air traffic control system, for example, some of the key abstractions include controller workstations, weather displays, aircraft tracks, communications system, and flight plans. Some of the operations associated with these abstractions include the creation of situation and tabular displays, algorithmic tracking and display of aircraft trajectories, and activation, distribution and closing of flight plans. These abstractions and operations are common to all ATC systems regardless of the complexity of the operations within a given airspace. They apply to small airport operations that only service general aviation aircraft, as well as to the major metropolitan airports such as LAX in Los Angeles, O'Hare in Chicago, and Heathrow in London.

The real-world objects can be refined and collected into classes that can be reused for a given system implementation. A class can, for example, be identified as Displays with subclasses of Situation Displays for depicting aircraft positions and Tabular Displays for arrival and departure lists. Objects can then be created as instances of a given subclass to satisfy a specific requirement for a system implementation. During the design phase these conceptual objects will be transformed into display objects using, for example, X Window. Individual systems can be tailored for specific customer requirements using the core of product line software components. How much tailoring will be required depends upon how different the current system is from the system perceived when the components were created, and how well the module interfaces have been designed.

5.5 DOMAIN ANALYSIS PRODUCTS

A number of products will be produced during the course of the domain analysis. The major products will include at least the following:

1. **System functional specification.** This document will specify the system requirements of the problem domain. It can use a formal format specified in a standard documentation series (e.g., US DoD Mil-Standard 2167A, [DOD88]) or an informal description. This document will serve as a precursor to a formal Software Requirements Specification document to be prepared during the requirements analysis phase. The functional specification can also serve as a marketing tool used by the sales force. Other information associated with this document includes size and costing data of the software components. Initial size estimates can be made based on existing modules. More exact information can be filled in as the components are created.

2. **Classes and objects.** This includes conceptual, high level abstractions of the major elements of the system. For an ATC system, for example, a class may be Radar Interfaces. An object within the class may be a particular Swedish, Russian, or American radar. The attributes associated with the object could include electrical interfaces, message types and content, and the radar scan rate. Operations could include the reception of radar data, sending track or plot messages, and sending radar configuration messages.

3. **Existing software.** A list of existing software for the corresponding functionality should be made for each set of class and object combination. The software should be evaluated for potential reuse with regard to programming language and available documentation. The evaluation should include a quantitative analysis of the estimated effort required for reuse, "lift" (reusing a software module without any associated documentation), redesign, or direct translation.

4. **In-house expertise.** It is highly likely that there are several individuals who are experts in different areas of the problem domain. This will include both systems and software engineers. These individuals should be identified with their particular area of expertise and potential availability for supporting the project. The availability of such a talent pool is extremely important for the success of the project, and a total lack of such individuals should weigh heavily in a decision of whether or not the project should be undertaken.

5. **Prototyping.** A number of high risk areas can be identified for potential prototyping. In a distributed system this could include the interprocess communication mechanism, fault tolerance, or database design. Another

important area is to determine display requirements with a flexible design to satisfy different personal preferences. The prototyping effort should not be associated with throw-away code. It should be carefully selected and implemented with well defined interfaces so that it can readily be integrated with the rest of the system that will be developed later.

The conclusion of the domain analysis serves as the starting point for the requirements analysis. At this time the functionality is well known, and reasonable estimates should have been obtained for the magnitude of the software development effort. The effort can then be divided among the prototyping tasks and the software development tasks. One team of developers can start the transformation process of existing software, and other teams can start the requirements analysis for the development of the new software required.

6

Requirements Analysis and Object-Orientation

The first phase of a software development effort is to analyze a set of requirements that describes the system to be implemented. This description is either in the form of a formal document according to a certain documentation standard such as Mil-Std-2167A [DOD88], or an informal report with either a system or an operational view of the application. If no such document exists, it should be created as a part of the requirements analysis phase and prior to the start of any design efforts.

In this chapter we will extend the object-oriented paradigms of OOP and OOD to include the analysis phase with the creation of high level, abstract objects: object-oriented analysis (OOA). The objective of OOA is to create classes and objects that can be transitioned to OOD classes and objects.

One of the most important results of the analysis phase is to convince the customer that we thoroughly understand the problem domain. This we can do best by providing a description with graphical illustrations and text in a language that the customer can readily understand. If we create object names that are close to real-world object names, the customer can easily relate to our requirements analysis effort, and agreement about the requirements should be easy to obtain. Heavy use of "computerese" will only tend to confuse a customer, with the possibility of lengthy discussions of what it is that we are planning to design and implement.

The OOA approach presented here includes modeling techniques presented in [BAI89, CHE76, COA91, and SCH88] and is used to create abstract objects that can be transformed to design objects via data abstraction. We are not

73

abandoning the transformation from extended structured analysis into real-time design techniques (SA/RTD) used for distributed real-time systems [NIE88, NIE90, WAR85]. OOA is used as an adjunct to these techniques in order to identify the major data structures within the real-time system. A transitioning phase is still required to determine the concurrent elements of the system. The transitioning steps that lead from requirements analysis to design are described in subsequent chapters.

There is significant controversy within the software engineering community about exactly what steps, characteristics, and notations are required for claiming that a specific analysis approach is truly object-oriented. Some of the approaches only deal with objects, methods, and attributes, others include classes. The creation of classes implies inheritance where subclasses can be formed from superclasses (metaclasses). One of the major problems with many existing OOA formulations is that the notation is extremely complex and it will require a significant investment in training a staff of engineers for a large project. We will attempt to create a relatively simple set of rules that can be employed without a major upheaval of existing approaches using familiar notations for graphical representations.

6.1 REQUIREMENTS SPECIFICATION

It would be virtually impossible to effectively design and implement a large real-time system without some form of document that specifies the requirements of the system to be created. If no such document exists, it should be written before any analysis work is even attempted.

A requirements document can be created after conversations with the customer, or from existing system descriptions or formal proposal requests. It can also be based on the domain analysis described in the previous chapter. In either case, it is extremely important that the customer reviews the document and gives a formal approval to the contents. This document provides the starting point for the software development activity. The more relevant detail contained in this document, the easier the design process becomes. A glaring lack of detail in a requirements specification provided by the customer usually means that the customer is not very certain of the exact functionality to be implemented, and could be taken as a warning sign that the requirements are likely to change. This in turn, probably means that the software development process will be chasing a moving target.

The situation is quite different when we are creating a set of common software modules from which future systems are to be composed. There may not be an actual customer yet, and a formal approval cannot be obtained. In this case we write the document based on the anticipated requirements derived from the domain analysis, and use this as a baseline for the analysis phase.

6.2 REQUIREMENTS ANALYSIS

A basic assumption here is that a detailed requirements document is available, and that we start our software development activity based on the stated functionality. In this section we demonstrate the primary differences between the extended structured analysis technique and an object-oriented approach using entities and entity-relationships.

6.2.1 Structured Analysis

One of the traditional development strategies is to use data flow diagrams (DFDs) to analyze a set of requirements. A functional decomposition is performed with a circle or "bubble" representing a subfunction or *transform*. A transform is sometimes used as a synonym for a *process*. In this book we will use the phrase *process* to describe a concurrent element. The top level view is described with a context diagram which shows a single transform and all the external interfaces. The single transform contains all the functionality for the software modules we are going to design and implement, and the rectangular boxes represent the external interfaces.

An example of a context diagram is shown in Figure 6.1 for an air traffic control system (ATCS). The annotated lines show the data that will be flowing between ATCS and the external systems. Plot data, track messages, and weather data, for example, will be entering ATCS from a radar, and flight plans, control messages, and meteorological data will be transmitted and received between the communication network and ATCS. Some ATCS systems are connected directly to external facilities and will be exchanging hand-off data (as an aircraft moves from one airspace sector to another), status messages, and flight plans.

The top level transform is decomposed into subfunctions as shown in Figure 6.2. This view represents a simplified version of an air traffic control system and the data flowing between the various functions. The primary emphasis throughout the analysis phase in the structured approach is on the data flows between the functions, with only a cursory view of the actual data structures. This is one of the major differences between OOA and structured analysis. During OOA, the primary emphasis is on discovering objects and determining the operations to be performed on these objects. Some of the objects will manifest themselves as data structures with certain attributes and a set of operations that will be necessary to create, update, and terminate data elements within the boundaries of the object.

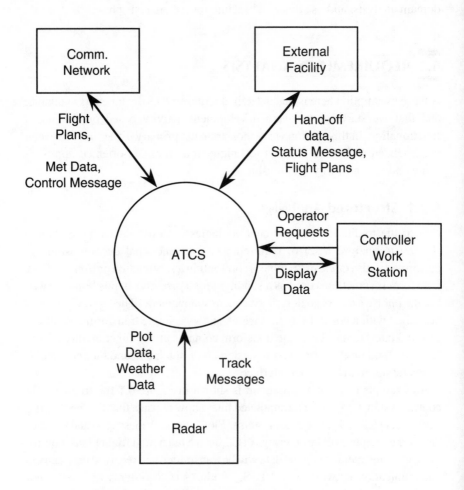

Figure 6.1 ATCS Context Diagram

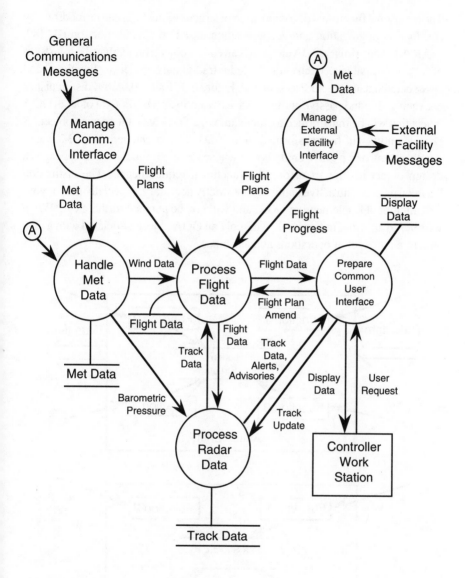

Figure 6.2 ATCS Top Level DFD

6.2.2 OOA Objects

The traditional functional decomposition of structured analysis can be modified by considering aggregation and decomposition based on data abstraction [BAI89, WAR89]. The primary OOA element is an entity (object) rather than the transform of structured analysis. Each entity includes traditional transforms (functions) and an associated data structure as shown in Figure 6.3. Bailin [BAI89] distinguishes between active and passive entities. An *active* entity can be thought of as an OOA object that will be transformed to, for example, a Track Manager design object. A *passive* entity will be transformed to an ADT, e.g., a Queue or List Manager. Another view of a passive entity is one whose (derived) function will appear as a design object in support of one the functional requirements. The distinction between passive and active entities is not strictly necessary, especially not for your first attempt of implementing OOA, and will not be pursued further here. When we refer to an *entity* in this book, we imply an OOA object associated with a data structure and a set of operations and attributes.

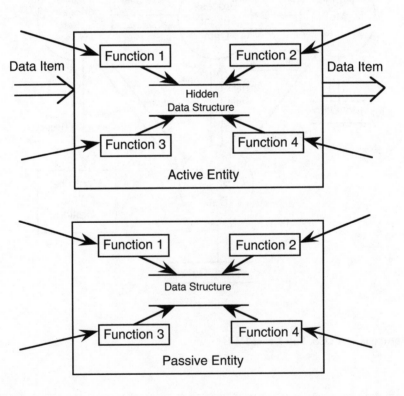

Figure 6.3 OOA Entities (Objects)

The two primary tools used to represent OOA objects and the flow of processing are entity-relationship diagrams (ERDs) [BAI89, CHE76, WAR89] and control and data flow diagrams (CDFDs) [NIE88, WAR85, WAR89]. ERDs are used to:

- Identify entities that translate to real-world objects (OOA objects).

- Analyze entities and their relationships to determine an abstract component view independent of processing flows.

- Identify ADTs as potential design objects.

- Determine hierarchical decompositions and inheritance relations that may lead to class and object creations.

- Present a logical view of a database structure.

The ERD presents a design model that identifies OOA objects that will be translated to design objects.

CDFDs are used to:

- Show the flow of data between the functional components (transforms).

- Show the control (stimulus-response) and sequencing of events of the functional components.

- Represent a system view of the operational approach.

- Decompose a system into lower level transforms.

- Identify the concurrent elements of a real-time system.

The CDFD presents a specification model of the operational system and becomes an important element of the transitioning step from analysis to design. A CDFD can also be considered a pictorial representation of the functional requirements, which are often written as a set of input-processing-output descriptions. We may also occasionally refer to a "DFD," i.e., strictly a data flow without any control flow.)

The OOA model of the ATCS example is shown in Figure 6.4. The rectangles shown in Figure 6.4 represent the top level entities (OOA objects) in an ATCS application and the relationships between them are depicted with diamonds. The relationships are used to determine subentities using verb phrases like "contains," "has a," "is a," "produces," "receives," etc. The identified entities and subentities can be implemented as database objects during the design phase using a logical view of the required data structures [BRA89]. They can be decomposed into subentities, and we may discover additional data structures during the decomposition. Note the different naming conventions used in ERDs and CDFDs. Entities in ERDs are all noun phrases, whereas the transforms in CDFDs are all verb phrases. This is another indication of the design (object) flavor of the ERD paradigm, and the processing flavor and system view of the CDFD of SA/RTD.

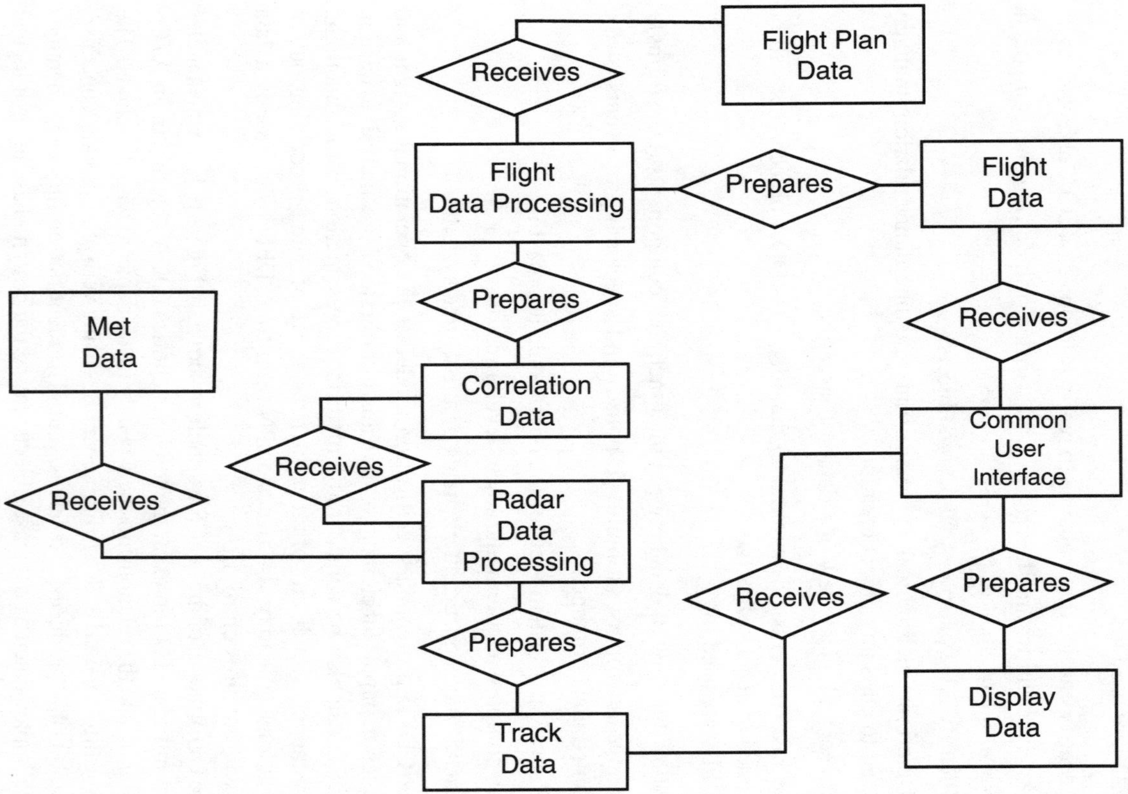

Figure 6.4 ATCS Entity-Relationships

The objects shown in Figure 6.4 are associated with a set of attributes and operations. These objects will later be transitioned to design objects with data types specifying the data structure, and subprograms representing the operations. Each design object will eventually be implemented with programming constructs, e.g., Ada packages or C++ classes and subclasses.

6.3 IDENTIFYING OBJECTS AND CLASSES

The most promising technique for identifying objects and classes is an iterative approach starting with the recognition of objects from the domain analysis. An initial collection of abstract real-world objects will lead to a class definition. The class will then spawn subclasses based on the attributes of the objects. Actual software design objects will occur during the implementation phase as instances of a given class or subclass.

The following set of categories is presented by Shlaer and Mellor [SCH88] as an aid in the identification of objects with a real-world view:

1. Tangible things.

2. Roles (operations performed or viewed by people).

3. Incidents (occurrences or events).

4. Interactions (transactions or contracts).

5. Specifications (inventory, manufacturing).

Tangible things that relate to an ATC system, for example, include aircraft, radars, displays, and controller workstations. Aircraft objects may include large passenger jets, cargo planes, and private planes. This may suggest a superclass of Aircraft that will define the operations common to all aircraft. Subclasses can be created for Large Jets and Private Planes with the additional operations for each subclass based on the respective aircraft characteristics (attributes).

Objects determined by a certain view could include aircraft tracks and callsigns, flight plans, velocity vectors, and weather data as seen by an air traffic controller. A pilot's view of the same system (for building an avionics system) would include communication and navigation frequencies, voice communication, navigational aid indicators, flight patterns, and airspace divisions. The roles played by different air traffic controllers, for example, could suggest a superclass of Controller with subclasses of Supervisor Position, Approach Controller Position, and Trainee Position. The implementation of the different positions will require different types of displays and functionality.

A real-world view based on events associated with an ATC system may suggest creating objects and classes from the various states of a flight such as departure, arrival, and en-route. A view based on interactions may include the reception or transmission of track messages or flight plans.

An analysis method that only includes objects and not classes is usually referred to as an information model approach, and is not considered strictly an OOA by the purists. The concept of classification and thus inheritance, is missing with this approach. This may be perfectly acceptable if the implementation language (e.g., Ada) does not support a class structure.

Coad and Yourdon [COA91] offer a similar set of rules for identifying a set of objects within a given problem space:

1. Structure (classification, including hierarchy, and assembly).

2. Other systems (systems and "external terminators" our system has to interface with).

3. Devices (external devices (other than "systems") we have to interface with).

4. Events remembered (timing of important events within the system).

5. Roles played (direct users, and models in which the system involve information handling about people).

6. Locations (particular site information that is important to the system, such as placing a radar site near the north pole).

7. Organizational units (grouping of people within the system).

A context diagram for a typical command and control processor (C2P) system is illustrated in Figure 6.5, and the associated top level CDFD shown in Figure 6.6. We usually include some graphical descriptions to get a better idea of the operational features of a system. One of the dangers of this approach is that we might get sidetracked down the path of a pure functional decomposition if we continue to refine the transforms depicted in Figure 6.6 without first looking for the objects and potential classes and introducing ERDs. The most important features to look for in the creation of objects and classes for this system are Other Systems and Devices. The other system that the Command and Control Processor (C2P) interacts directly with is the Combat System, and the devices include at least one Data Link Terminal (only one is shown here) and Peripherals such as a display terminal, disks, magnetic tape units, and printers.

With the C2P serving primarily as a store-and-forward message handler between the data links and the combat system, the human Role and Organizational Units are not important here. Even though there is a facility for an operator to enter data into the system, the role of that operator is insignificant compared to the role of a controller in an ATC system.

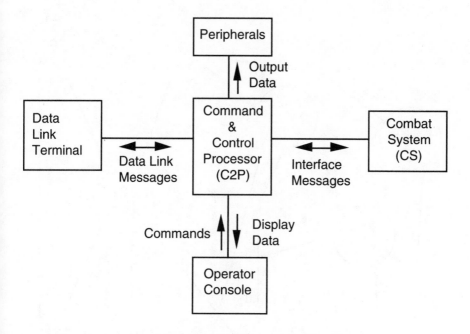

Figure 6.5 Command and Control System Context Diagram

Each C2P system will reside onboard a particular class of ships, and Location only enters into the determination of adaptation parameters and tailoring of the design to fit different hulls.

The type of Events that must be remembered in this system include the time tagging of messages received from the data links and from the combat system. The time tags are normally used in extrapolation of the estimated time a message would be transmitted over the data link.

No immediate Structure or Classification emanates from the two figures, but if additional data links were added, we could identify different link interfaces and sets of messages that could form class structures. Some of the objects associated with data structures emerging from the initial analysis include:

Data link interfaces — buffer areas

Data link messages — messages

Combat system interface — buffer areas

Combat system interface messages — messages

Local and remote tracks — tracks

Surveillance data (track file) — tracks

Operator console interface — commands

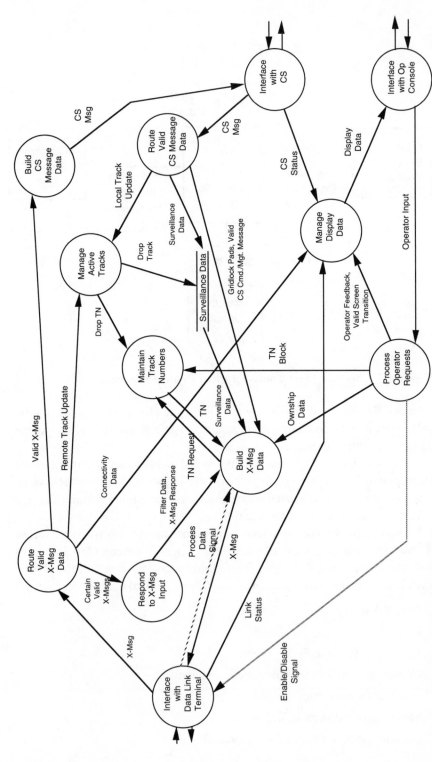

Figure 6.6 C2P Top Level CDFD

Console display — display data

Operator requests — requests

Time tags — synchronized time

Creation of classes from these objects suggests Interfaces, Tracks, and Messages as the most likely candidates.

6.4 ATTRIBUTES

Attributes are used to gain a better understanding of an object and describe its characteristics. For example, the attributes of a radar may include the following:

1. Location (a specific reference of where the radar is located in latitude/ longitude, (r, theta) or (x, y)).
2. Scan Rate (revolutions per second or minute).
3. Type (primary or secondary surveillance radar, or a combination of both).
4. Data (weather data, plots, or tracks)

In addition to getting a better understanding of the characteristics of objects, the list of attributes is used to determine if we have identified a proper object. If only a single attribute for an object appears, for example, it could mean that what we have called an "object" should really be an attribute. That attribute should then be found among the other objects identified, or should be added to the existing objects.

What we strive for in this phase is to identify a set of common attributes that will be valid for every specific instance of the abstract object. This is similar to constructing a relational data model where each row is an object and each column represents an attribute. We are not, however, making a conscious effort to "normalize" the data elements; we are initially simply collecting information about an object.

There are very few "how to" guidelines that can be made for the process of discovering and classifying attributes. The only commonality among them is that each attribute represents a characteristic of a data element that can be described in terms of enumeration values, state values, constants, and data types.

The ERDs described in Section 6.2 are sometimes referred to as ERA diagrams if attributes are included with each entity. This may tend to make the diagrams cluttered, however, and we will not include them in this book.

6.5 OPERATIONS

Among the important information about an object is its behavior. We need to know the actions that an object is required to perform, and potential actions that may be performed on the object by other objects. This type of behavior information can be used to determine the proper interfaces between the objects that make up a system.

The behavior of a given object is described as a set of operations. This is referred to as services and methods by other authors. The term "services" is quite different from anything referred to within structured analysis, and "methods" is too close to the classical OOP terminology. It is important not to consider the operations as software entities in the form of subprograms or processes during the analysis phase. We are still analyzing the requirements and trying to determine the "what" and not the "how."

Operations are identified for the required processing performed on data associated with the object or messages received or sent by the object. It is important to focus on observable behavior in the real-world view and not be concerned with derived requirements that will eventually emerge during the design phase. A strategy for identifying operations by a classification of actions has been suggested in [COA91, and LIS86]. The following list of categories can be used as a guide:

1. **Constructors.** Operations to Create new data elements.
2. **Modifiers.** Operations to Update existing data elements.
3. **Mutators.** Operations to Insert, or Delete.
4. **Observers.** Operations to return information about a data element, e.g., Empty, Full, Size, or Member. This could also include sending a signal when a given event is recognized.

6.6 NAMING CONVENTIONS

One of the important characteristics of an object is a unique identifier that is used to distinguish it from other objects. A set of naming conventions is necessary for the development of a large project where different groups of analysts are working on the various portions of the system. It is also important that the names of objects and classes created match closely with actual, real-world entities. Several authors [BOO91, COA91, FIR90] have offered guidelines for the proper naming of objects and classes. A synopsis of these suggestions follow.

1. **Objects.** Object names are formed from singular, proper, or noun phrases such as Primary Radar, Secondary Radar, Local Track, Remote Track, Tabular Display, or Situation Display.

2. **Classes.** Class names are formed from common (plural) noun phrases such as Radars, Tracks, and Displays.

3. **Attributes.** Attributes are identified by descriptive names and their values, e.g., Track Number, Radar Location, and Message Type.

4. **Operations.** Operations are identified by verb phrases that portray an accurate description of the function to be performed, e.g., Convert to Stereographic, Create Message, Prepare Tabular Display.

Names for objects, classes, attributes, and operations should be chosen carefully. Use names that are common within the problem domain and reflect real-world entities.

In general, the names we create should be readable without any unnecessary prefixes or suffixes. Avoid the creation of computer readable names like TR_Corr for a function that is really Track Correlation. The only time computer readable names could be used is if you have a database tool that is used for requirements traceability, and it requires the use of unique identifiers without any delimiters. Even then, maybe you should choose a tool that can understand ordinary descriptive names. We should never let a tool dictate our analysis or design approach!

6.7 TRANSITIONING TO OBJECT-ORIENTED DESIGN

The most difficult transformation to make for engineers who are OOA novices is the transitioning from OOA to OOD. One of the primary benefits of SA/RTD is the rich source of graphical material available in describing the functional capabilities of a particular system. Data flow diagrams extended with control information (CDFDs) are the primary graphics tools used, and convey a wealth of information. The transitioning steps include a concurrency analysis with a set of process abstraction rules for determining the concurrent elements of the system [NIE88]. A graphical notation is used where the functional capabilities map to concurrent processes, and also show the special interfaces between the processes. This is illustrated below and explored further in the case studies in the Appendixes.

The transitioning from OOA to OOD would be straightforward for a sequential system. Each functional capability identified as an object would map directly to a software component, and the operations associated with each object would become subprograms. Sequential programs are not our major concern here, however; we are primarily interested in distributed real-time systems.

A proper transitioning from OOA to OOD requires a concurrency analysis to determine a set of processes that represent the concurrent elements in the system. These processes constitute a set of abstract objects that can be implemented as software modules. This is consistent with the view of other authors that structured analysis and OOD are indeed compatible [WAR89, HEN91, SHU91, SHU92] and not orthogonal as advocated by others [COA91, FIR91].

The process abstraction technique is presented in Chapter 7 as the major step of transitioning from requirements analysis to design. Chapter 8 describes how data abstraction is used to implement the (data) objects identified during the requirements analysis.

Summary

The OOA paradigm has been included in our development process by identifying classes and objects during the requirements analysis phase.

The ERDs are used to describe a design model for real-world objects that can be translated to design objects during the design phase.

The CDFDs are used to present a specification model of the operational system.

Specific guidelines are given for the identification of classes, objects, attributes, and operations.

The OOA approach outlined here can be used effectively for a new product line effort to produce reusable components. It makes no sense, however, to add ERDs as documentation to a project that will be reusing large amounts of object-oriented software that was developed using a structured analysis approach. The primary emphasis of object-orientation is on the design objects themselves, and not on how they were developed. Software components that can readily be reused will exhibit a high degree of object-orientation regardless of the requirements analysis employed.

7

Process Abstraction

As we noted in the previous chapter, the primary problem of using strictly OOA/ OOD rather than OOA in combination with structured analysis and real-time design is the missing transitioning to the design phase for real-time systems that are inherently concurrent. A proper transitioning from OOA to OOD includes a concurrency analysis to determine a set of processes, i.e., process abstraction [NIE88, GOM84, SHU88b]. This could be a combination of, for example, Unix processes and Ada tasks, VMS processes and Ada tasks, or only Ada tasks, Unix processes, or VMS processes. These processes represent an intermediate set of objects that can be transitioned directly to a software implementation, but they have to be discovered first; they are not going to appear via hand waving or magic. We are thus combining OOA, SA, and process abstraction to facilitate the transitioning that is missing in the traditional OOA approaches.

The achievement of system reusability is highly dependent on how well the processes have been designed. If all of the process interfaces are closely coupled, it will be very difficult to create systems from the design objects that contain the process functionality. The objects must be designed with a distributed architecture in mind, such that they can be reconfigured for different hardware architectures without a major redesign.

The word "process" is used here as an abstraction of an entity that will be implemented as a software module that will execute concurrently with other processes. We will distinguish between an abstract process and a specific Ada task when that is appropriate. We will also refer to specific Unix or VMS processes when the cases arise.

89

7.1 PROCESS IDENTIFICATION

The identification of a set of processes originates with the data and control flow diagrams derived during the analysis phase and a set of process selection rules [NIE88, NIE90]. These rules are repeated here:

1. **External devices.** These devices normally run at widely differing speeds and usually require a separate process for each device or channel. These processes should be designed as simple device drivers with a minimum of executable instructions.

2. **Functional cohesion.** Transforms with closely related functions can be combined into a single process if this will reduce the expected run-time overhead compared to having each function as a separate process. The implementation of the set of functions as separate modules within the single process will contribute to functional cohesion (highly desirable) within each module as well as within the process.

3. **Time-critical functions.** Certain functions must be performed within critical time limits, and this implies a separate (high priority) process for such functions.

4. **Periodic functions.** Periodic functions should be implemented as separate processes that are activated at the proper time intervals. Such functions should not be combined into a single process, because it would quite likely be difficult to program more than one periodic function within the suspend/resume conditions of the process. In Ada, for example, we can specify a periodic interval with a delay statement. The Ada task will be suspended for (at least) the period specified, and it will be difficult to have more than one delay statement representing (accurately) different periodic functions within the single task. If periodic tasks compete for the use of a processor, they can be specified with a high priority to ensure a minimum latency for the expiration of the period.

5. **Computational requirements.** Transforms that are not time critical (and often computationally intensive) can be designed as background processes (low priority) that will consume spare CPU cycles.

6. **Temporal cohesion.** Transforms that perform certain functions during the same time period, or immediately following certain events, can be combined into a single process. Each function should be implemented as a separate module or set of instructions within the process. This contributes to functional cohesion at the module level, but only temporal cohesion within the process.

7. **Storage limitations.** Virtual storage limitations may dictate the creation of additional processes by splitting up any process that is found to be too

large. This limitation may apply to processors that use only 16 bits (or fewer) for virtual address calculations. Although not a conceptual issue of concurrent processing, this is frequently a practical issue for older processors. For our software-first approach, this will not be a problem since we will simply choose a modern 32-bit processor that can support the required amount of memory.

8. **Database functions.** Functions that need access to a shared database can be collected in a single process with mutual exclusion for the access mechanism, and the structure of the database hidden. This is the concept of a monitor [HOA74, NIE88], and can be implemented in Ada with a package that specifies the access routines. A task implemented with a selective wait statement can provide the required mutual exclusion.

9. **Asynchronous functions.** Functions (other than the external device drivers mentioned in 1 above) that appear independently and sporadically throughout the operation of the system should be separate processes. Examples of this type of function include (1) data recording that is activated and terminated at irregular intervals by an operator; and (2) an alert function that manages the queueing and display of alerts as they are received from the various processes.

10. **Minimizing communication.** The combination of functions into processes should be made such that the overall communication between the processes is minimized. When the processes are later distributed among a set of processors, this design consideration will result in a lower overall remote communication latency for the system. (This consideration is also brought up to a higher level when we later develop the virtual nodes.)

11. **Minimizing total number of processes.** Every effort should be made to keep the number of processes to a minimum. There is a significant amount of run-time overhead associated with each process in the form of context switching, scheduling, and dispatching. Too many processes can eat up valuable run-time resources.

To identify a set of suitable processes for the robot controller functions shown in the CDFD in Figure 7.1, we first use rule number 1. The functions interfacing directly with external devices are allocated as processes. This may be modified later if it is determined that functions that are closely related to the device drivers should be included with the driver based on rules 2 or 6. The processes identified for the robot controller are shown in Figure 7.2.

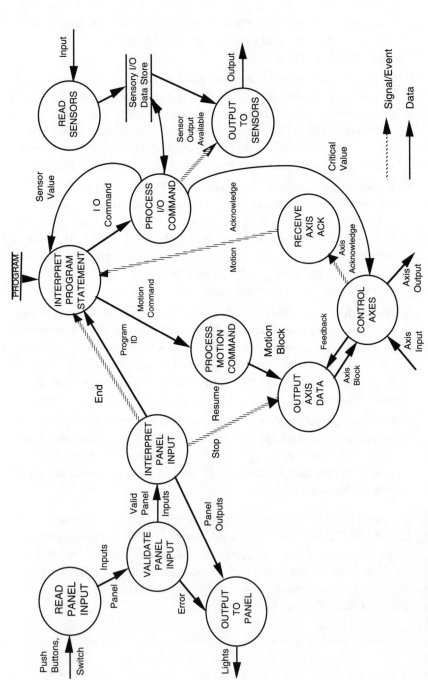

Figure 7.1 Robot Controller CDFD

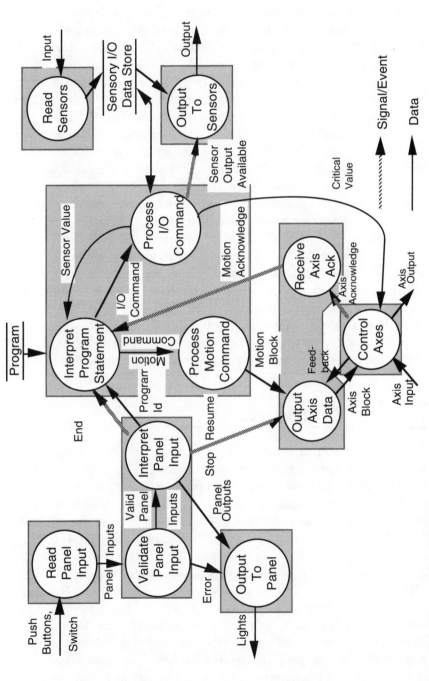

Figure 7.2 Process Identification

Rules 2 and 6 have been used to combine the functions Validate Panel Input and Interpret Panel Input into a process. The same two rules have been used in combining Interpret Program Statement, Process Motion Command, and Process I/O Command. Rule 6 has been used in combining Output Axis Data and Receive Axis Ack. Even though we have not explicitly used rule number 8 in Figure 7.2, we clearly note the data area Sensory I/O Data Store and the fact that it is accessed by three different processes. This data store must either be included with one of the other processes or encapsulated in a separate process. It is identified as an abstract object with the final design decision deferred until the interfaces between the processes have been established.

The identification of the system processes is a major step in the transitioning procedure from analysis to design. The abstract objects resulting from this identification are represented by the circles in Figure 7.3. The semantics of the circles is significantly different from the circles used in CDFDs where they are simply functions. The processes shown in Figure 7.3 are abstract design objects that will be implemented in software as, for example, independently executing Ada tasks, or Unix or VMS processes. Another significant aspect of the processes shown in Figure 7.3 are the connections between them. This is another important step in the transitioning from analysis to design.

The representation of the processes is illustrated in the Process Structure Chart. Each process depicts an independent node in a network; there is no hierarchy associated with this chart as is the case with traditional structure charts (depicting a subprogram calling tree). Each node represents an abstract object that will be converted to one or more design objects during the design phase.

7.2 PROCESS INTERFACES

Another important part of the transitioning phase is the determination of the interfaces between the concurrent elements represented by the process abstraction. The processes shown for the robot controller in Figure 7.3 are pairwise connected. These connections symbolize a particular coupling between each producer/consumer pair of processes. The producer CP Input Handler passes Panel Inputs to the consumer CP Cmd Interpreter, and represents a tight coupling. The producer is waiting (may be suspended) until the consumer has accepted the data. An even tighter coupling is illustrated by the producer Axis Manager, which passes the data Axis Block to the consumer Robot Handler. In this case the producer is not only waiting until the data is received by the consumer, it is also waiting for a reply (Axis Ack and Feedback). The loosest form of coupling is illustrated between the producer Program Interpreter and the consumer Axis Manager. The "pump" symbol shown between these two processes signifies that the producer does not want to wait for the consumer to

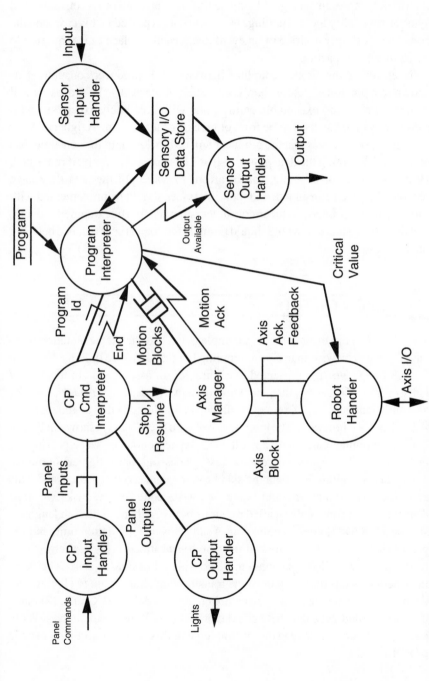

Figure 7.3 Robot Controller Process Structure Chart

accept the data (Motion Blocks), and the two processes are thus decoupled from each other. The "lightning bolt" (e.g., between Axis Manager and Program Interpreter) represents a signal being sent from a producer to a consumer and symbolizes a fairly loose coupling. No actual data is passed in this case, and the consumer is simply notified of an event that has taken place or is requested to perform a certain action.

Determining the proper coupling between each producer/consumer pair shown in a process structure chart is extremely important. The processes will be transformed into executable entities, and will most likely execute under a run-time system that uses some form of blocking mechanism. A tight coupling in such a system means that the producer will be blocked until the consumer has completed accepting the data passed to it and has prepared a reply, if requested. Device drivers, for example, can ill afford to wait until the data they have received has been consumed, and their interfaces should be implemented with a loose coupling. Each producer/consumer pair must first be examined in detail, and then the system as a whole should be analyzed for a proper balance between the processes.

7.3 DESIGN OBJECTS

A *design object* in this context is a complete, but abstract, representation of an entity that can be written in a programming language as code or PDL (Program Design Language) and presented to a compiler (or assembler). In the case of Unix or VMS processes, they can be written in, for example, Ada, C, C++, or assembly language. Each process will then be implemented as an independent Ada, C, or C++ program. The interfaces between the processes shown in Figure 7.3 can be implemented with a mailbox or asynchronous message passing for the loose coupling, and synchronous message passing for the tighter couplings.

Ada tasks communicate via the synchronous rendezvous mechanism. This is a blocking mechanism, and before we write code for any tasks we must determine the proper caller/called relations between them. The Ada language standard [DOD83] does not allow an Ada task as a compilation unit, and the circles shown in Figure 7.3 are still at too high an abstraction (even after we have made the caller/called decisions) to be considered design objects. The other intermediate steps that are part of the transitioning strategy are to (1) translate the processes from the process structure chart to an Ada Task Graph; (2) make the caller/called decisions between the tasks; and (3) encapsulate the tasks in packages. The packages can then be implemented as Ada design objects in code or PDL.

7.4 ADA TASK INTERFACES

The robot controller process structure illustrated in Figure 7.3 has been transformed to the task structure shown in the Ada Task Graph in Figure 7.4. The loose coupling between the producer Program Interpreter and the consumer Axis Manager has been implemented by adding the Ada buffer task Buffer_Motion_Blocks. Other intermediary tasks can be introduced to create the desired coupling between the processes [NIE88]. The data area Sensory I/O Data Store has been included in the added task Protect_Sensor_Data, implying that all data accesses will be made via entry calls to this task. The remaining interfaces will be accomplished with the rendezvous after a detailed analysis of the proper caller/called decisions.

7.5 CALLER/CALLED DECISIONS

The Ada tasking model includes a synchronization mechanism (rendezvous) for inter-task communication. This mechanism has a direct effect on the behavior of the tasks in the system, since it includes a blocking scheme. Calling tasks are blocked until a rendezvous is completed. If the called task is not ready to accept a call, the caller is blocked and placed on a queue until the called task is ready. It thus becomes necessary to perform a careful caller/called analysis before the tasks are coded in Ada. As an aid to this analysis, a set of conventions and heuristics [NIE88, NIE90] has been prepared to guide the analysts through the decision process. The caller/called decision rules are the following:

1. **Device drivers.** Device drivers can be pure servers or hybrids for interrupt driven devices. These drivers will contain entries for the interrupt handling, and, possibly, an entry for the interface with other application tasks. It may alternately make a call to the interfacing application tasks, and thus become a hybrid. For devices that require polling, hybrid tasks or pure callers are the most likely choice. These drivers will poll the devices via calls to see if they are ready for input or output. They may contain entries for the interfaces with the other application tasks, or they may make calls to these tasks.

2. **Controlling tasks.** Tasks that need to control a rendezvous are called. The control is typically implemented with guarded entries, nested rendezvous, exception handling with inner frames, and the use of the Count attribute.

3. **Busy tasks.** Busy tasks are called. "Busy" refers to tasks that can interact with several other tasks, i.e., there are several entries specified within a single task. If a busy task is allowed to make calls to other busy tasks, severe delays could be experienced for the calling task.

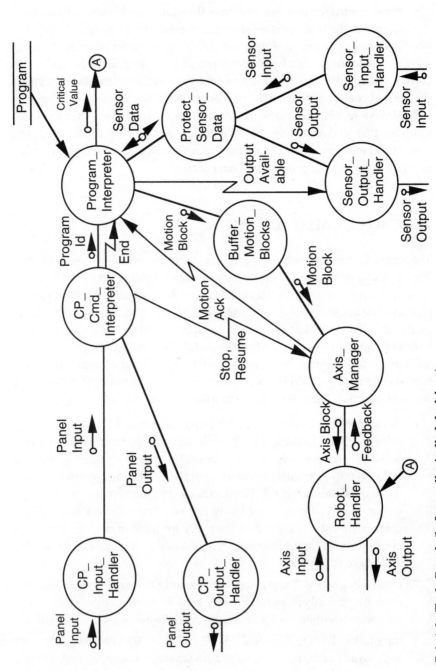

Figure 7.4 Ada Task Graph (before caller/called decisions)

4. **Complex tasks.** Algorithmically complex tasks are callers. This will reduce their complexity compared to making them called tasks. A call within a task represents an abstraction of a portion of the algorithm, and thus reduces the complexity of that task body.

5. **Service tasks.** Tasks with functions that provide the equivalent of executive services should be pure servers, like a buffer task used to store input or output data.

6. **Avoid hybrids, if possible.** If the choice (in conjunction with the heuristics given above) is between a hybrid or a pure caller or server, avoid the hybrid. This will enforce the notion of active or passive tasks discussed above and advocated by Pyle [PYL85] and Burns [BUR85].

7. **Minimize interprocessor communication.** A buffer task and data analysis task may be included with an I/O device driver to reduce message passing between processors. This could effectively reverse the caller/ called direction of entry calls derived for a uniprocessor design. The additional processing performed by the analysis task could be to strip off message headers and to check error codes. The amount of data crossing the communication medium could thus be substantially reduced.

8. **Allow polling.** In a uniprocessor design, polling implies "busy wait" which usually wastes resources. Active and passive tasks are carefully constructed to only allow polling where it cannot be avoided. In a distributed design, however, polling is of much less concern because there are fewer tasks per processor and busy wait is less important.

Using the rules listed above, the Ada task graph has been completed as shown in Figure 7.5. Each pair of tasks must first be subjected to the caller/called analysis, and then the overall task structure is evaluated for a proper balance. In completing the Ada task graph, we made use of some conventions that simplify the decisions somewhat: buffer and monitor tasks are always called (Buffer_Motion_Blocks and Protect_Sensor_Data, respectively). Similar conventions can be made for other intermediaries [NIE88]: transporter tasks should always be callers, and relays should be hybrids with one entry for accepting data and should act as callers to deliver the data to the consumer.

The final step of the transitioning from requirements analysis to design for an Ada development is the packaging of all the tasks shown in the final Ada task graph.

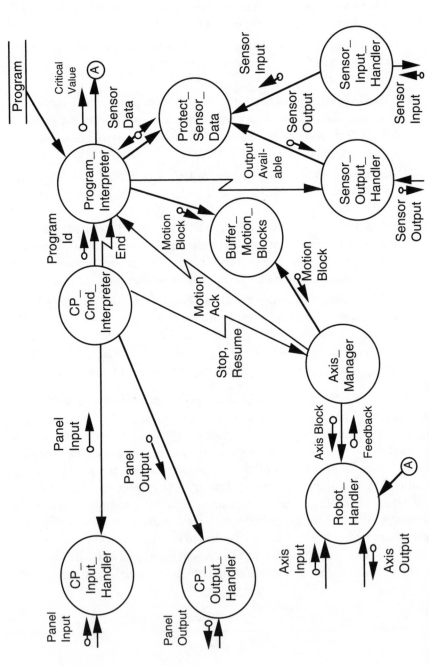

Figure 7.5 Ada Task Graph (after caller/called decisions)

7.6 ADA PACKAGING

Ada tasks must be encapsulated in either subprograms or packages before they can be presented to an Ada compiler. We will assume here that the proper encapsulation mechanism for the Ada tasks derived during the process abstraction phase is an Ada package. The Ada task structure shown in Figure 7.5 has been packaged using the following rules:

1. **Encapsulation module.** Tasks can reside in subprograms, tasks, and packages. Nesting of tasks is not recommended, since the debugging process can be extremely complex. This leaves us the choice between placing tasks in packages or subprograms. The only tasks recommended for placement within a subprogram are tasks used as simulators or for special debugging purposes. These tasks should then be placed in the main procedure for maximum control of the debugging process. The recommended placement of tasks is within packages, unless a specification requirement makes it mandatory to put a task within a subprogram.

2. **Functionality.** Tasks can be grouped within the same package if their functionalities are related, and it is not envisioned that the tasks will ever be distributed to different processors.

3. **Reusability.** Special purpose tasks, e.g., buffers, transporters, and relays, that can be used by several units within the program (or by other programs) should be placed in packages as library units. These packages should be generic, if possible, for maximum reusability.

4. **Coupling.** Tasks should be placed in packages such that the coupling is minimized with respect to data types, operations, and constants that are imported from the encapsulating package.

5. **Visibility.** The package structure should provide for minimum visibility of task entries. Task specifications should be hidden in package bodies, and entrance procedures provided for interactions between tasks that reside in different packages. Special consideration must be given to whether entrance procedures should handle conditional or timed entry calls, or if the task specification should be moved to the package specification to provide these services directly. The entrance procedures may also be required to interface with an interprocessor communication mechanism in distributed systems.

6. **Dependency.** The chosen package structure should result in a minimum dependency (use of *with* clauses) between the packages. It is desirable to confine *with*ing to package bodies, rather than package specifications.

7. **Recompilation.** The chosen package structure should result in a minimum amount of recompilation when any of the packages are changed.

This is closely associated with the dependency issue described above. Minimum recompilation will occur when the required *with*ing is performed by the subunits (for tasks or subprograms) rather than by the package specification or body that encapsulate the tasks or subprograms. This also implies that helper packages should not be nested within the application packages, but should be made independent library units. The use of the *separate* statement for task bodies declared inside a package body supports an incremental development strategy and minimizes recompilation.

8. **Object orientation.** Every effort should be made to construct application packages that represent objects that support encapsulation and loosely coupled modules.

9. **Data stores.** A data store that appears on a DFD and is accessed by two or more tasks applying non-atomic operations on the data should be protected by a monitor task which is encapsulated in a package.

The polygons shown in Figure 7.6 are Ada packages that encapsulate one or more Ada tasks. These packages are Ada design objects and correspond to the application packages described in an earlier chapter as part of the package taxonomy. The application packages represented graphically in Figure 7.6 will be coded in Ada as compilation units that will be configured as one or more Ada programs in a distributed real-time system. The functionality expressed within each application package can be traced directly back to a capability or subfunction specified in the software requirements document. To promote reusability, additional design considerations will be made to ensure that the design objects are not cognizant of the hardware architecture. This is described further in Chapter 11.

The determination of the set of Ada application packages (or Unix or VMS processes) that contain the functions listed in the requirements specification completes the transitioning phase from analysis to design. The final objects of this step are the graphical design objects from which code or PDL can be written in the implementation language. PDL is also written for the abstract data objects identified during the OOA phase. We see clearly from this how the transitioning phase and OOA are complementary pieces of the development strategy, and not orthogonal.

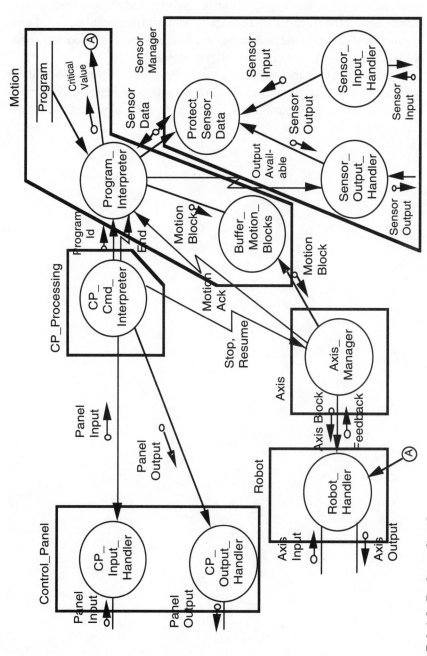

Figure 7.6 Ada Package Graph

Summary

A necessary step in the overall software development strategy for real-time systems is the transitioning phase from analysis requirements to design. This phase employs the process abstraction paradigm with the identification of a set of concurrent elements and their interfaces. These elements are nodes in a non-hierarchical network, and represent abstract design objects.

A strict OOA/OOD approach may create a similar set of objects, but with no consideration for concurrency. The proper interfaces between concurrent elements will have to be retrofitted into the objects, with a high likelihood of the necessity for costly design changes.

8

Data Abstraction

Proper design of objects identified during the domain analysis, data modeling, and process abstraction steps can result in a significant amount of reusability. This is accomplished by encapsulating only one major data structure as a type, and by carefully identifying all the operations associated with declared objects of that type. The resulting design objects support a loosely coupled system, and provides components that can be reused in the construction of different systems within the same problem domain. We also describe a hierarchy of data abstraction domains where modules can be reused across different problem domains.

There are a number of different ways to perform the data encapsulation and advantages and disadvantages associated with each approach. The various approaches and their tradeoffs are described in the sections that follow.

The objects described here are not restricted to those discovered during the analysis phase. They may also be discovered during the decomposition of other objects in the preliminary and detailed design phases.

8.1 DATA ABSTRACTION AS A DESIGN PARADIGM

The concept of data abstraction is based on the combination of procedural abstraction (calling subprograms with parameters) and abstraction by specification [LIS86]. A data structure, declared as a type, and the operations required to manipulate objects of the type are specified together and collected as a program module. The module represents an encapsulation of the type and the

105

operations, and the operations are considered an interface for affecting the behavior of objects of the type.

The complete specification of objects include the attributes (characteristics) associated with a particular object. For objects created with data abstraction, the attributes include the data elements that describe the object as a type. If, for example, the object is an instance of type Tracks, attributes will include such things as track number, position, altitude, and speed. These attributes will be visible as parameters in the invocation of the operations associated with the object. There may also be internal attributes (e.g., the size of a track file) that are hidden from the users. Some attributes may be implemented as Observer Operations, e.g., Empty, Full, Member_Of, etc. (see Section 6.5).

The paradigm of information hiding is closely associated with encapsulation. The object-orientation of an encapsulated module was described in Chapter 2, and is shown in Figure 8.1. The module boundary presents the interface to the users of the operations, but the actual data structure (e.g., components of a record) and the implementations of the operations are hidden from the users. As long as the interface remains the same, we may change the implementation (e.g., make it more efficient) without affecting the rest of the program modules.

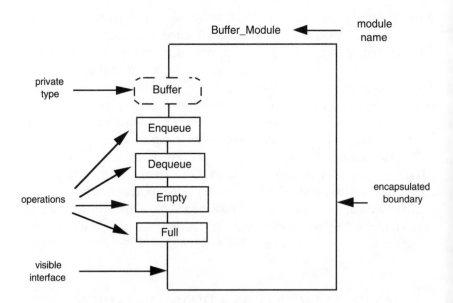

Figure 8.1 Object View of Encapsulated Module

An example of an abstract buffer type (for integers) using Ada is the following:

```
package Buffer_Module is
   type Buffer is private;
   procedure Enqueue
               (I : in  Integer; B : in out Buffer);
   procedure Dequeue
               (I : out Integer; B : in out Buffer);
   function Empty (B : in Buffer) return Boolean;
   function Full  (B : in Buffer) return Boolean;
   private
   . . .
end Buffer_Module;
```

The package Buffer_Module encapsulates the (private) type Buffer and the operations that modify and describe the behavior of objects of the type Buffer. The package specification presents the interface to users of this module, and the data structure of the private type is "hidden" in the private part. The implementation of the operations are hidden in the package body of Buffer_Module (not shown). In this case the operations Empty and Full can be considered attributes of the buffer objects and are visible on the module boundary. Other attributes include the type of the elements to be stored (Integer), and the size of the buffer (hidden from the users).

Another example of an encapsulated object is the following Stack abstraction implemented in C++:

```
class Stack {
private:
     long stackItems[50];
     int stackPtr;
public:
     void stackInit();
     long topOfStack();
     long pop();
     void push(long);
};
```

This represents the interface to users of the class with stackItems as the type, and stackInit, topOfStack, pop, and push the operations allowed on objects of the type. Attributes of instantiated objects include the size of the stack (fixed at 50 elements), and the elements to be managed (long integers).

The data abstraction paradigm can be utilized at different levels and during the different development phases. One way to describe these different views is by including a data abstraction domain hierarchy [BAI89]:

- Application domain. The specific problem domain such as air traffic control, robotics, satellite tracking, etc.

- Technology domain. Supporting domains such as communications (e.g., IPC), database management, and graphics interfaces.

- Computer science domain. List managers, stacks, queue managers, etc.

- Execution domain. Supporting domains for specific execution environments, e.g., storage allocation, process activation and termination, and error handling.

The ADTs shown above for the buffer module and stack manager belong to the computer science domain. An example of an ADT for the application domain is a Sensor_Manager object encapsulating the Sensory I/O Data Store shown in Figure 7.3:

```
package Sensor_Manager is
   type Sensors is private
   procedure Manage_Sensor_Data
                 (Sensor_Data : in out Sensors);
   procedure Output_Available;
   ...
private
   type Sensors is ...;
   ...
end Sensor_Manager;
```

The operations associated with this design object include Manage_Sensor_Data and Output_Available, with the latter representing a signal. The attributes associated with objects of type Sensors include the type of sensor data to be managed, critical values, and the size of the sensor data storage (hidden from the users).

Examples of data managers that fit in the other domain levels will be presented in subsequent chapters, e.g., an IPC module that belongs to the technology domain (see Chapter 11).

The advantage of using data abstraction as a design paradigm is that it supports the creation of highly modular design objects with a good opportunity for reuse. The well defined interfaces provide a loose coupling between the modules using the abstract data type, and changes can be made to the implementation without affecting the rest of the system. Abstract data types (ADTs) can be created for a number of common data structures, such as stacks, queues, and lists, as well as for the specific application domain, and reused from one project to another. If additional operations are required, the interface is modified for the new capabilities. The parts of the system that are using the data abstraction must be recompiled for the new specification, but they do not have to be redesigned.

A potential disadvantage with information hiding is that users are unable to extend the operations listed in the interface specification; the changes must be made to the encapsulated module.

8.2 IMPLEMENTING CLASSES AND OBJECTS

A number of data structures are usually identified during the requirements analysis. These are documented as objects and classes and listed with their associated attributes and operations. During the analysis phase these objects are abstractions, e.g., a track file, and during the design phase they are transformed to design objects, e.g., Track_File_Monitor. We may uncover additional data abstractions when we are performing the process abstraction analysis. The latter will be required to support the functionality of the application packages (or processes) and will be implemented as design objects in addition to the ones determined via the data modeling effort. The data abstractions discovered during these initial development phases will normally fall into the application and technology domains.

Numerous data structures are normally discovered during detailed design as the processes are decomposed, resulting in additional data abstractions that will fall into all four of the data abstraction domains.

How the abstract objects are implemented as design objects depends on a number of different variables, many of which were discussed in Chapter 4 describing the Ada package taxonomy. We will now review the relative merits of the Ada package objects with regard to data abstraction.

8.3 DATA MANAGERS

We described different forms of data managers in the discussion about the Ada package taxonomy. The choices were to use services, open or closed type managers, or an object manager. The least desirable of these, from a reusability standpoint, is the use of services packages (see Figure 4.3). This creates a tightly coupled system, and the degree of reusability will be quite low. A services package is simply a collection of operations that are specified separately from the associated type and data structure, and is not a good design object. Any changes in the type specification, for example, will require a redesign of all the application packages using that type. Services packages do not satisfy the strict definition of data managers and should never appear at the application domain level. They may be available as directly reusable program entities in the form of mathematical libraries, graphics interfaces, or bindings to communication interfaces or operating system services, i.e., at the technology, computer science, and execution levels.

A better implementation of a data abstraction is the use of an abstract data type (ADT) or type manager. The type of the data structure is specified in a package specification with the associated operations. The open type manager (see Figure 4.4) is not as desirable as the closed (use of a private type) type manager (see Figure 4.5), and should only be used if the clients using the type manager must have access to the components of the data type. The closed type manager represents the best design object for systems where more than one instance of the data structure is required. The data structure is then hidden from the users of the type managers, and the detailed implementation can be changed without affecting the rest of the system. The internal program object (variable declared in the user program) must be passed as a subprogram parameter to all type managers.

If only a single instance of a data structure, e.g., a track file, is required in a system, an object manager is preferred (see Figure 4.6) over a type manager. In this case, not only is the type of the data structure hidden, the instance of the (single) object is declared internally to the design object and is also hidden from the user. This represents very loose coupling between the modules in the system that require access to the single data structure. A high degree of reusability can be expected for reconfiguration of a system, or for constructing small, medium, or large systems within the problem domain: Since the internal program object is completely hidden from the user, it is never passed as a subprogram parameter to the object manager. This may also improve the run-time performance.

Data managers (type and object managers) will appear at all domain levels except execution. Many of these objects will be discovered during detailed design.

8.4 MONITORS

A monitor is a more complex design object than a data manager in that it also provides mutually exclusive access to the data structure in a real-time system. It is usually implemented with a set of operations that are accessed via procedure calls, and each call is handled in mutual exclusion with respect to the data structure access. A monitor will usually have more operations than a data manager to obtain the required data security. The actual implementation of the mutual exclusion is hidden to the user of the monitor, and could be designed with, for example, multiple accept bodies within a single Ada task:

```
with Track_Defs;   use Track_Defs;
package Track_File_Monitor is
   procedure Add_Track (Track_ID : out Track_Number;
                        X, Y     : in  Coordinates);
```

```
Track_Store_Full : exception; -- raised by Add_Track

procedure Get_Next_Track
                    (X, Y      : out Coordinates;
                     Track_ID : out Track_Number);
No_More_Tracks : exception;
                          -- raised by Get_Next_Track

procedure Drop_Track (Track_ID : in Track_Number);

procedure Update_Track
                    (X, Y      : in Coordinates;
                     Track_ID : in Track_Number);
end Track_File_Monitor;
```

The detailed implementation of this specification is hidden inside the task body of a task that is specified in the package body:

```
package body Track_File_Monitor is

   task Monitor is

      entry Add (Track_ID : out Track_Number;
                 X, Y      : in  Coordinates;
                 Full      : out Boolean);
      entry Get_Next (X, Y      : out Coordinates;
                      Track_ID : out Track_Number);
      entry Drop (Track_ID : in Track_Number);
      entry Update (X, Y      : in Coordinates;
                    Track_ID : in Track_Number);
      entry Correlate (X, Y : in Coordinates);
      entry Extrapolate;
   end Monitor;
   ...
end Track-File-Monitor;

with Track_Services; use Track_Services;
separate (Track_File_Monitor)
   task body Monitor is
      Track_Storage : Track_File;
                 -- this is the internal program object
      Last_Track    : Track_Count := 0;

   begin
      loop
         select
```

```
      accept Add (Track_ID : out Track_Number;
                  X, Y     : in  Coordinates;
                  Full     : out Boolean) do
         Full := Last_Track = Track_Count'Last;
         if Last_Track < Track_Count'Last then
            Last_Track := Last_Track + 1;
            Track_Services.Update
                    (Track_Storage X, Y, Last_Track);
         end if;
      end Add;
   or
      accept Get_Next
                  (X, Y     : out Coordinates;
                   Track_ID : out Track_Number) do
         Track_Services.Get_Next (Track_Storage,
                             X, Y, Track_ID);
      end Get_Next;
   or
      accept Drop (Track_ID : in Track_Number) do
            Track_Services.Drop
                    (Track_Storage, Track_ID);
      end Drop;
   or
      accept Update
                  (X, Y     : in Coordinates;
                   Track_ID : in Track_Number) do
         Track_Services.Update (Track_Storage,
                             X, Y, Track_ID);
      end Update;
   or
      accept Correlate (X, Y : in Coordinates) do
         Track_Services.Correlate
                        (Track_Storage, X, Y);
      end Correlate;
   or
      accept Extrapolate do
         Track_Services.Extrapolate (Track_Storage);
      end Extrapolate;
   end select;
 end loop;
end Monitor;
```

Calls to the monitor are intercepted by the entrance procedures listed in the package specification and relay the calls to the proper task entry. Each accept body in the task Monitor will execute as a critical section and guarantee mutually exclusive access to the data structure Track_Storage.

The structure and interfaces of data monitors are extremely important for achieving reusability. A complete set of operations and associated parameter types should be considered when the monitor is designed. The internal implementation must be carefully constructed to provide the required mutual exclusion. This type of object will usually be apparent at the application domain level, and possibly at the technology level.

8.5 DATABASE ISSUES

The primary choices to be made during the preliminary design phase (or as early as the analysis phase) include the implementation of the data structure using data managers and monitors, shared data, message passing, or database management systems (DBMSs). Each approach can be used, but there are significant run-time issues to consider. Shared data, for example, is usually efficient, but a locking mechanism is required for data integrity when non-atomic operations are performed. This mechanism is not promising for reusability because it is usually linked to operating system services (e.g., semaphores and Test and Set instructions). This also provides for extremely tight coupling between the modules accessing the data structure. A different problem is how the data should be represented in an architecture that includes heterogeneous processors. Data representations may be different among the processors, and additional run-time overhead will be expended with data transformations and copying.

A DBMS is very general and usually offers a high degree of reusability, but is (in many cases) very inefficient. Another potential drawback with DBMSs is that they may require a special interface as a layer between the application and the database manager, e.g., an Ada binding to SQL. If such a binding does not exist, it will have to be developed at additional expense. Some DBMSs may also be very restrictive in the number of data types they can handle. They may, for example, only be able to recognize integer, floating point, boolean, and strings as data types. This will be in serious contrast to the unlimited typing that can be created in Ada. One solution to the heavy overhead of a DBMS is to host it on its own processor. This will not compete for processing power with the applications modules, but it will increase the hardware cost and communication time. Additional database issues are considered in Chapter 12.

Data managers and monitors fall somewhere in between shared data and DBMSs. Closed type managers and object managers are excellent design objects for creating reusable systems, and can be made to execute efficiently. Special care must be paid to the design of monitors and the mechanism used to provide mutual exclusion. In the example shown above for the Monitor task, every access to an accept body is via a rendezvous. The rendezvous mechanism involves context switching and blocking of the callers that will directly affect the run-time performance. A more efficient monitor can be built within a package structure, provided an adequate locking mechanism can be provided. A monitor implemented with a task adds the overhead associated with context switching and task management. Home-grown DBMS objects will appear at the application level, whereas the reuse of an existing DBMS object will be at the technology level.

Summary

The use of data abstraction is a very important step for achieving design modules with a high degree of reusability. An object created with the data abstraction paradigm encapsulates a data structure, the operations required for managing the data structure, and a set of attributes.

The data abstraction paradigm is used during all of the different software development phases and represent different design views. These different views can be expressed with a data abstraction domain hierarchy:

• Application domain

• Technology domain

• Computer science domain

• Execution domain

The encapsulated objects we will design with data abstraction for real-time systems include type and object managers, monitors, and DBMS. The objects will appear at all levels of the domain hierarchy.

Besides the efforts required in creating design objects that provide loosely coupled systems, the designers should be on constant lookout for the possibility of using Ada generics. Parameterized type and object managers offer the highest possible potential for reuse. A considerable drawback with the use of generics can be in systems that employ restarts. The use of Ada generics may add significantly to the elaboration time and could prevent a timely restart procedure.

9

Modules and Interfaces

One of the most important aspects of designing for reusability is the creation of loose couplings between the software modules that represent the system requirements. This type of coupling is accomplished with a careful design of the interfaces between the modules. By "module" in this context we mean Ada packages and tasks, C++ classes and subclasses, Unix, VMS, etc. processes, and any higher level combination of these entities to produce a virtual node in a distributed system [NIE90]. A module can even be implemented as a complete Ada program within an operating system process.

9.1 ENCAPSULATION

We have seen examples of data managers as design objects where a type and its associated operations are completely encapsulated within an Ada package, e.g., a stack abstraction:

```
package Stack_ADT is
   type Stacks is private;
   subtype Elements is Natural range 0 .. 100;
   procedure Push (Stack : in out Stacks;
                   Item  : in      Elements);
   procedure Pop  (Stack : in out Stacks;
                   Item  : out     Elements);
   function Top_Of (Stack : in Stacks) return Elements;
```

```
Stack_Empty    : exception; -- raised in Pop
Stack_Overflow : exception; -- raised in Push
private
    -- code for type Stacks
end Stack_ADT;
```

We have encapsulated a stack abstraction with the private type Stacks and the operations Push, Pop, and Top_Of. The operations provide clean interfaces to this module, and the implementation details are hidden entirely within the package body of Stack_ADT. Every effort should be made to encapsulate major data structures within Ada packages with well defined interfaces. This promotes a high degree of reusability where modules can be reused not only within a current program, but also for programs in other problem domains. By well defined interfaces, we mean:

- Properly named operations.
- A complete set of operations for all expected users.
- Minimum and sufficient number of parameters in the parameter lists.
- Properly named exported exceptions.
- An indication of where exceptions are raised.
- Only user defined exceptions listed in the package specification will be exported out of the package.
- Use of *private* types whenever possible.
- All implementation details hidden in the package body.

9.2 ENTRANCE PROCEDURES

We extend the concept of making operations visible in the package specifications to the packages that contain the application tasks. These are the application packages referred to in our Ada package taxonomy, and we severely restrict inter-task communication between tasks residing in different application packages. Only tasks that are specified within the same application package (body) are allowed to interface directly via task rendezvous. By restricting inter-task communication we can distribute application packages, and tasks within an application package do not need to know anything about the hardware architecture hosting the Ada program(s). The interfaces for inter-task communication will be provided as *entrance procedures* visible in the package specification:

```
with Robot_Definitions;  use Robot_Definitions;
package Motion is
    procedure Start_Program (Id : in Program_Id);
```

```
procedure End_Event;
procedure Motion_Ack;
procedure Dequeue_Motion_Block
              (M_Block : out Motion_Block);
end Motion;


package body Motion is
  task Program_Interpreter is
    entry Start_Program (Id : in Program_Id);
    entry End_Event;
    entry Motion_Ack;
  end Program_Interpreter;


  task body Program_Interpreter is separate;


  procedure Start_Program
              (Id : in Program_Id) is separate;
  procedure End_Event    is separate;
  procedure Motion_Ack   is separate;
  procedure Dequeue_Motion_Block
          (M_Block : out Motion_Block) is separate;
end Motion;
```

We note that the task specifications are entirely hidden in the package body. The visible entrance procedures make the necessary entry calls, and the user of this package is not aware of the tasks. If someday we decide to implement the functionality encapsulated within this package without tasks, or by adding other tasks, this can be done without changing the module interfaces. This is in direct support of the reusability we are hoping to achieve. A graphical representation of the object Motion is shown in Figure 9.1.

9.3 MODULES IN DISTRIBUTED SYSTEMS

A concept similar to entrance procedures can be used in distributed systems. The entrance procedures for incoming access are augmented with "exit" procedures to intercept calls to subprograms that may reside in another process or processor. An "exit" procedure may be a part of an interprocess communication (IPC) mechanism that executes on behalf of the caller. The achievement of reusability in distributed systems is even more dependent on clean module interfaces than in uniprocessor systems. Processes are allocated among processors and should not have any knowledge about the actual hardware architecture. If the processes are tightly coupled, a redesign would have to be done each time a system is configured for a new hardware architecture, and reusability would be greatly curtailed. The recommended design of IPC mechanisms is treated in more detail in Chapter 11. The concept of an exit procedure is shown in Figure 9.2.

9.4 EXCEPTION HANDLING

If exception handling is implemented to provide error detection and possible recovery, it must be designed into the software solution. A loose coupling is realized when the exceptions are designed as part of the module interfaces. For data managers this is accomplished in Ada by declaring exceptions in the package specification, along with types and operations:

```
package Stack_ADT is
   type Stacks is private;
   subtype Elements is Natural range 0 .. 100;
   procedure Push (Stack : in out Stacks;
                   Item  : in      Elements);
   procedure Pop  (Stack : in out Stacks;
                   Item  : out     Elements);
   function Top_Of (Stack : in Stacks) return Elements;
```

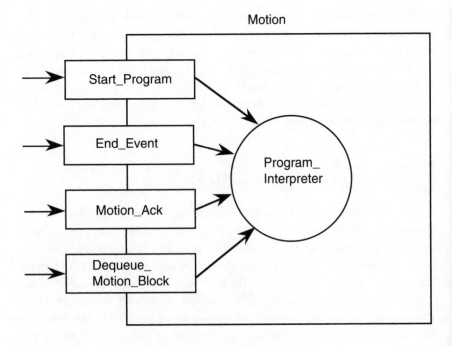

Figure 9.1 Calls to Visible Entrance Procedures

```
Stack_Overflow : exception;  -- raised in Push
Stack_Empty    : exception;
                        -- raised in Pop and Top_Of
private
  -- code for type Stacks
end Stack_ADT;
```

The user of this package should expect Stack_Overflow to be propagated as an exception when the operation Push is called, and Stack_Empty when Pop and Top_Of are called, and should prepare the necessary exception handlers.

For application packages the exceptions are declared with the entrance procedures:

```
with Robot_Definitions;  use Robot_Definitions;
package Motion is
  procedure Start_Program (Id : in Program_Id);
  procedure End_Event;
  procedure Motion_Ack;
  procedure Dequeue_Motion_Block
              (M_Block : out Motion_Block);
  Illegal_Motion_Command : exception;
                        -- raised in Motion_Ack
end Motion;
```

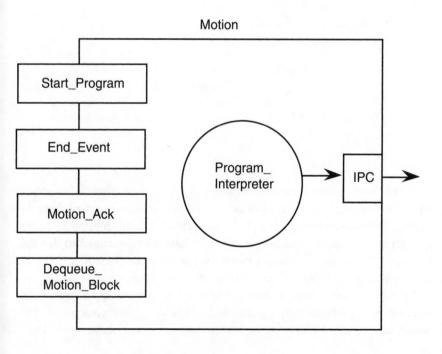

Figure 9.2 Call to Internal Exit Procedure

A user of any of these packages (by *with*ing) must include suitable exception handlers to capture the exceptions propagated from within the imported packages. It is up to the user to decide what recovery actions should be taken once an exception is captured in the handler.

A design rule to enforce compliance with the module interfaces is that no exception other than what is specified in the package specification should be propagated out of a package. This means that predefined exceptions, for example, that are detected within a package boundary must be handled locally, and not propagated out of the package. If an exception is to be reraised within a package, it can only be one of the exceptions declared in the package specification. These simple rules provide well defined interfaces and keep the modules loosely coupled.

9.5 GENERICS

An even higher level of reusability can be achieved by parameterizing Ada packages:

```
generic
   type Index_Type is range <>;
   type Element is private;
package Buffer_Module is
   type Buffer is private;
   procedure Enqueue
               (I : in   Element; B : in out Buffer);
   procedure Dequeue
               (I : out Element; B : in out Buffer);
   Buffer_Empty : exception; -- raised in Dequeue
   Buffer_Full  : exception; -- raised in Enqueue
private
   . . .
end Buffer_Module;
```

The parameters for this package are Index_Type for specifying the buffer size and Element, which is the type of item to be placed in or removed from the buffer. The module interfaces include the operations and exceptions, just as a non-generic package. The only things that have to be changed to use this package for a buffer of different length and buffer elements is to specify the index type and the type of elements to be stored in the buffer.

A generic package can easily be extended by adding parameters and operations, and keeping in mind that subprograms can be passed as generic parameters. This allows the creation of library packages that make calls to unknown consumers:

```
generic
  Size : in Natural := 20;
  type Item is private;
  with procedure Consumer (C : in Item);

package Buffer_Relay is
  procedure Enqueue (I : in Item);
end Buffer_Relay;

package body Buffer_Relay is
  task Buffer is
     entry Enqueue (I : in  Item);
     entry Dequeue (I : out Item);
  end Buffer;

  task Transporter is
    -- Calls
       -- Buffer.Dequeue
       -- Consumer
  end Transporter;

  task body Transporter is
    X : Item;
  begin
    loop
      Buffer.Dequeue (X);
      Consumer (X);   -- generic parameter
    end loop;
  end Transporter;

  task body Buffer is separate;

  procedure Enqueue (I : in Item) is
  begin
    Buffer.Enqueue (I);
  end Enqueue;

end Buffer_Relay;
```

An instantiation of this relay is illustrated as follows:

```
...
package New_Relay is Buffer_Relay
  (Size    => Max_Relay_Size,
   Item    => Relay_Elements,
```

```
Consumer => Imported_Package.Operation);
```

The call to the unknown Consumer inside the Transporter task will refer to the operation specified in the imported package as the actual parameter.

9.6 BINDINGS

If we want to access a set of modules that are part of a DBMS, we should create a layer between our application packages and the DBMS to provide a loose coupling between the modules requiring access and the implementation of the DBMS. This also applies if we want to use a set of routines written in another programming language, e.g., C routines to interface with xlib, TCP/IP or RPC (Remote Procedure Call). This layer is usually referred to as a "binding," and shields our application modules from the implementation details of the underlying DBMS, windowing approach, or communication mechanism. We are primarily concerned with Ada bindings, and they do exist for SQL, xlib, and TCP/IP.

The interface to the SQL Ada binding is made via procedure calls and the passing of parameters. One problem with using an Ada binding to SQL is the limited number of types that SQL can accept. The rich typing structure of Ada is lost, and parameters passed to SQL must be based on the primitives that SQL will accept.

Some of the Ada vendors provide packages that allow access to low level TCP/IP mechanisms. These packages come as modules with a complete set of interfaces for making connections to ports and sockets, for sending synchronous and asynchronous messages, and for receiving messages [TEL88]. Vendor packages are also available for interfacing with xlib and X Window.

The advantages of using an Ada binding as a layer between the application modules and the low level details are that a standard set of interfaces can be used throughout the system, and that a complete layer can be replaced without causing a major redesign of the system. A disadvantage is that the binding may be implementation dependent, and when we switch to another hardware architecture, a new binding is required, but may not be available and additional efforts or expenses are required. A different binding may require a different set of interfaces, and the calls to the binding will then have to be redone.

9.7 ADAPTATION PARAMETERS

Adaptation parameters are values used to initialize a program for a given hardware configuration. This may take place once every morning, or whenever a system is first started up, or repeatedly during normal operation as restarts are necessary to satisfy certain fault tolerance requirements. Examples of adaptation parameters include the number of tracks that can be handled in a tracking system, the hardware configuration for a small, medium, or large system within a certain problem domain, and periodicities for when certain data elements should be displayed on a screen.

The following three types of adaptation parameters are usually employed in real-time systems:

1. **Fixed.** Fixed adaptation parameters are unique for a given system, and do not change during execution of the program. Examples include number of tracks in a track file and time periods for updating a display. These parameters are treated as constants, and their values are established at compilation time. There are two basic methods of creating design objects to encapsulate these values: (1) all the adaptation values can be assembled in a single package that is globally visible; and (2) the adaptation values that belong to an application package or data manager are declared in the body of their respective packages. The first method makes it easy to locate a particular adaptation parameter, but whenever a value is changed, all the modules referencing the global package must be recompiled. The second method makes it harder to locate adaptation values, but provides a better design object. When an adaptation value changes, only the affected modules need to be recompiled, not the whole system as in the first case. The fixed adaptation values are usually set by an operator using off-line services.

2. **Variable system parameters (VSPs).** These are system parameters that can be changed by an operator on-line while the program is executing. An example of a VSP is the number of minutes after an estimated time of departure that an ATC flight plan should be brought up by the computer. The design will need to accommodate these requests dynamically without having to shut down the system. This can be accomplished with a module that runs as a separate process that accepts the request for change and distributes the changes to the affected modules. The adaptation module must be designed in consonance with the other application modules and provide the proper interfaces. This is especially important in a distributed system where the changed VSPs may have to be sent to different processors.

3. **Configuration parameters.** These parameters are set during start-up and for any restart that may occur. Examples of configuration parameters include the number of sensors that are on line for a data acquisition system, the number and mode of processors, e.g., active and standby for a specific hardware architecture, and the number of active LANs in a communica-

tion system. The values for these parameters are determined during program elaboration and cannot be changed after the system has (re)started. The simplest way to handle this case is for a configuration manager (Ada package) to include the necessary code in the executable part of its package body to reset the necessary values. The design must be carefully analyzed to make sure that tasks specified with the configuration manager are not already executing and attempting to use the values that need to be changed. (For details regarding the order of program elaboration and task activation, see [SHU88b, Chapter 11].)

The proper design of objects to encapsulate adaptation parameters will greatly influence the potential for reusability and fault tolerance. Small, medium, and large systems can be constructed by varying the adaptation parameters to fit the desired system. If some of the hardware elements become faulty, adaptation parameters can be used to reconfigure the system with the remaining hardware.

Summary

The structure of the module interfaces is *the* most important design aspect for realizing a high degree of reusability. If the modules are closely coupled, major redesign efforts can be expected when even minor changes occur. If the modules are created as well-encapsulated objects with clean interfaces, maximum reusability should be expected even in distributed systems.

Exception handling should be an integral part of module interfaces. Restricting the level of exception propagation can greatly reduce the complexity of a module interface, and will support the object-orientation of the design objects.

Another aspect of having a design with well defined interfaces is that it facilitates teams of developers working on parts of the overall system. After the different teams agree on the interfaces and the required Ada types for the parameter lists in the operations, each team can then continue to develop Ada PDL and use the interfaces to the packages developed by the other teams. This prevents significant amounts of redesign when the teams finally integrate their software modules into the complete system solution.

10

Layering of Objects

In the previous chapter we noted that one of the most important design features for realizing a high degree of module reusability was to provide well designed interfaces between the modules. It is also imperative that the functionality represented by a module is properly encapsulated and that the module design employs information hiding. If the hidden details inside a module are changed, only minor effects are inflicted on the other modules in the system.

The concept of loose coupling between modules can be expanded to include sets of objects that represent an abstract layer in a hierarchy of layers. This is of particular importance in real-time systems, which are inherently of a high complexity. A loose coupling between layers implies that if one or more of the modules in a particular layer is modified or replaced, it will only affect the layer above it.

The concept of layering was pioneered by Dijkstra in his description of the design for the "THE" - Multiprogramming System [DIJ68]. This system was designed to support a number of user terminals, and was organized in a hierarchy of multiple layers as shown in Figure 10.1. Each successive layer is viewed as an abstraction of layered machines to hide (abstract away) the details of the lower level layers.

We noted in some of the earlier chapters that one of the problems with a pure object-oriented development process for real-time systems is the difficulty in transitioning between the various development phases. One way to alleviate this difficulty is to envision a set of abstract layered virtual objects as the result of each step in the transitioning. We are thus expanding Dijkstra's layered notion here to include layers of abstract objects, even before the design phase begins.

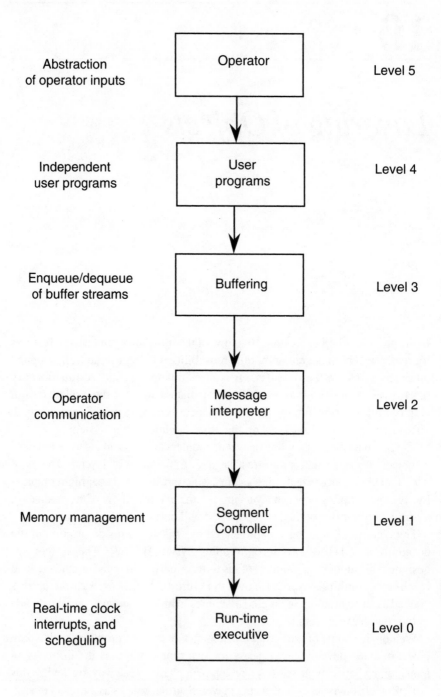

Figure 10.1 Layering in THE Multiprogramming System

This chapter describes a layered object-oriented development approach for real-time systems implemented in Ada. Objects are defined for each step of the development with a series of layered virtual "machines," which represent the objects through top level design. The approach is illustrated with the design of a simplified version of a robot controller.

10.1 DOMAIN ANALYSIS

The expanded view of layering is illustrated in Figure 10.2. The documentation used to collect the data for each layer is shown with an acronym to the left, and the development step to the right of the layer (parallelogram). The first layer is created during the domain analysis when the original abstract classes and objects are identified. The system functional specification (SFS) is used to create the products emanating from this step, which are the conceptual real-world classes and objects that represent the major functions of the application. Examples of these products include Radars, Radar Interfaces, Data Links, Temperature Sensors, Robot Joints, and Message Handlers.

10.2 REQUIREMENTS ANALYSIS

Control and Data Flow Diagrams (CDFDs) are created from the software requirements specification (SRS) to identify the major functional transforms and the data flows and control flows between them. The transforms illustrated in the DFD shown in Figure 10.3 for a robot controller represent a layer of abstract functional objects. The data flows and control logic illustrate the interfaces between the objects shown on the CDFD. At the end of the requirements analysis we have a set of abstract data objects, and the transforms representing the major functional decomposition. The major data abstraction shown in Figure 10.3 is the Sensory I/O Data Store. The transforms and associated data structures must be subjected to a concurrency analysis before they can be transformed to actual design objects.

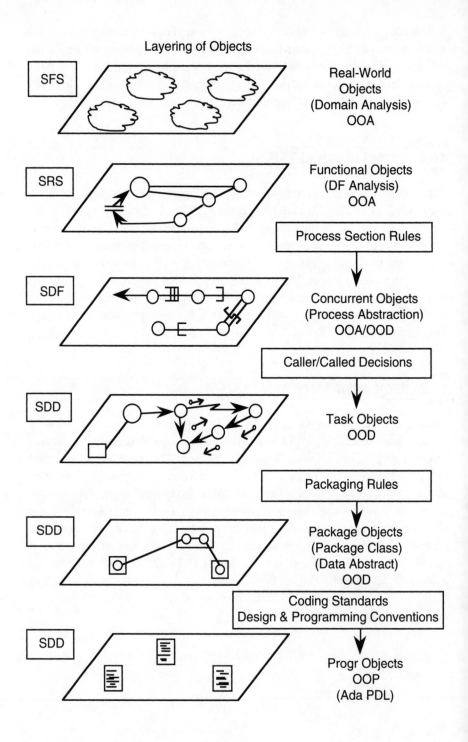

Figure 10.2 Vertical Layering of Objects

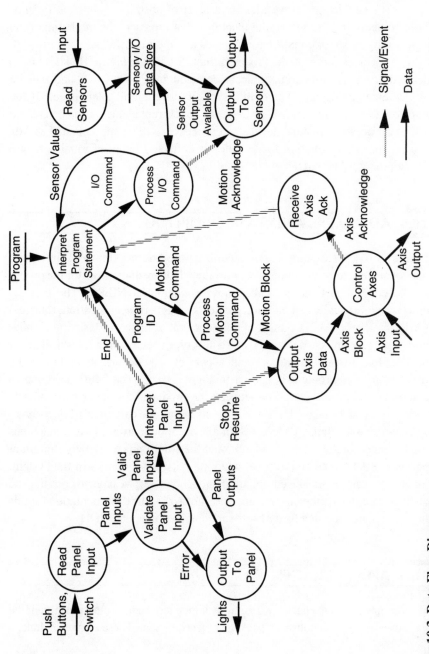

Figure 10.3 Data Flow Diagram

10.3 CONCURRENCY ANALYSIS

Using the CDFDs and a set of heuristics for combining functions into concurrent elements (see Chapter 7) we identify a layer of abstract *concurrent objects*. These objects are virtual parallel machines that represent the modeling of the problem into a set of concurrent processes and their interfaces.

The processes shown in the Process Structure Chart in Figure 10.4 have been derived from the functional objects depicted in Figure 10.3, and can be implemented as design objects in a specific programming language. If the implementation language is C or C++, the concurrent elements can be created as Unix processes. In Ada, the abstract processes will be implemented as Ada tasks. The documentation for this step is collected in an informal software development folder (SDF).

10.4 ADA TASKS AND TASK COUPLING

From the process structure chart we determine the Ada tasks that will implement our concurrent solution model. We introduce intermediary tasks for the proper level of coupling between *producer* and *consumer* tasks [NIE86]. The intermediary tasks are usually instantiations (objects) of generic specifications (classes) for buffers, relays, and transporters. Identical application tasks are implemented as task objects declared using a task type specification (class). The set of Ada objects (tasks) that represents a layer of one concurrent solution to the robot controller problem is shown in Figure 10.5. The heuristics used to determine the proper coupling between the producer/consumer pairs of Ada tasks were listed in Chapter 7 when we discussed the caller/called decisions.

The circles in Figure 10.5 represent a layer of concurrent, virtual machines implemented as Ada tasks. This view of the solution is extremely important because it determines the overall coupling between the tasks in the system. Since Ada tasks cannot be compilation units, however, we have to continue the analysis one step further and encapsulate the tasks. The documentation for this layer is maintained in a formal software design document (SDD).

10.5 ADA PACKAGES

We saw in Chapter 4 a package taxonomy which represents a classification of the various ways we can construct package objects in Ada. These classes include:

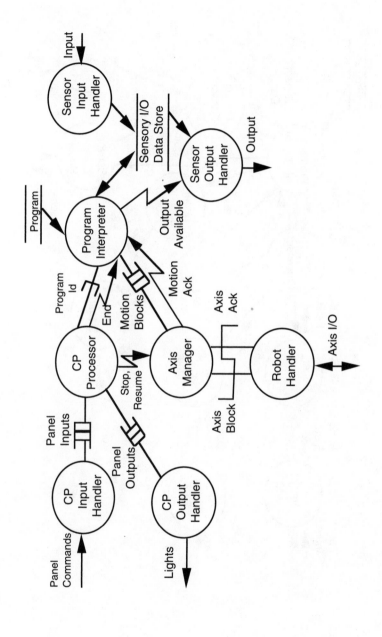

Figure 10.4 Process Structure Chart

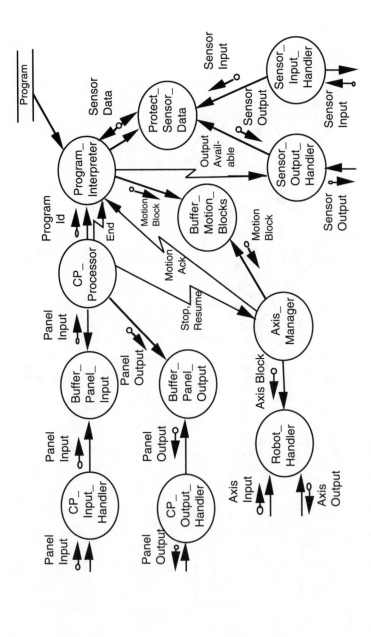

Figure 10.5 Ada Task Graph (after caller/called decisions)

1. Application packages.
2. Communication packages.
3. Helper packages (including Definitions, Services, Open and Closed Type Managers (Abstract Data Types), and Object Managers).

We can, for example, implement an open or a closed package (object) as an abstract data type (class), or we may choose an object manager instead. Some of these packages are created as instantiations (objects) of generic specifications (classes). The recommended technique for encapsulating Ada tasks is to declare them in package bodies and provide entrance procedures for inter-package task access. This provides a loose coupling between the tasks and supports reusability both in uniprocessor and distributed architectures.

The Ada application packages shown in Figure 10.6 portray the top level design objects for the robot controller. This layer represents the actual design objects that can be written in Ada PDL or code, and is a *module* view rather than a *machine* view shown for the abstract processes and Ada tasks. During the packaging we are concerned with the creation of modules, their interfaces, and how to document them. When we create the processes and tasks, we are constantly evaluating the design decision made with regard to run-time performance, potential for deadlock, producer/consumer coupling, etc. The documentation for this layer is also maintained in the SDD.

10.6 LVM/OOD

The process abstraction effort culminates with a concurrency model that includes a set of cooperating Ada tasks encapsulated in Ada packages. Each of these tasks has a single thread of control (although they may declare nested task objects dynamically during system operation). Each application task represents a major portion of the system requirements, and may have too large a functionality to be expressed as code statements within its task body. Each task body will by convention be limited to a certain (approximate) number of lines of Ada code statements, and will have to be decomposed if the approximate line count is exceeded.

This section describes the Layered Virtual Machine/Object-Oriented Design (LVM/OOD) approach [NIE88] to decomposing large Ada tasks into packages and subprograms to support the functionality of a given task. This is a continuation of the packaging described in Section 10.5, and relevant documentation is maintained in the SDD.

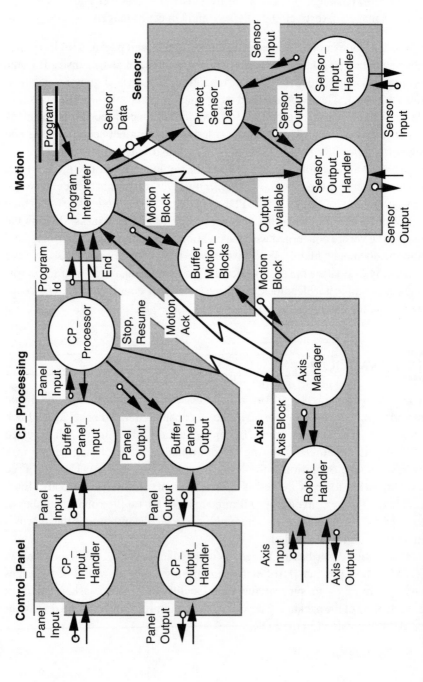

Figure 10.6 Ada Package Graph

Layered virtual machines can be created at different levels of abstraction. We have already seen examples of layered virtual machines in the form of cooperating sequential processes as Ada tasks based on process abstraction (see Figure 10.5). For our purposes, we will be employing functional and data abstraction in parallel during the decomposition of the large Ada tasks. The functional abstraction will result in a set of layered high level "instructions," i.e., procedure calls and function invocations, that will support a hierarchy of layered virtual machines. A virtual machine in this context will consist of a set of abstract instructions that will solve a given problem, i.e., support the implementation of the functionality of the specific virtual machine. The instructions will consist of lower level virtual machines (subprogram calls) and operations on objects.

In addition to the functional abstraction that will create the hierarchy of layered machines, we must also take data abstraction into account. Data abstraction is concerned with data types, data values, and operations on instances of objects of the given types.

To decompose large Ada tasks we have a parallel concern for functional abstraction with a resulting hierarchy of layered virtual machines, and data abstraction with a resulting set of packages that encapsulate that abstraction. This parallelism is illustrated in Figure 10.7 and shows the intimate linking between the virtual machines and the operations on objects. The left side of this figure shows the layered virtual machines, and the right side the objects that represent the data abstraction. The virtual machine instructions make use of the operations visible on the object (Ada package) boundary. A given object may use lower level objects to support its operations, but this would be invisible to the virtual machine instructions. This relationship is shown in Figure 10.8.

The approach to the decomposition of large Ada tasks is to develop, in parallel, the hierarchy of virtual machine instructions and the objects and their operations that support these instructions. The functional decomposition proceeds according to the guidelines of traditional structured design, and the resulting hierarchy is illustrated with structure charts. Every effort is made to organize the instructions (Ada subprogram calls) that support a higher level virtual machine in horizontal layers. This will allow only a minimal impact on the virtual machine if any of the instructions are modified. The data abstractions used to support the virtual machine instructions are created with Ada packages in the form of the data managers listed in Figure 4.1. Services packages may also be used to support the virtual machine instructions. The operations are declared in the package specification, and the implementations are hidden in the package body. The actual data objects may be internal to the package for object managers or declared externally by the user of the object for open or closed ADTs.

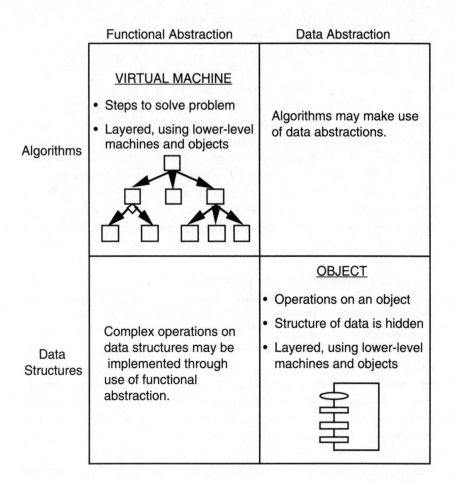

	Functional Abstraction	Data Abstraction
Algorithms	**VIRTUAL MACHINE** • Steps to solve problem • Layered, using lower-level machines and objects	Algorithms may make use of data abstractions.
Data Structures	Complex operations on data structures may be implemented through use of functional abstraction.	**OBJECT** • Operations on an object • Structure of data is hidden • Layered, using lower-level machines and objects

Figure 10.7 Functional and Data Abstraction

This is the lowest level layering in the development hierarchy, and the particular step involved is detailed design. Depending upon the size and complexity of an individual task, each task decomposition may result in several layers to include all the virtual machines.

A potential disadvantage of using the LVM/OOD approach is that the layering may become too finely grained, resulting in many very small subprograms. A large number of subprogram calls may increase the run-time overhead during execution, unless the compiler optimizes the calls with in-lining. This may also be accomplished by using the pragma *Inline*, but now the system solution is compiler dependent. Another disadvantage of a large number of compilation units is the increased effort required for configuration control.

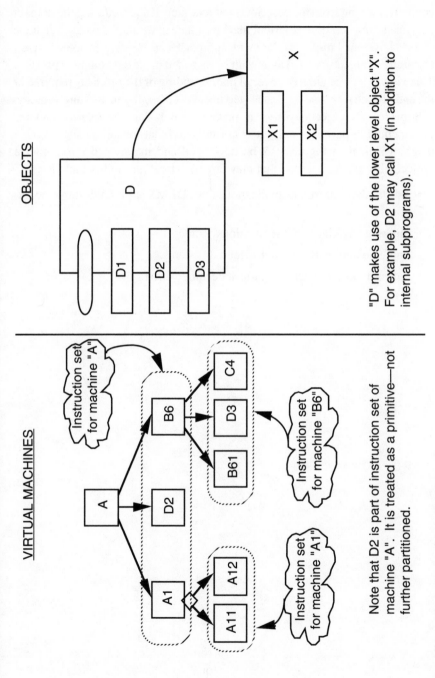

VIRTUAL MACHINES

Instruction set for machine "A"

A

D2

A1

A11   A12

Instruction set for machine "A1"

B6

B61   D3   C4

Instruction set for machine "B6"

Note that D2 is part of instruction set of machine "A". It is treated as a primitive—not further partitioned.

OBJECTS

D

D1

D2

D3

X

X1

X2

"D" makes use of the lower level object "X". For example, D2 may call X1 (in addition to internal subprograms).

Figure 10.8 Virtual Machines and Objects

Summary

We have seen how the concept of layering can be used in many different contexts, ranging from the description of real-world objects during the domain analysis to the creation of virtual machines during detailed design. We have shown how our entire development approach can be viewed as a layered hierarchy of objects created as a result of each step in the development process. This view is a great aid to an overall understanding of the products required at the end of each step, and how each step fits in the overall transitioning strategy.

Some of the object layering is primarily of pedagogic interest and for documentation purposes only; it is not intended that the composite layering diagram shown in Figure 10.2 be developed and maintained throughout a project. The object layering that may directly affect reusability includes:

- Ada bindings to isolate applications from DBMS or graphics implementations.
- Implementation of communications protocols.
- Implementation of IPC in distributed systems.
- Layered virtual machines for task decomposition.

11

Objects in Distributed Systems

One of the major design issues in a distributed real-time system is how well the details of the communication mechanism can be hidden from the application modules. If a high degree of reusability is to be realized in such a system, it is imperative that module interfaces be carefully constructed to allow redistribution of major application functions to different processors. In a large ATC system, for example, the modules performing the flight data processing and tracking functions could reside on separate processors. In a smaller system, however, these same functions may have reduced functionality and will reside in the same processor.

An additional dimension has been added to the design complexity by the distributivity requirements. The programming objects that are deemed to be distributable should have direct knowledge neither of other processes within their local processor, nor of processes residing on the other processors in the distributed system. If all interprocess communication is hidden from the programming objects that make up the application packages, these packages can be distributed among processors without major rippling effects throughout the system.

This chapter describes various design approaches that may be taken to profit from maximum reuse of software components that can be distributed among processors without a major redesign effort. The focus is placed on employing standard communication protocols and models that are publicly available, and avoiding proprietary approaches.

11.1 DISTRIBUTED REAL-TIME SYSTEMS

Tremendous advances have been made in processor technology during the last few years, and modern microprocessors are used in a wide range of complex real-time systems. Most of these real-time systems are inherently concurrent, and efficient solutions are designed using the parallel architecture of distributed heterogeneous processors and other hardware units that are connected via a network. Examples of such systems include air traffic control, process automation, remote sensing and data acquisition, and robotics. Distributed systems also include multiple workstations that are connected to one or more file servers, but they are of less interest here.

The primary advantages of using distributed architectures in real-time systems include a highly modular design with major functional areas allocated to different processors, a high degree of extendibility, and the potential for fault tolerance. An example of a distributed system is shown in Figure 11.1. A processing element (PE) may have its own local memory (M), or it may have access to shared memory. The processing elements can be homogeneous or heterogeneous and are connected via a network. The network will usually consist of a combination of buses for processing elements that reside within the same chassis, and local area networks (LANs) or wide area networks (WANs) for processing elements that are physically separated. The specific communication mechanism chosen depends on the physical distance between the processors and the bandwidth required. Shared memory can be used for processors that are in close physical proximity, but considerable care must be exercised to maintain data integrity.

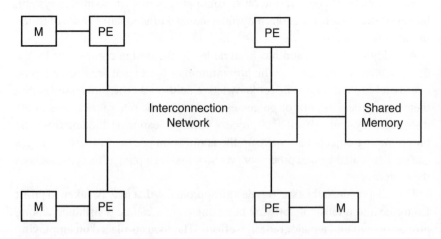

Figure 11.1 Distributed System of Processing Elements (PEs) with Local Memories and Shared Memory

The key to a successful distributed architecture solution is an implementation of an efficient interprocessor communication (IPC) mechanism. This requires a combination of effective message protocols and sufficiently high bandwidths within the network to sustain the message traffic. The IPC is probably the most important design element in a distributed software solution for a real-time system. It does not matter how fast the individual processors are if they cannot communicate efficiently. An inefficient IPC may suffocate a distributed system and create a communication bottleneck regardless of how fast the individual processors may operate. The design of the IPC is also crucial for the realization of maximum reusability when a new system is built. If the IPC does not effectively shield the applications from the details of the communication mechanism, a major redesign should be expected when a new system is composed for a different hardware architecture.

11.2 DESIGN ISSUES

The primary design issues for reusability concern the structure of the communication software and the granularity of units to be distributed. The design of the application modules follow the general guidelines outlined in earlier chapters, but we now have a new dimension in attempting to shield the application modules from the details of the communication mechanism.

To enhance the opportunity for reuse of components, we expand the communications considerations to include interprocess communication, in addition to interprocessor data exchanges. This will permit a looser module coupling if any of the components are reconfigured to another processor in a system restart. This is illustrated in Figure 11.2, where the IPC mechanism is shown as an interface both within as well as between the processors. If, for example, the Ada rendezvous was used between two packages residing in different processes, a significant amount of redesign would have to take place if one of the packages was moved to another processor and a remote rendezvous was not available. (It is not included in the LRM [DOD83].)

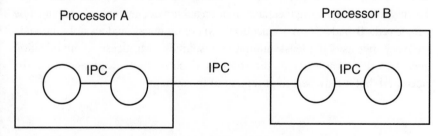

Figure 11.2 Interprocess Communication Mechanism

To achieve transparency of the interprocess communication mechanism, the predominant design paradigm is to create the software modules in layers and to use standard protocols. The layering will provide a degree of information hiding where a complete layer can be replaced and only affect the layer above. It is highly recommended that only publicly available protocols be used to avoid becoming locked into certain vendors' implementations. These choices may, for example, include the Open Systems Interconnection (OSI) or Transmission Control Protocol/Internet Protocol (TCP/IP). An example of protocol layering is shown in Figure 11.3 for the OSI and a DoD protocol. If we choose the OSI model, the software modules will have specific interfaces between each layer, and the modules in each layer will only need to support the functionality of its respective layer. The OSI model implements all seven layers, whereas the DoD protocol only uses four of the seven.

A distributed system can be implemented with shared data as the communication mechanism between application modules. This can lead to major problems, however, and message passing is the preferred method of transferring data in a distributed system. If shared data is used, it must be protected with a locking mechanism to provide data integrity via mutually exclusive access by concurrent elements. Another problem is that data representations are different for heterogeneous processors. Data transformations will have to be provided at the application level, and will reduce the level of reusability that can be accomplished with message passing. In the latter case, data transformations can be implemented in a lower layer and made transparent to the application modules. The major advantage of using shared data is higher efficiency if care is taken to avoid repeated copying of the data elements.

Regardless of the communication mechanism chosen, every effort must be made to minimize the amount of data transformation taking place. There should be no transformations made for data passed between homogeneous processors in a heterogeneous system.

A significant design issue is the choice (or combination) of point to point, broadcast, and multicast communication. This choice is dependent on the security of the system. The use of point to point connection will guarantee delivery of a message, but uses lots of resources, and may be slow since either a synchronized blocking mechanism or an acknowledgement scheme must be employed. Broadcast (or connectionless) communication does not guarantee delivery, but uses the least amount of resources. Multicast communication increases the complexity of the solution since multiple destinations can be specified, but it may be a requirement of the system.

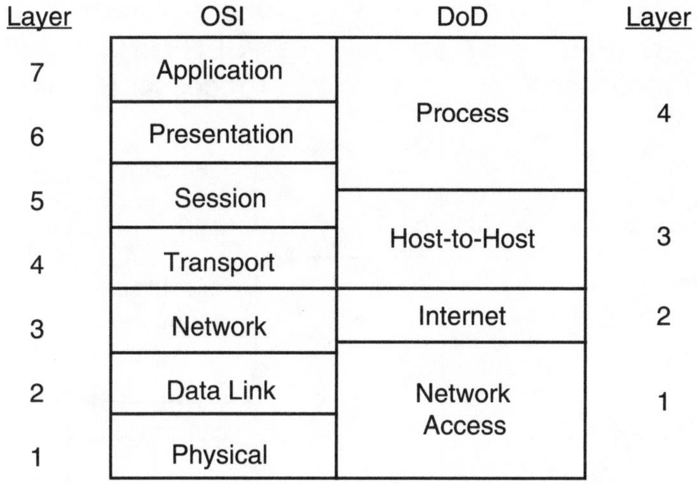

Layer	OSI	DoD	Layer
7	Application	Process	4
6	Presentation		
5	Session	Host-to-Host	3
4	Transport		
3	Network	Internet	2
2	Data Link	Network Access	1
1	Physical		

Figure 11.3 Protocol Layering

11.3 REMOTE PROCEDURE CALLS (RPC)

The basic idea behind RPC is to make the interprocess communication an extension to the programming language by furnishing a set of software modules callable from the application program. This provides a *uniform* method for communication between processes in a network. The approach applies to processes that reside on the same processor as well as to those that reside on different processors. This method is well proven and is documented in numerous publications [SUN86, COU91, COR91]. The primary design feature that distinguishes RPC from message passing is that an application using RPC is calling an actual operation. When an application is using message passing, the message type determines the operation to be performed. Another difference is that the caller is usually blocked until the call is accepted, but not necessarily completed. Message passing can be implemented with or without a blocking mechanism.

The basic RPC communication paradigm is based on the client/server model illustrated in Figure 11.4. The calling program is a *client* and resides on one processor. The *server* resides on another processor and executes a procedure call on behalf of the client. The processors are connected by a network or a bus, and the interprocessor communication mechanism is completely transparent to the application program.

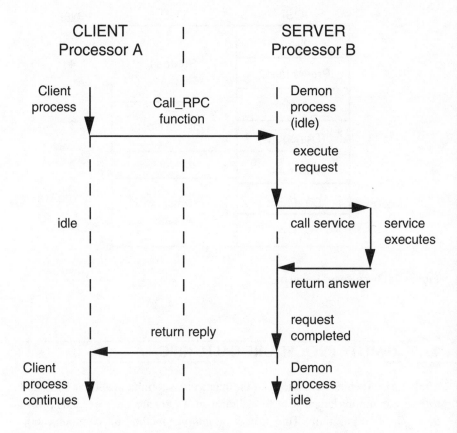

Figure 11.4 Client/Server Model for Remote Procedure Call

The low level protocols can be implemented with Transmission Control Protocol (TCP), User Datagram Protocol (UDP), Open Systems Interconnection (OSI), or any other suitable protocol. The application is completely insulated from the details of the implementation of the communication services. Parameters are passed between the client and the server in both directions on the network. Calls can be made for either synchronous or asynchronous communication. In the asynchronous mode, control is returned to the caller without a reply. The caller will subsequently make an inquiry about an expected reply.

In order to make the remoteness of the RPC call transparent to the user of the service, the server is copied on the client machine with a "stub" code. This code has exactly the same interface as the actual server on the server machine, but instead of performing the requested service, it simply passes the parameters in the procedure call to the server over the network. The server stub on the server machine is implemented as a demon process. It passes the parameters in the remote procedure call to the actual server and returns parameters to the client. The local and remote RPC subprogram call looks the same to the calling program, and this program does not realize (or care) that its request is actually forwarded to another processor. This approach provides for the lowest coupling between the application and the communication services, and provides a level of layering that supports a high degree of reusability. RPC will be implemented as layer 5 (session) in the OSI model shown in Figure 11.3.

The major disadvantage of the RPC approach is that appropriate services have to be established for each function required. In a distributed system with a large number of different services to be provided across the network, it may be more advantageous to implement a message passing system. It would then be easier to add a message type than a service as an RPC. The RPC mechanism is illustrated in Appendix A for an Add function implemented in Ada.

11.3.1 Sun Microsystems RPC

Sun Microsystems has designed an RPC as an open standard for remote procedure calls [SUN86]. The standard has been placed in the public domain, and support software is distributed free of charge. The Sun RPC is both machine and language independent, and defines a network standard for RPCs.

Using this standard, a "program" can be exported to the network. Each program has a program number as its own unique identifier. A program may have one or more procedures that will be accessed via RPCs. Each procedure within the program is given a number, typically in the order in which they appear in the program specification.

Sun RPC is built on top of UDP, and a special "portmapper" [COR91] is necessary to take care of the mapping between RPC program numbers and UDP port numbers. The portmapper can be called as a remote procedure and is the only RPC program with a fixed UDP port number. A *port* is an address or reference to a specific program on a remote processor.

11.3.2 External Data Representation

The distributed architectures utilized in many real-time systems employ heterogeneous processors. Data transferred from one processor to another must be transformed to the internal data representation of the receiving processor if the data is to be interpreted correctly. This may also preclude the use of shared data since memory references could be ambiguous. The data transformation from one format to another may represent a significant run-time overhead and must be performed efficiently. One way to implement this is to send the data over the network in a standard format and have each receiving processor transform the data to its proper internal format.

One of these network representations has been created by Sun Microsystems and is called XDR (eXternal Data Representation) [SUN86]. XDR defines how basic data types such as integer, boolean, etc. are represented on the network. This facilitates the connection of heterogeneous processors with different internal data representations and byte orderings. The type conversions can be made transparent to the application programs, and reusability is realized via the standard data format.

Figure 11.5 illustrates a model for the transformation that takes place between the standard representation and the representation on the respective client and server machines in a heterogeneous environment. Before data is sent over the network, it is translated to the XDR format. This means that a module receiving data from the network does not need to know anything about the processor that sent the data. The receiving module only has to translate from the standard XDR format to the internal representation of its associated processor. This provides a reasonable solution to the problems with the different byte orderings and unique data representations.

The modules required for the client/server functions and the data transformations should be implemented with a layered approach. XDR will represent layer 6 (presentation) in the OSI model shown in Figure 11.3.

The discussion up to this point has not considered language dependent program implementations. The most commonly used programming language for RPC implementations is C. The sections that follow will focus on task communication and synchronization in Ada and how RPC can be implemented for Ada programs.

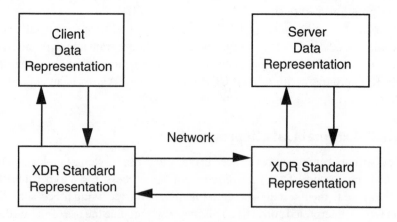

Figure 11.5 Transformation via Standard Data Representation

11.4 ADA AND DISTRIBUTED SYSTEMS

Since its initial language standardization in 1983 [DOD83], Ada has gained world-wide recognition as a suitable programming language for real-time systems. The language specification does not include any constructs or services for an IPC mechanism for task communication between tasks that reside on different processors, or for programs in different processes. Such an IPC mechanism will have to be developed as a part of a distributed software application, or obtained as a set of service routines that have already been created. This section describes the development of suitable IPC mechanisms for distributed real-time systems developed in Ada.

An example of a distributed real-time system is shown in Figure 11.6 for a remote temperature sensor system used to control the temperatures of a set of remote furnaces. The sensors are driven by a set of microprocessors that send the data they receive to the control unit (remote temperature controller). The latter microprocessor accepts commands from the host computer, and returns sensor data in the form of data packets. The host computer can be a mini, mainframe, or microprocessor depending upon how much processing has to be done on the data received. Multi-microprocessor systems offer low cost and programming flexibility for a variety of data acquisition systems.

The significance of a distributed Ada software design for a real-time system is that the distributed software modules represent the totality of the required functionality of a *single* application. The modules residing in the various processors have the need to communicate, and this necessitates an efficient IPC mechanism between the processors.

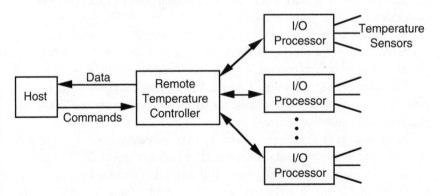

Figure 11.6 Remote Temperature Control System

11.4.1 Ada and Remote Communication

The normal Ada entry calls are not defined across processor or process boundaries. The concept of timed and conditional entry calls only have semantic definitions within a processor with a single system time. An "immediate" rendezvous for a conditional entry call across processors would have to have a specific time reference to the caller's or server's processor. The time spent during communication would also have to be accounted for. The same problem exists for a timed entry call regarding how the expiration of the delay time should be determined.

A model for remote entry calls (RECs) in Ada is shown in Figure 11.7 and is based on an approach reported in [ATK88]. The standard communication interface (SCI) can be replaced by an RPC layer and completely shield the application from the IPC mechanism. A remote rendezvous layer, the SCI, and the communication layer are all separating the application modules from the actual communication primitives, which could be implemented by TCP or UDP.

Here is yet another example of layering to promote loose coupling between modules and a high degree of reusability. The two remote rendezvous layers can be replaced by corresponding RPC layers without a major redesign of the software modules in the application layers. Remote conditional and timed entry calls used in the REC mechanism would not be allowed in an RPC approach.

11.4.2 Implementing RPC in Ada

The original Sun RPC services were intended for C programs executing under the Unix operating system. One implementation of the corresponding RPC services for Ada has been developed by the Swedish branch of TeleSoft AB, and is referred to as AdaLAN RPC [TEL88].

The unit of distribution in Sun RPC is a "program" with associated type declarations and procedures. The equivalent unit of distribution in Ada is a package, which consists of a specification part containing visible entities and a body containing hidden entities. A single Ada program may thus correspond to several RPC programs, since a typical Ada real-time program will consist of multiple application packages.

The entrance procedures (in the visible part of the package specification) are implemented in the (hidden) package body to either access an RPC service or make a local procedure or entry call. The internal mechanism is completely hidden from the users of the package, and the stub code for RPC can be implemented by a modified package body, i.e., a package body which performs RPC calls.

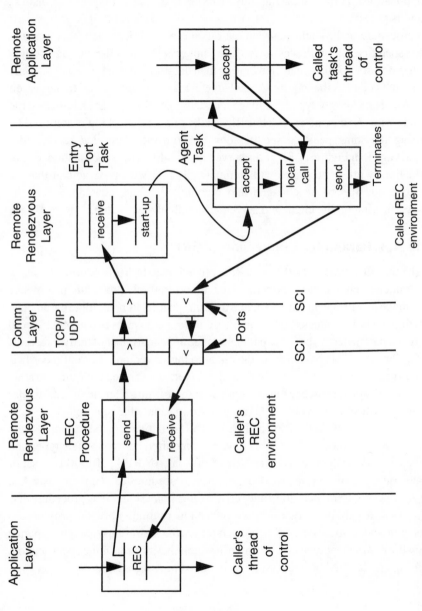

Figure 11.7 Remote Entry Call Model

The AdaLAN RPC concept is illustrated in Figure 11.8. The package body for P has been replaced by code which calls the server on Processor B. The application on Processor A has only visibility to the package specification of P, and is not affected by the calls to the server. The package P_RPC server calls a procedure in the package specification on Processor B, which is the same as the specification on Processor A. The implementation in the package body P on Processor B is the "real" body rather than the stub code on Processor A. Only the stub code has the required knowledge to make the remote call to the server.

Ada is a strongly typed language and does not allow programmers to write code with mixed data types. For RPC calls, this type checking is achieved by using the same package specification on both the client and server sides (package P in Figure 11.8). If the server side modifies the specification, one of the library utility programs will automatically notify the programmer that the client side has to be changed and recompiled. This guarantees that the specification on the client and server sides will always match.

11.4.3 Parameter Conversion (XDR)

The Sun RPC protocol defines an RPC procedure to be a procedure with one *in* parameter and one *out* parameter. Ada allows multiple procedure parameters of mode *in*, *out*, and *in out*. To match the Sun specification, multiple parameters will have to be collected into one record for *in* parameters and another record for *out* parameters. The *in out* parameters can appear in either of the two records. The "in record" is passed from the client to the server, and the "out record" is returned to the client as a reply from the server. The protocol requires exactly one in-parameter and one out-parameter. If there is no parameter in a particular direction, a special "void" type can be used to satisfy the requirement.

The parameters in the RPC call are sent on the network in the format defined in the XDR protocol. The type conversion required between Ada's types and the network XDR types is taken care of in AdaLAN RPC [TEL88] by a set of generic type conversion procedures. These procedures can convert basic Ada types such as enumeration, integer, floating point, etc. If a procedure has composite parameter types, new conversion routines must be provided to accommodate these types. The conversion routines for composite types operate on the component types in the order in which they appear in the specification. An example of XDR conversions is included in Appendix A.

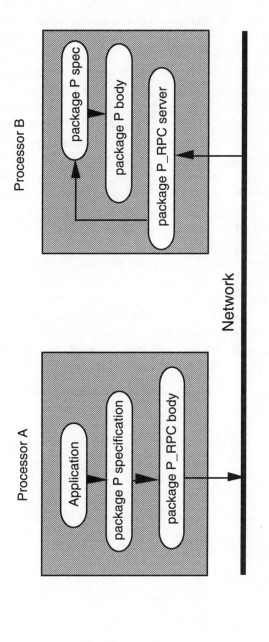

Figure 11.8 RPC in Ada

11.5 DESIGN PARADIGMS

One of the design paradigms employed for distributed real-time systems implemented in Ada, is to make the interprocessor task communication mechanism transparent to the tasks themselves. The only direct task-to-task interface allowed is between tasks that are encapsulated in the same master [SHU88b, BAR89], e.g., in the same Ada package. Packages are the basic building blocks of distributable *virtual nodes*, and tasks specified in the same package must necessarily reside on the same processor. A virtual node contains one or more Ada packages required to form an executable program unit on a given processor. The virtual nodes are mapped to physical processors with special software development tools. (A complete design methodology for distributed Ada systems is presented in [NIE90].) Conditional and timed entry calls are prohibited (by a design convention) between tasks residing in packages that may be distributed to different processors. This is only allowed for tasks residing within the same package.

We saw in earlier chapters that communication between tasks that reside in different packages is done via a protective layer of procedure calls; we called these procedures *entrance procedures*. This extra layer provides for transparency of local or remote entry calls. The entrance procedures will intercept calls to other application packages and determine whether the calls are local or remote. An example of the use of entrance procedures is shown with Ada PDL for a portion of a robot controller as follows:

```
with Robot_Definitions;  use Robot_Definitions;
package Axis is
  procedure Stop;
  procedure Resume;
  procedure Take_Block (B : in Motion_Block);
end Axis;

with Robot;
with Motion;
package body Axis is
  task Axis_Manager is
    entry Stop;
    entry Resume;
    entry Take_Block (B : in Motion_Block);
  end Axis_Manager;

  task body Axis_Manager is separate;

  procedure IPC_Remote is separate;
```

```
procedure Stop is separate;
procedure Resume is separate;
  procedure Take_Block (B  :  in  Motion_Block)  is
separate;

end Axis;
```

The task Axis_Manager is specified in the package body, and cannot be called directly. The entrance procedures Stop, Resume, and Take_Block in the package specification (visible part) transfer the calls to the task entries for local task communication. The entrance procedures may alternatively invoke REC, RPC, or other IPC services for remote task communication using the standard client/server model.

A client portion of a client/server model is illustrated graphically in Figure 11.9. The entrance procedures are pictured at the package boundary with the tasks hidden inside the package "wall." Calls made by the task Axis_Manager are directed to the "exit" procedure IPC_Remote, who will determine where these calls should be sent.

11.6 INTERPROCESS COMMUNICATION MECHANISM

The overall design objective of an IPC implementation is to insulate the application software from the details of the communication mechanism. This will provide for a portable solution, and will also allow improvements in the IPC implementation without affecting the design of the majority of the application modules. The most promising approach for achieving the design objective is to create layers of software services. The fewer layers the application software has to interface with, the less the impact on the application software when changes in the IPC mechanism are made. The sections that follow describe different IPC approaches with decreasing levels of coupling between the application modules and the IPC layers: (1) direct calls to low level communication primitives; (2) message passing; and (3) remote procedure calls.

11.6.1 Low Level Communication Primitives

One way to implement a distributed application is to use the communication primitives included with the operating system or executive controlling the program. If there is no operating system or executive (as in embedded Ada applications), communication primitives must be integrated with the application code. It is preferable that the chosen set of primitives belong to a standard protocol to make the code more portable.

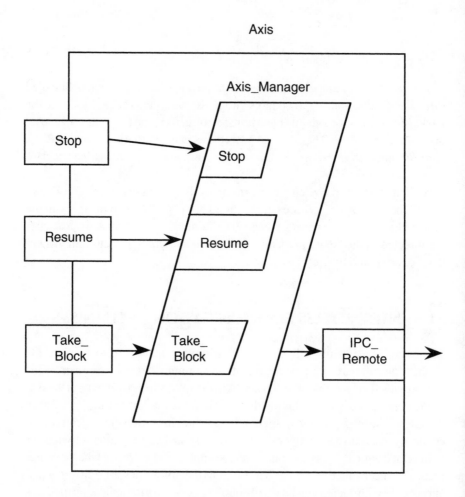

Figure 11.9 Entrance Procedures and IPC

Two commonly used standard protocols are the Transport Control Protocol/ Internet Protocol (TCP/IP) and the User Datagram Protocol/Internet Protocol (UDP/IP). They both utilize the same type of addressing where communication is thought to occur between *sockets*. A socket is a transient object used for interprocess communication. UDP uses *datagram* sockets, and TCP uses *stream* sockets. (The primary differences between UDP and TCP are described below.) The sender and receiver both have sockets allocated with respective associated addresses, i.e., the communication takes place between a pair of sockets. An Internet (IP) address determines the node (processor) in the network, and a *port* number identifies the particular socket on a given node. The IP address is a world-unique 32-bit number, and the port number is a node-unique 16-bit number. This is illustrated in Figure 11.10 with two nodes and two sockets per node. Each socket S has a port number bound to it. To properly address socket S4, both the IP address 10.3.5.124 and the port number 145 must be specified. The same port number can be used on different nodes since the IP address to reach the node is unique.

UDP and TCP port numbers can be bound to sockets either by having the programmer specify the mapping, or by letting the system pick any free port number currently not in use by any other socket.

11.6.2 Virtual Circuit (TCP)

TCP is a virtual circuit protocol which implements a reliable connection between two sockets. When TCP is used, a connection must be established between a sender and receiver before any data is transmitted by the sender. When the connection is established, the communication is symmetric, allowing both sides to send and receive data. The data is in a *stream* format with 8-bit bytes. Either sender or receiver may close the connection at any time.

TCP is typically used in a distributed application where it is natural to use the file concept of communication for large data transfers. It is not suitable in applications that utilize relatively short messages, because of the large amount of time spent on establishing the virtual circuit.

TCP does not offer any transparency to the application code. All of the services are hard-coded in a single layer, and the application is closely coupled to these services.

11.6.3 Datagram (UDP)

UDP is a protocol which sends data packets between unconnected sockets. It has been designed to be as fast as possible, but since there is a trade-off between speed and reliability, this protocol is potentially unreliable. Connections are not established prior to the sending of a data packet, and packets may get lost in the transfer. Neither the sender nor the receiver is notified when packets are lost. The level of reliability achieved with UDP depends on the particular network used and the buffering capacity of the processors utilized.

UDP is an asynchronous protocol. The sender may resume the transmission of the next packet without any indication of whether or not the previous packet arrived successfully. The sender may also end up sending a packet before the receiver is ready to receive. Multiple incoming packets may be buffered at the receiving processor to simplify the operations of the receiver, and to increase the reliability of successful data transfers.

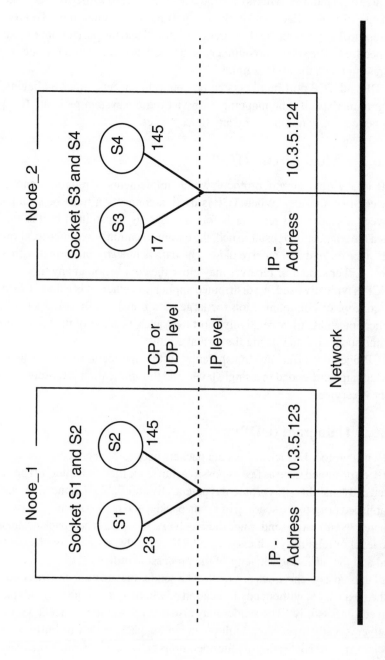

Figure 11.10 TCP/IP and UDP/IP Addressing

This protocol is fast and typically used for small data packets that must be transferred quickly. The speed, however, is obtained at the expense of a potentially unreliable system.

If the UDP service programs are accessed directly by the application program, a tight coupling is established, just as for direct access to TCP services. In the next section we describe a message passing mechanism that adds a layer between the services of the communication protocol.

11.7 MESSAGE PASSING

One way to overcome the problems with using the low level primitives directly is to implement a message passing mechanism as a layer between the application and the primitives. This layer will also, typically, handle the required data typing translation for data transfers between heterogeneous processors.

An illustration of the extra layer provided between the application program and the communication primitives is shown in Figure 11.11. The extra layer shields the application from the details of the chosen protocol, and the message passing scheme can be tailored specifically to the application. The design decision to choose message passing over RPC will probably be based on the relative effort of adding another message type vs. adding another operation. Another consideration is whether or not a non-blocking mechanism is required. If it is, the choice will be message passing since RPC uses a blocking scheme for making the remote calls. Asynchronous RPC requires additional operations.

A disadvantage of the message passing mechanism is that it has to be implemented for a specific problem domain, and the message structure throughout the system must be known. This can be implemented with a unique identifier for each message type, and could reach several hundred messages in a large system. There is also the potential for multiple copying of messages as they are transferred from one processor to another. This could be overcome with the use of shared data, but that presents another class of problems, e.g., memory references in a heterogeneous architecture and data integrity. It is still an improvement, however, over a design that accesses the communication primitives directly. An uncoupling has been achieved between the application and the primitives by introducing the message passing layer between them.

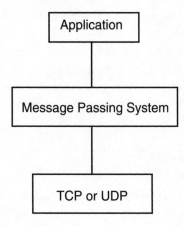

Figure 11.11 Message Passing Layer

Summary

The implementation of an efficient interprocessor communication mechanism is the key to a successful architecture of a distributed real-time system. With our prime concern for reusability, it is of utmost importance that well defined interfaces and layering of modules be designed carefully. The client/server model can be used to uncouple the application modules from the communications details. The use of standard protocol models and implementations such as OSI and RPC are highly recommended. This will go a long way toward achieving our desired reusability goal.

Message passing can be used to implement asynchronous process communication. A potential disadvantage with this approach is the likelihood of an excessive number of unique messages required in a large system.

12

Database Design

The two primary choices to be made regarding the design and implementation of large data structures are, first, whether to use home-grown data managers or available databases, and, second, if the choice is to use available databases, which type, e.g., relational, hierarchical, network, or object-oriented.

One of the basic assumptions we have made about object-oriented design for real-time applications is that the object-orientation will produce flexible, highly reusable systems that are easy to port to other hardware architectures, and that maintenance is reduced compared to other design paradigms.

After a brief description of database structures, the sections that follow will provide an overview of design features associated with traditional relational and hierarchical database design. Object-oriented data managers will then be described and compared to typical object-oriented database management systems. General Ada bindings will be discussed, followed by an illustration of how we can obtain an Ada binding to SQL. Database issues associated with the use of shared data will be discussed with emphasis on providing concurrency protection. This chapter concludes with a recommendation for a general database design strategy.

12.1 DATABASE STRUCTURES

The first step in the creation of a software design for a data structure is to perform some kind of data modeling. This may be done as simply as laying out a fixed number of components within a record, or it could be a complex set of tables related by certain rules. It is extremely important that this type of design analysis take place for a large system to promote reusability among applications. A hard-coded database program tailored for a single application cannot be reused without a significant redesign for another application, or even within the same problem domain.

There is usually a layering scheme included in a database design where the logical view (external representation) is presented to the users with the physical view (internal representation) hidden. Some of the criteria that can be used in the evaluation of a database design include [BLA88]:

1. **Performance.** Users must be able to access the required data quickly, and the access mechanism must be implemented in such a manner that the database does not become a bottleneck for the overall system. There must be a balance of the full range of services offered by a DBMS and efficient execution of the operations.

2. **Integrity.** The database structure must guarantee that the data stored and retrieved is correct (correctness is defined uniquely for a given application). Other features required include protection against unauthorized access and illegal system logons.

3. **Understandability.** The database structure and how to use it must be easy to understand for the clients (application users) and other software engineers who may want to include or expand the database in a different design.

4. **Extensibility.** The database design should be easy to extend for use in other applications or expand with extended features in the current application without disruptions for the current users. This is usually accomplished by separating the logical view and the physical view of the data organization.

5. **Availability.** The services provided must "always" be available, with only minimum delays after an unexpected failure. Backup and restart features are considered part of the normal operations offered by a full-service DBMS.

There are numerous choices available in the selection of how databases should be structured for a given application. Hopefully, the method we choose is appropriate for our application with regard to correctness, efficiency, ease of use, degree of reusability, and ease of maintenance.

The use of the word "database" implies a collection of (usually) large amounts of data organized in such a way that their data structures can be accessed and manipulated from within an application program. Access for retrieval and updating of specific data elements can be gained by calling a set of subprograms directly, or through a special interface such as Structured Query Language (SQL) [ANS89a, ANS89b]. Another implied assumption about databases is that they are protected against misuse to keep the data persistent.

We will only consider transaction oriented databases, where a *transaction* is a request for a certain set of operations to be performed on a portion or all of the data contained in the database. Examples of transactions include a request to read a record or a file, or an update of a record or a file. A single request may trigger several internal operations, and the transaction is only completed when all the required operations have been performed. A transaction can also be described as a unit of work, where the unit can be measured in particular primitive operations or a duration of time.

The primary data models used in structuring databases include hierarchical [TSI76], relational [COD70, DAT81], entity relationships [CHE76], and network [COD69]. This is not intended to be an inclusive list, but represents the majority of design paradigms of interest to us. We shall narrow the selection further and only discuss hierarchical and relational database structures.

The hierarchical model is used in a large number of applications, including real-time systems, and lends itself to a tailored implementation for a single application where the data is fairly unique to that application. The relational model is often used as a generalized database that can be used by several different applications.

One of the early choices in the database design phase is to decide whether to develop the system from scratch or adopt a commercially available system. The primary advantage of incorporating the use of commercial databases in the design of real-time systems is that they offer:

multi-user access

backup data recovery in case of disk crashes

multi-application access

data security through access control

data integrity via mutually exclusive access in a concurrent environment

extensibility for adding data and applications

There are several disadvantages associated with using commercial databases for real-time systems:

they are generally inefficient

they offer a limited set of data types

programming is required for access

there is usually a hefty license fee for their use

they may not provide all the required services for our application

Most databases are accessed via a mechanism usually referred to as a *schema*. This is sometimes represented as a *view* to the users. A *logical* view would be the mechanism used to access the database system from an application. A *physical* view would be details of how the data structures are organized and would not normally be visible to the users.

Some form of programming is required to establish the data that is to be manipulated by the DBMS. This interface to the DBMS can be very tightly coupled as shown in Figure 12.1, where the applications make direct calls on the DBMS services. A preferred access mechanism is where the applications enter the DBMS via an external schema as shown in Figure 12.2. The external schema can be considered an interface layer and can be implemented with a query language such as SQL. This type of interface will be discussed further in a later section of this chapter.

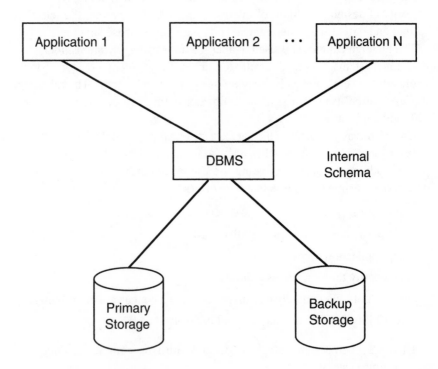

Figure 12.1 Direct DBMS Access

The choice of a particular DBMS is sometimes based on the desire to perform *ad hoc* queries, as opposed to a fixed set of pre-programmed queries. This may include, for example, a request for all the radar targets located within a certain geographic area. Many DBMSs cannot accommodate such a request because the data is not organized according to geographical areas, or there is no traversing mechanism for finding the data.

The requirement for ad hoc queries may drive database designers to create their own home-grown data managers to support the various data structures. The query mechanism is then built in a flexible way, or additional queries can easily be added without affecting the rest of the application.

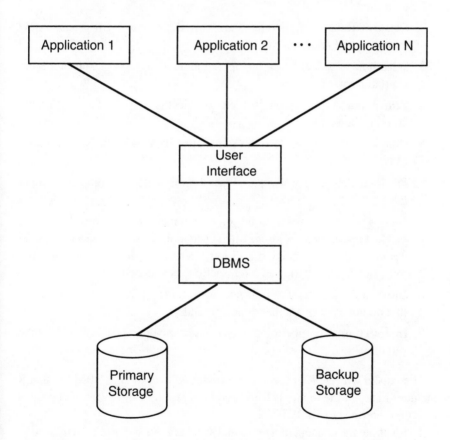

Figure 12.2 Layered Schema Architecture

12.2 RELATIONAL DATABASES

Relational database management systems (RDBMSs) are organized according to a relational model as originally defined by Codd [COD70, COD82]. This model has a sound foundation in mathematics, and is based on set theory and formal logic. Codd's mathematical representation of data structures can be expressed through relational algebra. Some of these algebraic relations can be summarized as follows [NAE89]:

1. **Relations.** A relation is the primary structure in an RDBMS and includes a set of rows and columns. The collection of rows and columns is referred to as a table.

2. **Closure.** Relational operations are closed, i.e., they will produce new relations, and relations can be nested.

3. **Selection.** A selection is an operation that chooses a subset of the available rows in a table.

4. **Projection.** A projection is used to select a subset of the available columns in a table.

5. **Union.** A union is used to concatenate two tables with the same number of rows.

6. **Product.** A (cross) product produces a combined table from two operand tables.

7. **Join.** The result of a join is the combination of selection, projection, and product operations. A join is often used as a measure of how efficiently a transaction is executed, e.g., 3 joins per transaction, 0.05 seconds per join, and an expectation of 5 transactions per second.

8. **Difference.** A difference is a "not" operation that finds rows in one table that do not exist in another table operand.

9. **Intersection.** This operation finds rows in two operand tables that are the same.

The reason why SQL is such an important adjunct to an RDBMS is that it includes many of the relations listed above as program structures, and creates a natural interface to an RDBMS.

To illustrate the concept of a relational structure, we will use a small portion of the data required for the handling of flight plan data in air traffic control (ATC) systems. (An overall object-oriented design treatment of an ATC system is included in Appendix B.) Most modern ATC systems consist of the two major processing portions: radar data processing (RDP) and flight data processing (FDP). Other processing functions in ATC systems include system monitoring and control, display, simulation, recording, and training.

The primary requirement for data storage and handling within RDP is the tracking of aircraft as they travel in designated airways. The amount of storage is relatively small compared to that required for FDP. The data required for FDP comprise flight plans, including repetitive flight plans (RPLs) for regularly scheduled flights; maps of en-route areas and areas surrounding an airport; weather data; airport layouts for ground control; aircraft characteristics of all aircraft expected to enter the controlled airspace; graphical and textual display data; and track data for determining the location of the aircraft that are being serviced.

A busy airport may handle a landing and departure every other minute for a single runway, in addition to the constant movement of aircraft, fuel trucks, and baggage handling vehicles on the ground. This all adds up to a tremendous amount of data handled on any given day, and the structure of the database for an automated ATC system becomes extremely important.

As an example in this section, we will take a narrow focus and illustrate the layout of the data describing aircraft characteristics. Aircraft characteristics data is used to determine en-route flight trajectories, provide spacing of aircraft for landing approaches and departures, issue warnings to support collision avoidance, and advise general aviation pilots of potential wake turbulence from larger aircraft. Individual data elements will include:

aircraft id (callsign) [primary key]

type of aircraft

weight class (wake turbulence indicator)

climb rate/descent rate

angle of climb

cruising speed

fuel capacity

fuel consumption

Flight plan data will include:

flight plan id [primary key]

aircraft id (callsign) [foreign key]

route

   legs

fixes

departure airport

destination airport

estimated time of departure (ETD)

estimated time of arrival (ETA)

Weather data will include:

weather location

type of report (forecast or observed)

validity period

wind data

    altitude

    direction

    speed

temperature and dewpoint

barometric pressure

cloud ceiling

visibility

All of the data listed above is used in an ATC system during the different stages of execution. The three different sets of data are not required in isolation; there are certain relations between them. An aircraft with a certain cruising speed at a given altitude flies a given route, and to be able to calculate the ETA we need to know the wind conditions to determine the true ground speed. A head wind component will add to the estimated time, whereas a tail wind component will reduce the time. There are thus certain relations established between the attributes of the aircraft, the route the aircraft is following, and the wind conditions along the route. The required data for these calculations must be organized in a manner that provides for efficient searches during the execution of the ATC program.

There is a direct connection between the organization of data managed in a relational database and object-oriented design. Relational data is usually laid out in a table format with rows and columns. Each row corresponds to an instance of an object, and the columns intersecting that row represent attributes of the object. For the ATC data illustrated above, we can construct three separate tables as shown in Figure 12.3. The first table is constructed for the aircraft characteristics, the second for the flight plan data, and the third for the weather data. Each table has a primary key and may have secondary (foreign) keys that are used to establish the relations between the tables. The keys are used in searching for the requested set of values that are to be modified or returned to the requestor.

Aircraft Characteristics

aircraft id	aircraft type	weight class	• • •	cruising speed

Flight Plan Data

flight plan id	aircraft id	route	• • •	ETA

Weather Data

weather location	type of report	validity period	wind data	• • •	visibility

Figure 12.3 Table Layout of ATC Data

An important design feature of the relations used in an RDBMS is the relationship between the data fields contained in the rows of the tables. This relationship is described in terms of normal forms [DAT81, BLA88]. We will only give a short description of the first three normal forms here:

1. A relational table is in first normal form if each attribute value (column in a given row) is atomic and does not include a repeating group.

2. A table is in second normal form if it satisfies the first normal form and each row has a unique key.

3. A table is in third normal form if it satisfies the second normal form and every non-key attribute depends directly on the primary key.

Examples of relational tables using third normal forms are shown in Figure 12.3. The table including aircraft characteristics has Aircraft Id as the unique key, and the other attributes depend on this key. The table including flight plan data has Flight Plan Id as the primary key, and all the non-key attributes depend on this key. Aircraft Id is a key attribute and represents a foreign key. This key refers to the aircraft characteristics table and illustrates how we can navigate between relational tables.

The use of normal forms in designing relations represent guidelines for database design. Normal forms improve data integrity by preventing update anomalies. They can also be used to speed up the required traversing of tables by employing more efficient searching and hashing mechanisms. A set of tables are "normalized" during the database design to arrive at the most suitable normal forms. Minimum data redundancy and inconsistencies are usually accomplished with the tables arranged in third normal form.

12.3 HIERARCHICAL DATABASES

The structure of hierarchical databases is well known to most programmers. A record or table, for example, is something we have all used in programming languages such as Ada, Pascal, C, Cobol, or Fortran. A table is created as a record with components where each component may consist of another record. In Ada the components of a record can be of any user defined type, and are not restricted to the primitive types such as integer, float, or boolean. This structure is fairly simple to create and understand, even when we make use of nested structures.

A hierarchical data model is created as a tree structure with a *root* as the highest node. The nodes attached to the branches of the tree are referred to as children of a parent node in the level above. Each parent node can have many child nodes, but each child has a unique parent. Every node, except the root, must be accessed through its parent.

Hierarchical data structures are fixed, unlike the relations created for RDBMSs. The search mechanisms are simpler and more efficient for hierarchical databases, but reprogramming is necessary when new queries are required. The primary advantage of using a hierarchical data model is that the data structures are well known, and it is fairly easy to predict the performance of a given set of relationships. The primary disadvantage is that it is difficult to modify the data structures without redesigning the system. If we want to delete a parent, we automatically delete all its children. The only way to access a child is through its parent.

An example of how data structures can be modeled hierarchically is shown in Figure 12.4. A field within a flight plan points to a wind area, which points to a set of altitudes. Wind data is then obtained for the given altitude corresponding to a certain route. This structure is inflexible and will not allow the construction of ad hoc queries. A hierarchical data model can be used in the design of data managers, but a relational model may have to be used where the schemas of data access are expected to change frequently.

12.4 OBJECT-ORIENTED DATA MANAGERS

A choice we can make for real-time systems is to create independent data managers for all the major data constructs without using commercial databases. This requires the construction of object managers, type managers, and monitors, as described in earlier chapters.

Ada is an object-based language with support for data abstraction. The package construct is used to create abstract data types (ADTs), and supports the object-oriented paradigms of encapsulation and information hiding. A package to encapsulate a stack for a small range of integer values, for example, can be written as:

```
package Stack_ADT is
   type Stacks is private;
   subtype Elements is Natural range 0 .. 100;
   procedure Push (Stack : in out Stacks;
                   Item  : in      Elements);
   procedure Pop (Stack : in out Stacks;
                  Item  : out     Elements);
   function Top-Of (Stack : in Stacks) return Elements;
   Empty-Stack : exception;
private
   -- code for type Stacks
end Stack_ADT;
```

The package specification includes the private type Stacks and subtype Elements. The only operations allowed on objects of type Stack are the procedures Push and Pop, and the function Top-Of (aside from the predefined operations for assignment and comparison of equality). The exception Empty_Stack is returned to the caller if an attempt is made to pop an element off an empty stack and is an integral part of the design object. The implementations of the operations are contained in the package body, and are not visible to the user of the package. This is especially evident in Ada with separate compilations of package specifications and bodies.

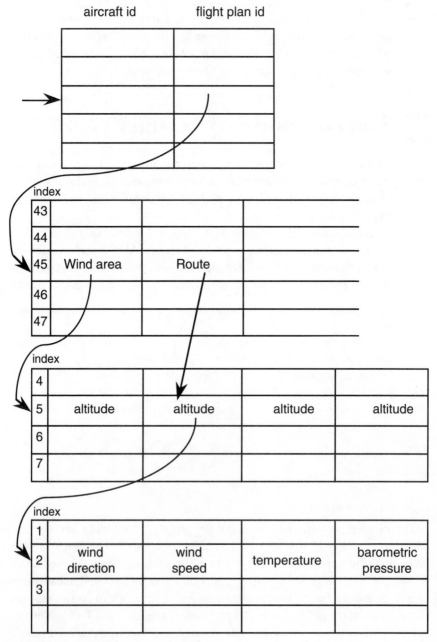

Figure 12.4 Hierarchical Linking

A program that requires the creation and manipulation of a data structure for a stack, imports the package Stack_ADT and declares a local stack object:

```
with Stack_ADT;
procedure Using_Stack is
  Local_Stack    : Stack_ADT.Stacks;   — stack object
  Local_Element  : Stack_ADT.Elements;
  . . .
begin
  . . .
  Stack_ADT.Push (Local_Stack, Local_Element);
  . . .
end Using_Stack;
```

For the ATC data listed in Section 12.2, we can create data managers for the aircraft characteristics, the flight plan data, and the weather data. An example of one of these data managers is a package encapsulating the flight plan data:

```
with Ac_Characteristics;
with Weather_Data;
package Flight_Plan_Manager is
  type Flight_Plan_Data is private;
  procedure Activate_Flight_Plan ( ... );
  procedure Amend_Flight_Plan ( ... );
  procedure Calculate_Time_Enroute ( ... );
  ...
private
  ...
end Flight_Plan_Manager;
```

This data manager is tailor-made for the problem domain and can be reused for a range of system requirements. If the interface (package specification) is inadequate for future systems, other types and operations can be added or modified for the changing requirements.

The use of object-oriented data managers is preferred in the construction of reusable components. The components can be carefully designed to accommodate a range of requirements, and interface changes can be made without affecting the design of the rest of the system (except for recompilation). In Ada, for example, the level of abstraction for reusability can be raised by the use of generic packages, and variant records can be used to accommodate a wide variety of structures for the same data type.

It is important to realize that the use of data managers does not automatically include the services normally expected from a DBMS, such as data protection, error control, backup, and concurrency control. These features will have to be built into the design as required for each problem domain. When the programming language used is Ada, concurrency control and mutual exclusion can be designed with Ada tasks and monitors. Error control can be accommodated with the use of Ada's exception handling. There is nothing inherent in the language, however, to support fault tolerance. If backup of critical data is required, this will have to be included as a part of the overall design.

12.5 OBJECT-ORIENTED DATABASE MANAGEMENT SYSTEMS

We have seen how we can design object-oriented data managers, e.g., abstract data types, monitors, or object managers using Ada packages. The creation of an object-oriented DBMS (OODBMS) combines the object-oriented features of encapsulation and information hiding available in a programming language with the services of a DBMS.

The primary difference between a data manager and an OODBMS is that the latter provides general services such as data security, error handling, concurrency control, and data backup. It may also include some undesirable restrictions such as a limitation on legal data types and the number of characters in a variable name. Another significant difference is that a relation or node is accessed by an index value in a DBMS, and by a unique identifier in an OODBMS.

The general features of an OODBMS can be described as follows [BUT91]:

1. **Data modeling.** The object model supports encapsulation, i.e., both a data structure (type) and the operations associated with the manipulation of objects declared of that type. The internal behavior of the data structures is also encapsulated within an OODBMS. The visible operations provide the only access to the data. This, in turn, implies that operations associated with data encoding that were previously performed by an application, using a traditional DBMS, are now performed inside the OODBMS.

2. **Integrity.** Any DBMS is responsible for providing data integrity at two levels: (1) structural integrity to protect the database from hardware or software failures; and (2) logical integrity to supply constraints via a set of rules or conditions for how a user can access the data. Structural integrity does not necessarily have a unique implementation for an OODBMS. Logical integrity, however, is implemented with a fixed set of operations for an OODBMS, and with relations, tables, and row restrictions for an RDBMS. The encapsulation and information hiding which is implicit in an OODBMS provide the required logical integrity. Only the operations declared in a visible specification can be used to access the data structures. This has the disadvantage that additional operations must be added when new constraints are required, and the same constraint may have to be repeated in several operations.

Another distinguishing feature of an OODBMS is that it can easily be implemented in distributed systems. Since the data structures are designed with object-oriented paradigms, individual objects can be allocated to different processors without redesigning those data structures. This will be much more difficult to implement for a monolithic DBMS when different portions of the data need to be allocated to different processors.

The requirements for an object-oriented relational database management system (OORDBMS) design is that the data is organized with a relational schema and a normalized form [DAT81], and that this design is implemented with an object-oriented programming language. The connection between objects and relations is that each row in the table represents an object, and the column values are the attributes of the given object. A collection of rows in a relational table can thus be considered a set of object instances within the class described by the table.

A significant amount of material is available in the literature describing relational databases and relational database management systems (RDBMSs). Publications illustrating the proper design of OORDBs are just starting to emerge. The OORDB technology is immature and it does not appear that a consensus or standard treatment of its design is forthcoming in the near future. The only agreement seems to be that the creation of an OORDB represents the intersection of RDBMS concepts and an object-oriented programming language [PRE90].

A few commercial OODBMS products are available [LIV90], but there are no standard interfaces. Some of the products can be accessed via C or C++, others through a version of SQL. There is also no industry agreement on how to create interoperability between OODBMSs and RDBMSs. The issue here is whether or not an organization that has been using an RDBMS can adapt it and use it in cooperation with an OODBMS, or if the RDBMS must be scrapped altogether.

An example of a commercial OODBMS is GemStone [MAI90]. GemStone combines a relational data model with the object-oriented programming language OPAL, an extension to Smalltalk. The primary concepts of the data model and language include object, message, and class. The object has a unique identifier and responds to messages (procedure calls) via OPAL methods (procedure bodies). A class corresponds to a record structure in a data manager or relational table. Data integrity is provided by periodic backup and data shadowing with multiple on-line copies of the database, which are updated for every transaction. Other examples include Vbase [AND90] and O_2 [LEC90]. In-depth descriptions of various OODBMS models and implementations are presented in [ZDO90].

12.6 ADA BINDINGS

Commercial DBMSs provide an interface to their services via procedure calls and function invocations as suggested in Figure 12.5. This type of interface locks an application into the use of that particular DBMS and offers a very low degree of reusability. A different application within the same problem domain must be reprogrammed with new calls, and a very tight coupling is created between applications and DBMS services.

The structured query language (SQL) can be used as an interface between an application and a commercial DBMS. This isolates the application from the internal schema (physical view) implemented by the DBMS, and offers a high degree of reusability if we later decide to use another DBMS that also supports SQL. This type of binding was illustrated in Figure 12.2 with the user interface replaced by SQL.

Bindings similar to SQL can be used as a layer to separate an application from the details of any collection of services (other than DBMSs), e.g., X Window and an Ethernet connection. The creation of any one of these bindings requires a number of steps, and we will first analyze the effort to create bindings in general, then we will focus on the use of SQL and interfacing to DBMSs.

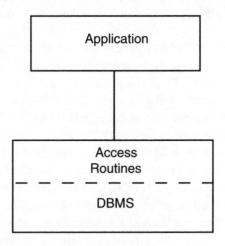

Figure 12.5 Direct Interface to DBMS

12.6.1 General Approach to Bindings

A general binding is usually created through the use of a programming language such as assembly or C, or a special programming language such as SQL. One approach for the creation of general Ada bindings has been suggested by McCoy [MCC90]:

1. **Create Ada data types.** Ada types must be created to match those supported by the particular binding. This may require the use of an Ada representation clause to map a user type to one of the primitive types available in the binding language.

2. **Declare an interface to the external routines.** Ada subprogram specifications are first written to match those of the interface language. A proper interface is then declared to map the Ada templates to the binding routines. This may be accomplished by using the pragma *Interface*. Typical interface languages supported via this pragma are C, assembly, and Fortran.

3. **Provide an interface to external data.** This may require the development of special routines which return the required data objects as parameters in the proper format.

4. **Provide a link to external libraries.** If, for example, a set of C routines collected in one or more libraries are to be used in the interface, a proper linkage must be established to reference these routines.

12.6.2 Ada Binding to Ethernet Connections

To illustrate the method suggested for general bindings, we present an Ada binding to a set of Ethernet C routines that implement a specific communication protocol. Even though this is not directly related to database design, a similar strategy can be used to interface to a commercial DBMS. As shown in Figure 12.6, the Ada application interfaces with the Ada Ethernet routines by *with*ing the package specification(s) that contain the required data managers. The application is shielded from the underlying C code by two full layers: the Ada Ethernet interface and the actual Ada binding to the C code.

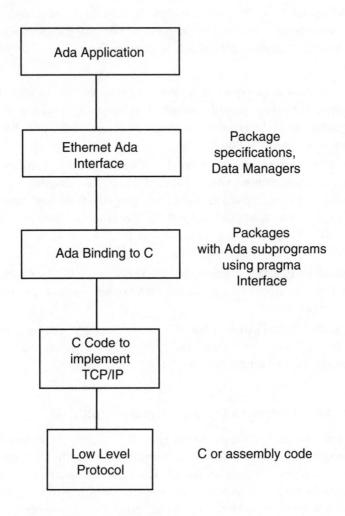

Figure 12.6 Ada Binding to C Code

The actual binding can be implemented as shown in the following Ada code fragments:

```
with TCP_IP_Types;  use TCP_IP_Types;
package Ethernet_Binding is   -- Ada/C binding
   ...
   function Get_Host_Address
    (Host_Name : Host_Address) return Internet_Address;
   pragma Interface (C, Get_Host_Address);
```

```
function Create_Socket
   (Address  : Integer_32;
    Socket   : Integer_32;
    Protocol : Integer_32) return Socket_Descriptor;
pragma Interface (C, Create_Socket);

function Bind_Address_to_Socket
   (Socket      : Socket_Descriptor;
    Socket_Adr  : Internet_Address;
    Adr_Length  : Address_Length) return Status;
pragma Interface (C, Bind_Address_to_Socket);

    ...
end Ethernet_Binding;
```

The use of pragma Interface will connect the Ada functions with equivalent C functions that will be linked in with the Ada code. One potential problem with this approach is that the parameter passing mechanism between Ada and C may not be compatible, and additional routines will then have to be created to perform the data transformation. Another problem is that some compiler vendors have implemented their own versions of the pragma to link the Ada subprogram name directly to a C name. This requires the use of a second pragma, and the code is no longer portable. If the low level protocol is implemented in Ada rather than C, the pragmas can simply be removed from the Ethernet_Binding package, and the low level Ada subprograms are then linked in with the rest of the Ada code.

The two layers that separate the application from the low level protocol implementation is accomplished via Ada's *with*ing mechanism:

```
with Ethernet_Binding; use Ethernet_Binding;
package Ethernet_Interface is -- application interface
   ...
   function Get_Host_Address ( ... )
                         return Internet_Address;
   function Get_Host_Name ( ... )
                         return Host_Name;
   procedure Create_Stream_Socket ( ... );
   procedure Initiate_Socket_Connection ( ... );
   procedure Write_to_Stream_Socket ( ... );
   procedure Read_from_Stream_Socket ( ... );
   ...
end Ethernet_Interface;

with Ethernet_Interface;  -- using the interface
use Ethernet_Interface;
```

```
separate (Application_Package)
task body Application_Task is
  -- local declarations
begin
  ...
  Get_Host_Address ( ... );
  Create_Stream_Socket ( ... );
  Write_to_Stream_Socket ( ... );
  ...
end Application_Task;
```

A similar type of binding as shown above can be used (in principle) to interface with a commercial DBMS, or we can create an interface to SQL if it exists for the chosen database. It is not quite as straight forward, however, as we will see in the next section.

12.7 ADA BINDING TO SQL

SQL has emerged as the primary interface to a commercial RDBMS, and an ANSI standard has been proposed [ANS89a]. The major problem with creating an SQL binding is that the developer of real-time application software is now phased with two entirely different programming paradigms [SEI91]. The real-time application is strictly procedural and functionally oriented, whereas the SQL part is used to model the relational algebra required for the database queries. SQL does not support the strong typing employed in Ada, and the Ada programmer either uses the limited set of types, or a transformation of types must be made. In the Ada interface we illustrated in the previous section for a binding to C code, the only potential problem was the compatibility of the parameter passing mechanism of the two languages.

Three basic methods of creating an Ada binding to SQL have been proposed [SEI91, DON87]:

1. **Embedded SQL.** This approach includes SQL statements in the Ada application code to express the relations required for accessing the DBMS. A standard Ada compiler cannot process SQL statements, and a pre-processor is thus required. The pre-processor will convert the SQL statements to equivalent Ada procedure calls that will actually make the queries to the DBMS.

2. **All-Ada binding.** This method does not require a pre-processor. SQL queries are modeled with standard Ada statements. As an example, a relation normally expressed in SQL as a table will be created as an Ada

record type. Some of the SQL keywords, e.g., *select* and *all* are the same as Ada reserved words, and will have to be renamed in the Ada model.

3. **New language.** To avoid the mixing of Ada programming and SQL query paradigms, a new programming language has been proposed [SEI91]. This language is called SQL Ada Module Description Language (SAMeDL) and is intended to bridge the gap between Ada application oriented programming and SQL DBMS accesses.

Each of the three methods listed above have advantages and disadvantages, and we must choose the most appropriate approach for our implementation. From an object-oriented perspective, SAMeDL seems, at first, to offer the best solution. Ada applications are written without any mixed SQL statements, and SAMeDL modules are written to model the SQL queries. This can provide a nice separation of design concerns, and support a clean interface to the DBMS. There is a major problem associated with this approach, however, SAMeDL is merely a proposal, and someone will have to write a language processor that is commercially available. The whole purpose of interfacing Ada code to a DBMS is that there are a number of commercially available DBMSs, and the reusability we are striving for should be accomplished by simply replacing the Ada binding.

The all-Ada binding has the advantage that it does not require any other compilation tools besides a standard Ada compiler. This method is dependent on trickery, however, e.g., choosing non-standard SQL constructs to avoid conflicts with the Ada reserved words. This will provide a very low level of reusability as each implementation will be tailored specifically for a narrow portion of the application.

Using embedded SQL statements requires the use of a pre-processor, but may still be the preferred method for applications to be implemented in the near future. Many of the commercially available DBMSs provide an SQL pre-processor for a particular base language, including Ada. SQL standardization efforts are underway [ANS89a and ANS89b], but are not strictly adhered to by the DBMS vendors. Reusability may still be limited as we switch from one DBMS to another, but at least we are using a commercially available binding with a commercial DBMS.

12.8 SHARED DATA

Global data structures can be implemented using shared data. The primary advantage of this approach is the high run-time performance that can be achieved compared to the use of data mangers or formal DBMSs.

There are two major problems associated with the use of shared data in a distributed real-time system composed of heterogeneous processors. The first is a requirement to protect the shared data from simultaneous access by concurrent processes. Data integrity cannot be guaranteed if the elements in a shared data area are updated without mutually exclusive access. If the actions that perform the updates are not atomic (indivisible), part of a record may have updated values, while the remainder of the record may contain old values, and the resulting data is no longer persistent.

Another problem associated with the use of shared data is memory address references made between heterogeneous processors. The data representation in one processor is quite likely different from that of the other, and a data transformation must take place. The main areas of concern are for processors with different word lengths and different byte orderings.

The problem with data integrity can be solved by providing a suitable environment for mutual exclusion. This can be designed using locking mechanisms (e.g., test-and-set instructions), semaphores, and special compiler directives (e.g., pragma Shared in Ada). In some limited cases unprotected shared memory can be used if we are convinced that the data cannot be compromised through simultaneous access.

12.8.1   Unprotected Shared Data

There is one class of data structures that can be shared without protection if they are accessed by exactly two concurrent processes. This is a circular buffer where one task manipulates the insert pointer, and the other task manipulates the remove pointer. This can be implemented with a generic Ada package as follows:

```
generic
   type Index_Type is range <>;
   type Element_Type is private;

package Buffer_Module is

   type Buffer is limited private;
   procedure Get (B : in out Buffer;
                  E :    out   Element_Type);
   procedure Put (B : in out Buffer;
                  E : in       Element_Type);
   function  Empty (B : in Buffer) return Boolean;
   function  Full  (B : in Buffer) return Boolean;

   Underflow : exception;
   Overflow  : exception;

private
   type Buf_Type is array(Index_Type) of Element_Type;
```

```
type Buffer is
   record
      Head  : Index_Type := 1;   -- remove
      Tail  : Index_Type := 1;   -- insert
      Buf   : Buf_Type;          -- array of elements
   end record;
end Buffer_Module;
```

This use of shared data without mutual exclusion protection is only justified when exactly one task manipulates the remove pointer Head, and another task manipulates the insert pointer Tail. If more than two tasks access this type of data structure, concurrency protection must be provided. The primary advantage of using unprotected shared data is that it avoids the overhead associated with the various locking mechanisms described in the next section. A case study using unprotected shared memory is presented in Appendix D.

12.8.2 Concurrency Control

A general mechanism to provide concurrency control can be implemented as illustrated in Figure 12.7. A number of clients make transaction requests through a server. The server is responsible for the required integrity of the data elements affected by each transaction. The net effect of the control is that the transactions are executed serially. This implies a potential wait period for transactions other than the one currently being executed.

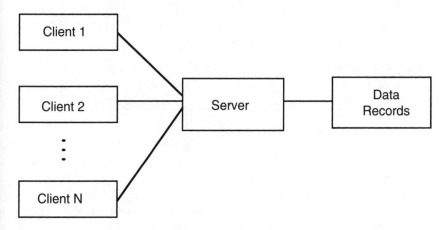

Figure 12.7 Concurrency Control of Shared Data

Several different methods of concurrency control are possible with various trade-offs in run-time efficiency and the potential for deadlock. Three of these methods are [COU91]:

1. **Locking.** The data elements to be used in a given transaction are locked and unavailable to other transactions. The locking is done before the transaction starts, and stays in effect during the entire transaction. The lock is removed when the current transaction is completed, and the next transaction is then selected. How much of a file is locked is an important design decision. A given transaction rarely requires the use of a complete file, and a partial lock that would allow other transactions to access the unlocked portions is probably preferred.

2. **Optimistic concurrency.** With the theory that the probability that two transactions require the exact same data elements are very low, an "optimistic" approach can be implemented. This will allow a read request to be performed immediately, whereas a write request is performed in two phases. The first phase is in a tentative form, which is invisible to the other transactions. The second phase is performed to determine if the write transaction can be accomplished as requested, or if it has to be aborted because the requested data entity is locked.

3. **Timestamps.** Each transaction is validated and timestamped when it is initiated, and if the request cannot be validated, the transaction is aborted immediately and put in a queue to be restarted later. A write request is deemed valid only if the data elements involved were last written and read by an older transaction. A read request is deemed valid only if the data was last written by an older transaction.

Which one of these three or other suitable methods is selected for a given application is an important design decision that will have to be considered carefully. A locking mechanism in Ada can be implemented as follows:

```
package Lock_Manager is
   type Locks is limited private;
   type Lock_States is (Free, Read, Write);
   function Is_Locked (Lock : Locks);
   procedure Request_Lock (Lock  : in out Locks;
                           State : in Lock_States);
   procedure Unlock (Lock : in out Locks);
private
   subtype Reader_Count is Natural range 0 .. 100;
   type Locks is
      record
         State   : Lock_States  := Free;
         Readers : Reader_Count := 0;
```

```
      end record;
end Lock_Manager;
```

The locking variable may have to be associated with a test-and-set instruction executed within the operating system for the implementation to be safe. Some vendors (e.g., DEC and Verdix) supply a special pragma for this purpose:

```
task body Application_Task is
  Lock : Lock_Manager.Locks;
  pragma Volatile (Lock);
  ...
begin
  ...
end Application_Task;
```

The implementation of a locking mechanism may require the use of semaphores to set a lock and to free it when the transaction is completed. Here is an example of a generic semaphore package [BUR90], that can be used in combination with a generic buffer package:

```
generic
  Initial : Natural := 1;
package Semaphore_Mgr is
  type Semaphores is limited private;
  procedure Wait   (S : in out Semaphores);
  procedure Signal (S : in out Semaphores);
private
  type Semaphores is
    record
      Sema : Natural := Initial;
    end record;
end Semaphore_Mgr;

generic
  Size : in Natural := 64;   -- default size
  type Item is private;
package Buffer is
  procedure Enqueue (I : in  Item);
  procedure Dequeue (I : out Item);
end Buffer;

with Semaphore_Mgr;
package body Buffer is
  subtype Index_Type is Positive range 1 .. Size;

  Buf    : array (Index_Type) of Item;
  Insert : Index_Type := 1;
```

```
   Remove : Index_Type := 1;

   package Mutual_Exclusion is new Semaphore_Mgr;
   package Not_Empty_Condition is new Semaphore_Mgr
                        (Initial => 0);
   package Not_Full_Condition is new Semaphore_Mgr
                        (Initial => Size);
   Mutex            : Mutual_Exclusion.Semaphores;
   Item_Available   : Not_Empty_Condition.Semaphores;
   Space_Available  : Not_Full_Condition.Semaphores;

   use Mutual_Exclusion;
   use Not_Empty_Condition;
   use Not_Full_Condition;

   procedure Enqueue (I : in  Item) is separate;
   procedure Dequeue (I : out Item) is separate;
end Buffer;

separate (Buffer)
procedure Enqueue (I : in Item) is
begin
   Wait (Space_Available);
   Wait (Mutex);
   Buf (Insert) := I;
   Insert := (Insert mod Buf'Last) + 1;
   Signal (Mutex);
   Signal (Item_Available);
end Enqueue;

separate (Buffer)
procedure Dequeue (I : out Item) is
begin
   Wait (Item_Available);
   Wait (Mutex);
   I := Buf (Remove);
   Remove := (Remove mod Buf'Last) + 1;
   Signal (Mutex);
   Signal (Space_Available);
end Dequeue;
```

The design objects Semaphore_Mgr and Buffer have a high degree of reusability and are developed at the computer science level in the domain hierarchy. The buffer implementation makes use of three different semaphores: one for guaranteeing mutual exclusion if there are simultaneous accesses to the buffer, another for ensuring nothing is returned from the buffer if it is empty, and the third for ensuring that nothing is added to the buffer if it is full.

Locking mechanisms incur a significant overhead in most applications, but may be required where the request for data transactions are highly concurrent. Any code including the setting and freeing of locks and semaphores must be carefully reviewed to make sure that the state variables have been released properly. Special deadlock avoidance mechanisms must be included in the design of the locking approach.

The major problem associated with the implementation of a locking mechanism is to ensure that the programmers comply with the specified coding conventions. The most common programming error in this area is to forget to release a lock when it is no longer needed.

In applications where the transaction requests are expected to occur with a low probability of simultaneous access, the second phase of the optimistic approach will proceed immediately without any significant overhead. This can be chosen as a more efficient implementation than the locking mechanism.

12.8.3 Using Pragma Shared

Ada provides the special compiler directive

```
pragma Shared (<variable>);
```

This can be used to protect shared variables, but has severe restrictions and may not be very useful in database design. It can only be applied to shared data elements of scalar and access types; arrays and records are specifically excluded. The large data structures usually associated with database design do not lend themselves to be of scalar or access types, and the type of concurrency control suggested in the previous section will have to be implemented, rather than make use of a simple pragma.

12.8.4 Heterogeneous Environments

The design of databases in distributed real-time systems presents special problems for architectures employing heterogeneous processors. Different data representations on different processors require the design of special software to perform the necessary data transformations. This is usually done by maintaining a standard internal representation as messages are passed between processors, with the necessary conversion performed at the receiving side. Special care must be taken that conversions are not performed between homogeneous processors. One example of this type of data transformation is illustrated in Appendix A, and represents the eXternal Data Transformation (XDR) approach implemented by Sun Microsystems [SUN86].

12.9 GENERAL DATABASE DESIGN STRATEGY

A general strategy for the design and acquisition of data management capabilities must be determined during the early stages of a project. If the choice is to develop the data managers from scratch without the use of commercial DBMSs, the effort must be costed and scheduled. If, on the other hand, the choice is to make extensive use of commercial database systems, less software has to be developed, but the cost of each system to be built must reflect the expense of software licenses and the development of suitable interfaces.

A middle of the road approach to the database issue is to create object-oriented data managers for the real-time system and to use a commercial DBMS for off-line functions such as:

Playback of data recorded on-line

Data reduction

Creation and modification of adaptation data

Report generation

Preparation of a demonstration program

This will usually only require a single site license, and will not add dramatically to the cost of the system. The efficiency of the chosen DBMS is not critical since all the functions are performed off-line. The degree of reusability should be expected to be high with the same DBMS used for similar functions regardless of the system size we are creating. The only possible additional cost for a large system will be extra disk and backup storage space for the larger volume of data.

One consideration for the use of a commercial DBMS is how the data is stored. In some systems, indexes used to traverse the data are stored in memory and the data elements are stored on disk. This can speed up the searching operations significantly compared to systems that keep both the indexes and the data on disk.

A real-time system can be designed with the type of object-oriented data managers illustrated in earlier chapters. We have seen examples of object managers, abstract data types, and monitors. These are tailored to the applications in the specific problem domain. A high degree of reusability is designed into the modules by carefully implementing the interfaces between the components. The use of Ada's generic capability enhances reuse by selecting formal generic parameters that can be instantiated for a wide range of similar functions.

Areas suited to generic functionality are discovered by listing common requirements, the attributes, and operations of identified objects. Requirements to be considered should include fault tolerance such as the periodic saving of *safe data* to be used in a switch-over to a standby processor. The type of data to be saved should only include critical data that is not quickly restored in a real-time system. In a tracking system, for example, the track store is relatively transient and may not need to be saved periodically, but adaptation and recording data should be saved. This is especially true of data required for historical purposes such as billing of customers and statistical data.

The reusability of tailored object-oriented data managers is realized by sharing both design and code. This includes both requirements and design documentation, as well as the PDL developed during the top level and detailed design phases.

P A R T 3

OBJECT-ORIENTATION AND REUSABILITY

In this part we focus on the approaches that will allow us to maximize reusability of software components to be developed for a given problem domain.

The traditional top-down waterfall model is not considered appropriate for an object-oriented development approach. We will suggest a combined top-down and bottom-up mechanism that can accommodate both the concurrency analysis and the use of object-oriented components.

The major theme throughout this book is how we can create reusable components. Recommendations are made regarding object-oriented evaluation criteria and component design to allow system scalability. The results of our reusability effort are collected in a parts catalogue that will contain the software components and the associated documentation.

One of the most important features required for a successful reuse effort is the ease with which the reusable components can be retrieved. Recommendations are made for configuration control and a retrieval system for the reusable software components.

This part concludes with a summary of the steps required for the domain analysis, requirements analysis, transitioning from analysis to design and the creation of design objects.

13

Top-Down vs. Bottom-Up Design Approaches

Traditional software development approaches are based on a top-down strategy where larger abstractions are decomposed into smaller subsets. This usually starts with the requirements analysis and flows into the top level and detailed design phases. The decomposition continues until software modules of a certain approximate size have been identified, e.g., 50 to 100 source lines of code (SLOC) for the given implementation language, in our case Ada.

A strict top-down development is an idealized concept that rarely happens in practice, because the size and complexity of real-time systems usually dictate an iterative approach. The way we document our software designs may give the illusion that we have followed a top-down approach, but several iterations and interludes of bottom-up work have actually taken place. (See Parnas's article "A Rational Design Approach—How and Why to Fake It" [PAR86].)

The combination of a top-down and bottom-up approach becomes inherent when using object-oriented analysis and design paradigms. The abstract objects may be identified in a top-down fashion, but the actual design objects are created and refined in a bottom-up manner. This chapter describes the natural blending of top-down and bottom-up efforts used to create reusable software components.

13.1 WATERFALL APPROACH

The traditional waterfall model for software development has been in use for a long time, and is one of the most prominent methodologies specified in a

191

formal customer/contractor relationship. This methodology specifies a series of development phases: (1) requirements analysis, (2) preliminary design, (3) detailed design, (4) unit testing, (5) integration testing, and (6) formal acceptance testing. Each phase has a requirement for certain documents to be produced, and there is usually a formal review signifying the completion of each phase.

The implication of using the waterfall method for software development is that each separate phase is completed in the proper sequence before the next phase is started. The completion of each phase concludes with a customer review to ensure that the requirements have been implemented properly. If discrepancies are uncovered during the review, the contractor is instructed to correct the problems before the next phase is started.

There is usually a partial payment plan associated with the various phases of the waterfall model. The contractor may be paid a portion of the total contract price, for example, when the preliminary design phase is completed, and another at the end of the detailed design phase. The acceptance of a formal review by the customer will constitute an approval for the partial payment, and the contractor is entitled to receive a certain sum within a given time period following the acceptance.

A typical waterfall model is pictured in Figure 13.1. During the requirements analysis phase, the application is analyzed and decomposed into manageable functional areas. The data flows between those functional areas are established and their interfaces described. A software requirements specification (SRS) is created and includes a detailed description of each functional area and the data elements and control flows expected between the functions. A separate interface requirements specification (IRS) is sometimes created to describe the interfaces between major subfunctions of a large system. Analysis tools produced in this phase include data and control flow diagrams, state transition diagrams, and interface diagrams. The SRS was traditionally created by systems engineers and, in the strict waterfall approach, was "thrown over the wall" to the software engineers for the software design and implementation. This idealized process assumed no changes to the requirements, and no feedback to the application users until the software was tested and certified.

There are some major problems associated with using the waterfall model for a large and complex real-time system:

1. **Incomplete requirements specifications.** It is very difficult to accurately specify all the requirements of a large system with sufficient detail to create an adequate design and implementation.

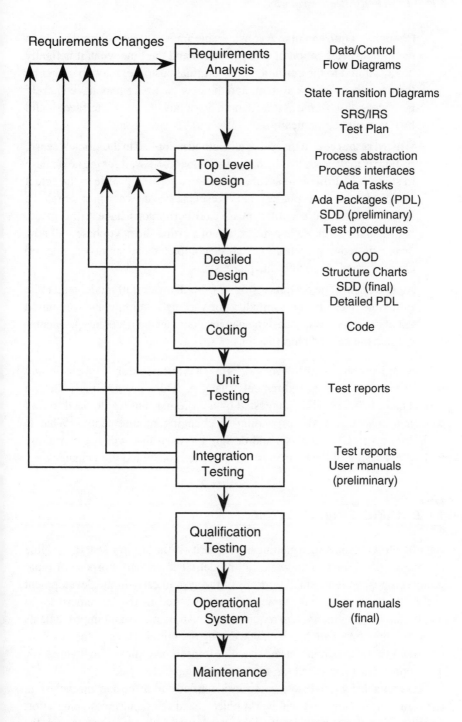

Figure 13.1 Waterfall Model

2. **Changing requirements.** A considerable amount of time elapses between the initial specification of a large system and the time when it is finally demonstrated to the customer. The original customer may no longer be the beneficiary of the system, and the new customer may have entirely new ideas of what the system should do or how the user interface should be represented graphically.

3. **Wasted resources.** If the waterfall method is applied in the strictest sense, resources may be wasted by having staff members wait for the next phase to start. It is difficult to accurately match a staffing profile to the actual events of the various phases. This is especially true when problems have been found at the end of a phase and corrections have to be made. Additional staff hired in anticipation of starting the next phase will now be idle until the corrections have been completed and approved, since no charges are allowed until the phase starts.

4. **Rigid design.** The designs resulting from the waterfall model tend to be inflexible and difficult to modify for varying requirements or required enhancements. Major design changes may then be necessary to accommodate the needed modifications.

The major problem with this method is that it is inflexible and unrealistic, and we do have to allow for requirements changes. This does not imply that we should cater to every whim suggested by a customer, but we do need to find some reasonable way of responding to changing requirements. What is desirable is a flexible analysis and design approach that will not constantly require a redesign of the entire system to accommodate required changes.

13.2 RAPID PROTOTYPING

Rapid prototyping has been gaining in popularity in the last few years as a viable alternative or adjunct to the waterfall model. The primary purpose of rapid prototyping is to create small portions of the system early in the development cycle. These portions are, typically, demonstrated to the customer/user to identify and clarify the system requirements. Adjustments and improvements in the requirements can then be made during the initial stages of the development cycle without major cost and schedule impacts, as indicated in Figure 13.2. This represents a combined top-down, bottom-up technique.

Areas suitable for rapid prototyping are identified during the domain analysis in terms of functionality and real-world objects, and the rapid prototyping effort operates in parallel with the rest of the development phases. Even though the waterfall and rapid prototyping methods are different, they are not incompatible.

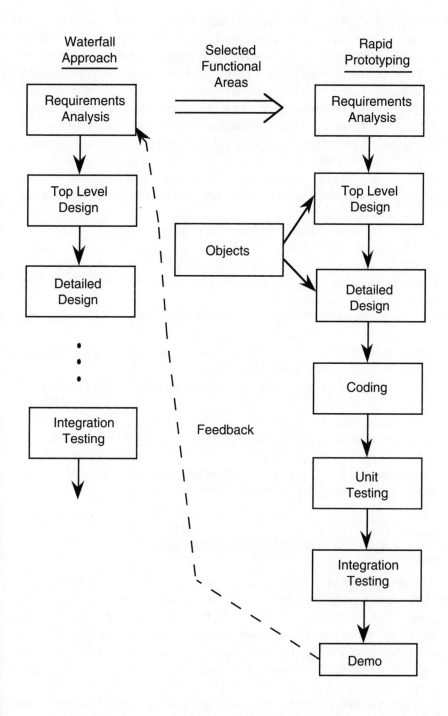

Figure 13.2 Modified Waterfall Approach with Rapid Prototyping

We can easily structure the process of rapid prototyping within the confines of the waterfall model or other suitable development technique, e.g., the "spiral" model [BOE88, SHU92]. A partial development effort of requirements analysis, preliminary design, detailed design, and unit testing can be employed to the portions of the system where the requirements are most likely to change. This portion is demonstrated to the customer as soon as possible with ensuing discussions of how the eventual system should appear. The overall system, meanwhile, is being developed using the normal waterfall method (or other method of choice) modified with the object-oriented paradigms. Before the system is turned over to the customer, the demonstrated portion is formally tested and integrated with the rest of the system, and is exercised during customer acceptance testing.

The portion to be demonstrated must be chosen carefully, with the limited scope clearly defined. It is preferable that the chosen piece be a part of the overall design to minimize the impact on the complete system. A major purpose of rapid prototyping is to support an incremental development process within the context of the overall preliminary design.

There are definitely some potential pitfalls to the use of rapid prototyping. Software may be created that will later simply be thrown away. Software that ends up in the final system may be poorly documented and "hacked" together without following design guidelines and coding standards. It is important that, at least, a minimal set of quality measures be applied to all software developed in a prototyping effort.

Rapid prototyping can also be applied to testing design paradigms in support of reusability concepts, such as an interprocess communication (IPC) mechanism. The creation of flexible software components in a distributed system is dependent upon an efficient IPC implementation, and the proper mechanism should be determined during the initial development phases.

13.3 OBJECT-ORIENTED DEVELOPMENT

A development approach that depends on a high degree of reusability does not fit the strict top-down model, since the objective is based on using software components that are used as building blocks for the new system. The building block approach is primarily a bottom-up strategy similar to the construction of a computer system using CPUs, buses, and memory chips that have already been built. We perform a mapping of abstract objects into design objects, i.e., software modules.

A top-down view from the system level is usually required to determine a balanced set of processes in a concurrent application, and how the components should be distributed among the various processors. The resulting development approach is a combination of top-down and bottom-up paradigms.

The transitioning from analysis to design is accomplished in a top-down fashion with the culmination of Ada application packages. In parallel with the transitioning we develop the data managers that were identified as abstract objects during the analysis phase. These objects were originally described with a minimal set of operations and attributes, and will have to be refined before they are implemented as proper data managers.

13.4 TOP LEVEL DESIGN

An Ada top level design consists of application packages, communication packages, and the helper packages as shown earlier for the package taxonomy. The graphical representation of the abstract design objects expressed as application packages is created top-down at the end of the transitioning period. These application packages will be written with Ada PDL to take advantage of the compiler's interface and type checking capabilities. Before the application packages can be compiled, however, the communications and helper packages must be developed bottom-up. If these packages are not available in the Ada library, none of the application packages can *with* them as required.

The creation of definitions packages and services packages should be carefully scrutinized to determine if they can be combined into proper data managers. The operations provided in the services packages require certain global types, and if these types can be removed from a definition package, we can instead implement a data manager.

When the data managers are created they should be analyzed to see if they can be made generic, and if the set of operations are complete. A method for refining the structure of objects has been suggested in [BUL91]:

1. **Single abstraction.** A data manager should only encapsulate a single data structure. If two or more data structures are described within the same data manager, the manager should be decomposed into one manager for each data structure.

2. **Unique objects.** Two or more objects should not encapsulate the same data structure. If this condition is discovered, the operations of the various data managers should be combined into a single data manager.

3. **Add inverse operations.** For each set of operations add the inverse set to make the object more reusable. Examples include add/delete, expand/contract, and start/stop.

4. **Add complementary operations.** Another way of making objects more reusable is to add complementary operations to the ones determined for

the current requirements. One potential problem with the addition of expected, future operations is that a compilation system may not optimize away the operations that are not referenced in the program. This may result in additional elaboration time and increased memory requirements.

One way to increase the reusability of Ada components is to look for the possibility of using generics. This creates a higher level module interface with a template (class) that can be instantiated with a set of compile-time parameters.

A design implication of using generics is that our methodology will not be strictly top-down. The generic units must be in the Ada library before we can instantiate them in our application programs. Generic units for a given application program will be created bottom-up before we proceed top-down with the application program that instantiates them. An example (taken from the case study in Appendix D) is shown below for a generic buffer module which is created bottom-up:

```
generic
   type Index_Type is range <>;
   type Element_Type is private;

package Buffer_Module is
   type Buffer is limited private;
   procedure Get
            (B : in out Buffer; E : out Element_Type);
   procedure Put
            (B : in out Buffer; E : in  Element_Type);
   function  Empty (B : in Buffer) return Boolean;
   function  Full  (B : in Buffer) return Boolean;
   Underflow : exception; -- raised in Get
   Overflow  : exception; -- raised in Put

private
   type Buf_Type is array(Index_Type) of Element_Type;
   type Buffer is
      record
         Head : Index_Type := 1;  -- remove
         Tail : Index_Type := 1;  -- insert
         Buf  : Buf_Type;         -- array of elements
      end record;
end Buffer_Module;

package body Buffer_Module is
   procedure Get
                (B : in out Buffer;
                 E : out    Element_Type) is separate;
```

```
procedure Put
            (B : in out  Buffer;
             E : in      Element_Type) is separate;
function Empty (B : in Buffer)
                    return Boolean is separate;
function Full (B : in Buffer)
                    return Boolean is separate;
end Buffer_Module;
```

The following application package (created top-down) uses the generic Buffer_Module to instantiate a buffer:

```
with Sys_Rep_Spec;   use Sys_Rep_Spec;
with Buffer_Module;

package ACI_Buffer is
  -- ACI_Buffer contains param specs and
  -- instantiation of the hdw buffer handler.
  ...

  type ACB_Index is new Integer
                    range 1 .. ACI_Size + 1;

  type ACB_Element is
    record
      Char   : Character;
      Kbd_Nr : Kbd_Index;
    end record;

  package ACB is new Buffer_Module
                    (Index_Type   => ACB_Index,
                     Element_Type => ACB_Element);
  ACB_Buffer : ACB.Buffer;
end ACI_Buffer;

package body ACI_BUffer is
  -- Task specifications for the ACI handler (for
  -- the hdw interface).  This task gets chars from
  -- the hdw buffer to the user interface buffers.

  task ACI_Handler is
  end ACI_Handler;

  task body ACI_Handler is separate;
end ACI_Buffer;
```

The generic design object Buffer_Module represents the highest level of reusability for design objects in Ada, and has been instantiated here with a size implied by the type ACB_Index and elements to be stored as ACB_Element. This clearly illustrates the natural combination of top-down and bottom-up paradigms, and how it benefits our development strategy.

13.5 DETAILED DESIGN

The detailed design for Ada programs will usually take place top-down since we can use the *separate* clause to defer details from the packages created during top level design. The subunits prepared during detailed design include subprograms and tasks that were declared in the application packages and the helper packages identified during top level design. The following subunit is an implementation of the task ACI_Handler which was deferred by a *separate* construct in the example in the previous section (see Appendix D for the complete case study):

```
with Text_IO;  use Text_IO;
with User_Interface;
separate (ACI_Buffer)

    task body ACI_Handler is
       Lost : array (Kbd_Index) of
                            Natural := (others => 0);
                -- Number of chars lost for each kbd

       procedure Process_Char is separate;

    begin
       Put_Line ("Start of ACI_Handler");
       loop
          if ACB.Empty (ACB_Buffer) then
             delay 0.010;
                    -- Wait 10 msec if hdw buffer empty
          else
             Process_Char;
                    -- Get char & kbd-number; put them
                    -- into intermediate buffer
          end if;
       end loop;

    exception
       . . .
```

```
end ACI_Handler;
```

The design object ACI_Handler is prepared in a top-down fashion during detailed design as an independent component and thus supports the incremental development strategy.

Some of the tasks declared within the application packages will be quite large and may include functionality that requires thousands of lines of code to implement. These tasks have to be decomposed into subprograms and additional data managers. This will usually be accomplished in a top-down fashion for the functional decomposition and with a parallel object creation for the data managers. This was illustrated in Chapter 10 and labelled layered virtual machines for the decomposition, and object-oriented design for the construction of the objects (LVM/OOD).

Summary

We do not advocate a strict top-down waterfall development approach. A more reasonable method is to combine a top-down approach for decomposing a large system into its functional areas and a bottom-up technique for the creation of objects. Nor do we recommend a completely bottom-up approach. The former ignores the use of objects, and the latter does not account for concurrency considerations. The two approaches should be employed as complementary development techniques. This will result in a flexible design with a high degree of reusability. It also embraces the rapid prototyping technique for demonstrating unproven user requirements and high risk implementation areas. Some customers may have to be convinced that the old waterfall approach is not cost effective. This can usually be done by tailoring of contractual documents that specify a development approach, and by demonstrating operational concepts early in the development cycle.

14

Reusable Components

The primary objective for using an object-oriented development approach is to create robust software modules for real-time systems that are easy to port to other hardware architectures and that provide a high degree of reusability. The ability to reuse software components is considered the most important aspect of staying competitive in the software business. It has been suggested that we should measure the productivity of our software engineers by how much software they reuse, not by how many lines of new code they produce per month [AUE89].

In this chapter we will look at the criteria that can be used to evaluate how components should be constructed for maximum reusability. Ada component design and tailoring of Ada systems from reusable objects are described, and the importance of adequate documentation is emphasized.

14.1 EVALUATION CRITERIA

The following criteria can be used by the developers during the design stages and by reviewers for the software evaluation analysis of component construction for maximizing reusability

1. **Modularity.** Every component should be highly modular with high internal cohesion and well defined interfaces for minimum coupling with the other system components. This includes *definition* and *package*

coupling for Ada packages [HAM85, NIE88], and *data, stamp, control, common,* and *content* coupling [PAG80] in order of decreasing desirability for Ada subprograms. The loosest form for coupling between Ada task bodies is the use of *in* or *out* parameters and small accept bodies for entry calls [NIE88]. The cohesion within each component that represents a subprogram should satisfy the normal cohesion rules, preferably *functional* or *sequential* [PAG80, NIE88]. Ada task bodies without selective wait statements and accept bodies should satisfy the same cohesion rules as Ada subprograms. Task bodies with several accept bodies may have a mixture of high cohesion within each accept body, but looser cohesion at the task level [NIE88].

2. **Single capability or abstraction.** Each component should encapsulate a single functional capability or data abstraction. If we are creating application packages, the tasks declared should represent a single, major functional requirement. The capability should be sufficiently small such that it can never be envisioned to be split across processors. In the case of data managers, they should only contain one major data structure and associated operations.

3. **Independence.** Software components should be designed without dependencies on a particular operating system, hardware architecture, compiler, or run-time environment. Each component should be sufficiently robust to be able to be adapted by other software organizations without redesign or reprogramming efforts for that component. For major functional capabilities, components should be combined through a common "binding" mechanism, e.g., for X Window graphics or SQL database interfaces. Each component should be designed to be independent of the execution order of any other component.

4. **Scalability.** Software components should be designed to accommodate a variety of system loads in the form of a variable number of processors and other hardware devices. This can best be accomplished by including a set of adaptation parameters.

5. **Fault tolerance.** Critical software components should be designed to be distributed across redundant processing elements, including backup storage for critical data on a hot standby processor. Software fault tolerance should be built into the design by including an exception handling mechanism. Run-time error checks created by the compiler should be left on, unless the overhead is too high and the software can be shown to be safe without them.

6. **Tailorability.** The set of reusable software components should be designed to accommodate small, medium, and large systems in the same problem domain without major modifications and redesign. Different

size systems can be tailored from the available set of components. This is best accomplished by building in a set of adaptation parameters for all attributes that depend on system sizing and capacities.

7. **Network extensibility.** Individual software components should be constructed according to established distribution guidelines. The Ada package is a natural unit for allocation to a given processor, and should be the primary encapsulation mechanism. The software components should be designed to form distributable entities, i.e., virtual nodes (VNs). More than one component may be combined into a VN. Each VN should not be aware of the processor it resides on, nor should it depend on any of the adjacent processors [NIE90]. This implies the use of a highly efficient and independent IPC mechanism (see Chapter 11).

8. **Descriptiveness.** Each software component must have adequate documentation to describe the functional capability it performs, and the design and programming techniques used to implement the component. The documentation will usually be found in formal requirements and design documents, and in the code in the form of module prologues and comments. The documentation must be placed under configuration control, and all coding and PDL must conform to the same project coding standards. It is important that test cases used in the debugging, validation, and qualification of the software be saved and made available in a central location.

9. **Traceability.** A thread of traceability must be established from the code level back through the design documentation and to the requirements description. The information can be contained in cross reference tables that are kept on electronic media.

14.2 COMPONENT DESIGN

The primary building block for creating reusable Ada components is the package structure. Subprograms could be used, but we would end up with, literally, thousands of individual Ada units that would have to be placed under configuration control. Subprograms also do not support the object-orientation, since each subprogram is only an operation and would not normally encapsulate a major data structure. Ada tasks by themselves cannot be components since they are not library units, but they form an important part of the application packages that contain embedded tasks which execute portions of the given problem domain functionality.

A classification of Ada packages was described in Chapter 4. This taxonomy serves as an initial guideline for the creation of reusable components. Packages are first created as logical units within a given category, and are then designed and implemented as physical Ada components in accordance with the evaluation criteria described in the previous section. All of the first seven criteria should be considered in the component design without any particular order of importance. The latter two are, of course, also important, but primarily from a user's point of view.

14.3 COUPLING AND COHESION

Specific guidelines for the creation of object-oriented abstract data types and object managers were offered in Chapters 8 and 9. These data managers should provide only the necessary and sufficient services required to implement a specific data structure. A module that imports one of these packages would utilize all or most of the services provided in it.

The desirable design concepts of loose coupling and strong cohesion were introduced for traditional structured design of subprograms before Ada packages and tasks were available in a programming language. It has been proposed [HAM85] that the traditional coupling concepts be extended to include the use of Ada packages as follows:

1. **Definition coupling.** Two components are definition coupled if they use a common definition that is global to both of them. This would be the case if they both *with* the same package, or use a resource that is defined in the package that contains both components.

2. **Package coupling.** Two components are package coupled if they both import the same package (by *with*ing), but do not use any common elements within the package.

Of these two new forms of coupling, the former represents a better (looser) interdependence than data coupling, since data may not actually be shared. Two or more modules may simply import a common type from the same package. Package coupling appears to offer the ultimate in loose coupling since neither data nor types are shared by the two modules importing the package. It is questionable, however, that this is a desirable way to structure a package. It should probably be split up into two or more packages, and have each module *with* the package that contains the elements it needs. An exception to this guideline is a widely used, very general purpose package such as a package of mathematics or graphics operations.

Cohesion has traditionally been applied to sets of code statements within individual executable units such as subprograms or tasks. We can extend the notion of desirable cohesion for object-oriented design by considering the operations and data encapsulation within data managers.

Suggestions for good package design have been made in [BOO87] and include the modeling of abstract data types. Such packages should provide only the necessary and sufficient services required to implement the specific model. A module that imports one of these packages would utilize all or most of the services provided in it. Guidelines for constructing packages that will minimize the overall coupling of the program include [BOO87, p. 228]:

1. **Named collections of declarations.** Objects and types are exported, but not other program units. This corresponds to our Definitions packages.

2. **Groups of related program units.** Program units are exported, but not objects or types. This is equivalent to the Services packages defined in the package taxonomy.

3. **Abstract data types.** Objects, types, and their operations are exported. This corresponds to our Data Managers, including Object Managers.

4. **Abstract state machines.** Objects, types, and their operations are exported. State information is maintained in the package body (or in a task body contained within the package body). This can be implemented within an Ada task body using a select statement, or a case statement inside a subprogram.

The above guidelines can be used as an aid to a qualitative evaluation of package designs for maximizing reusability.

14.4 APPLICATION PACKAGES

A set of heuristics can be used as an aid in creating the primary design objects, i.e., the application packages that contain the primary functional requirements. The first six rules listed below apply to how a task or group of tasks should be packaged. The last two apply to packaging in general. The rules are the following [NIE88]:

1. **Encapsulating module.** The Ada syntax rules [DOD83] allow tasks to reside in subprograms, tasks, and packages. Tasks cannot be implemented as compilation units, however, and this leaves us the choice between placing tasks in packages or subprograms. The only tasks recommended for placement within a subprogram are tasks used as simulators or for special debugging purposes. These tasks should then be placed in the main procedure for maximum control of the debugging

process. The recommended placement of tasks is within packages, unless a specification requirement makes it mandatory to put a task within a subprogram.

2. **Functionality.** Tasks can be grouped within the same package if their functionalities are related, and there is virtually no chance that the tasks will ever have to reside on separate processors.

3. **Generics.** General purpose tasks, e.g., buffers, transporters, and relays, that are likely to be used in many of our systems should be placed in packages as library units. These packages should be generic, if possible, for maximum reusability.

4. **Coupling.** Tasks should be placed in packages such that the coupling is minimized with respect to data types, operations, and constants that are imported from the encapsulating package. The rendezvous mechanism should only be used directly between tasks if they are declared in the same package body.

5. **Visibility.** The package structure should provide for minimum visibility of task entries. Task specifications should be hidden in package bodies, and entrance procedures should be provided for interactions between tasks that reside in different packages. Special considerations must be given to whether entrance procedures should handle conditional or timed entry calls, or if the task specification should be moved to the package specification to provide these services directly. Task specifications may also have to be moved to the package specification if required by certain OS services (e.g., the use of the AST mechanism in VAX/VMS).

6. **Data stores.** A data store that is accessed by multiple tasks should be created as a monitor design object with an encapsulated task to provide the required mutual exclusion, or other suitable locking/synchronization mechanism.

7. **Dependency.** The chosen package structure should result in a minimum dependency (use of *with* clauses) between the packages. It is desirable to confine *with*ing to package bodies, rather than package specifications, and to task body subunits where the *separate* statement has been used to defer details.

8. **Recompilation.** The chosen package structure should result in a minimum amount of recompilation when any of the packages are changed. This is closely associated with the dependency issue described above. Minimum recompilation will occur when the required *with*ing is performed by the subunits (for tasks or subprograms) rather than by the package specification or body that encapsulate the tasks or subprograms.

The guidelines listed here will provide a high degree of reusability because the module design satisfies the object-orientation described earlier, and the design considerations are tailored for a possible distribution of the components among multiple processors.

14.5 ADA GENERICS

Generic packages and subprograms in Ada are used as templates from which programs of similar functionality can be constructed. These templates are written only once, but are used repeatedly by each program that needs a specific kind of functionality. We have already seen examples of generic functions for performing buffering, relaying, transporting, and the management of semaphores. Other examples include sorting, message handling, and finding roots of various mathematical functions. The advantages of using generics in Ada include (1) a higher probability of correctness—there is less code to write and test—and (2) easier maintenance—changes are made only in the generic units rather than throughout the program. The new instantiations are automatically created when the program is recompiled (if we don't change the formal generic parameters).

Reusable software, in the form of generic packages or subprograms, is obtained from an Ada library and instantiated with the proper actual generic parameters in the application program being designed. An ideal design situation would be to construct our whole application program from generic units, similar to the way hardware is designed. A potential caveat is that a significant elaboration time may be experienced on a restart in a system that has certain fault tolerance requirements for restarting after software or hardware faults have been detected.

Extendibility pertains to the ease with which software can be modified to reflect changes in the requirements. Generic Ada units can be extended by making the necessary modifications, and replacing the old generic library units with the modified units. The old application programs that use the generic units will have to be recompiled, but not redesigned. The instantiations need not be modified, unless the generic parameters have been changed.

14.6 ADAPTATION PARAMETERS

One of the most important (and usually most neglected!) design decisions to be made for reusable components is how the adaptation data will be handled. This data determines sizes and capacities of a particular system and should not be hard coded. Examples of adaptation data include maximum number of tracks that can be handled, maximum number of workstations connected, and the number of active sensors in a data acquisition system. The number of adaptation parameters varies greatly between systems, with a range of from 10 to 20 for a small system up to several hundred for a large system.

A flexible design can only be accomplished if the handling of the adaptation data is carefully designed in the software architecture from the start of the development process. The major functions involved with this type of data are creation, initialization, modification, and distribution. One solution to the creation, initialization, and modification of adaptation data is illustrated in Figure 14.1. An off-line system allows an operator to create and modify the values for a list of published adaptation parameters via a DBMS. The DBMS updates the required fields in the database which will be used during startup of the operational system.

Some of the adaptation parameters, referred to as variable system parameters (VSPs) are allowed to be modified on-line when the system is executing. Examples of VSPs in an ATC system include a weather report that is considered valid for VSP hours, and a flight plan to be activated VSP minutes prior to scheduled departure.

A mechanism to accomplish on-line modification of adaptation parameters is shown in Figure 14.2. An operator requests modification of certain values from an Adaptation function. This function evaluates the requests and returns either a positive acknowledgement or an error message depending on whether the request meets with success or failure. After a successful update of one or more adaptation parameters, the Adaptation function distributes the new values to all the functional capabilities that need them.

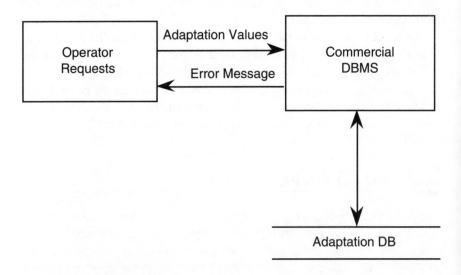

Figure 14.1 Off-Line Adaptation Requests

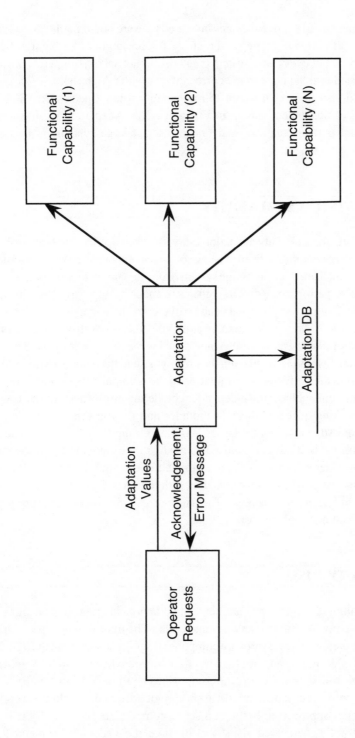

Figure 14.2 On-Line Adaptation Requests

If mechanisms such as the ones indicated here are not implemented as part of the overall software strategy, the strive for reusability can be significantly hampered. For every new system created, another set of parameters must then be inserted into the code in the correct places with a high risk of inaccuracies. It would also be very difficult to implement on-line updates of VSPs. The abstract design object shown in Figure 14.2 as Adaptation is an extremely important part in creating small, medium, and large systems from a set of reusable components.

14.7 SYSTEM SCALABILITY

The criteria for scalability and tailorability are directly related to how well a new system can be composed from existing software components. We are envisioning building small, medium, and large systems from the same components, but initially we have no performance data to guide us in choosing appropriate architectures.

The lack of performance data can be overcome by using the steps illustrated in Figure 14.3. Areas suitable for prototyping and the construction of a nominal demonstration program are determined during the domain analysis. The sizing and timing results obtained from the prototypes and the demonstration program are fed into the performance evaluation of the nominal system. Other inputs to this evaluation include any independent modeling efforts performed, as well as benchmarking of the application modules and the run-time system (e.g., the ACM SIGAda Performance Issues Working Group (PIWG) tests). The combination of this input can be used to evaluate the estimated performance of scalable systems. This data can be applied in choosing suitable architectures for a wide range of customer demands with regard to functionality, processing power, and network interfaces. The data can also be utilized in the preparation of proposal material and costing data.

14.8 COST ISSUES

Undertaking a project to create reusable components represents a significant corporate investment and an associated risk. The most obvious risk is that the effort to create reusable software components will cost more than the traditional method of designing and implementing each system from scratch. Another risk is that the task of maintaining the components gets bogged down with configuration control problems, and the users cannot adequately build their systems. The proper approach to building a set of components successfully is to plan ahead for the perceived risks and to have the necessary implementation mechanisms in place before they are needed.

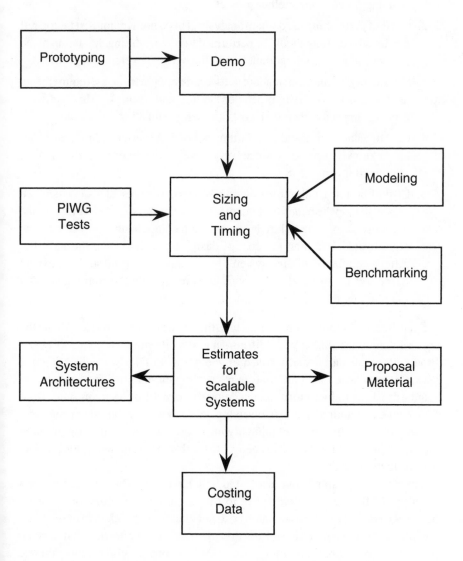

Figure 14.3 System Scalability

General cost factors for establishing a set of reusable software components include the following:

1. Up-front costs of setting up and running the software development organization. This includes the hiring and training of a software develop-

ment staff, unless the staff can be transferred from an organization that is winding down from another project.

2. Costs of performing the domain analysis. This is not a major cost factor, but the domain analysis should be performed very early during the startup of the project and is a very important step in the overall development process.

3. Costs of performing the standard software development tasks (requirements analysis, top level design, detailed design, and testing). Most software organizations have their own cost factors for estimating these tasks.

4. Cost of establishing and maintaining software libraries. This is probably an unknown parameter since very few software organizations have attempted this in the past.

5. Cost of building tailorable systems from components. This is where we expect to reap the benefits of our effort to create the software components. The cost of creating tailored systems from components is expected to be significantly less than the cost of designing each system individually. After a number of tailored systems have been created and sold, we expect to recover the original investment spent in creating the components and maintaining the software libraries.

Specific cost factors to consider include the software productivity rate and the cost reduction associated with "lifting" and transitioning available software. Productivity rates are usually based on the number of software lines of code (SLOCs) produced per unit time, e.g., per person-month, and include the standard tasks. Productivity numbers reported for real-time systems range from 50 to several hundred per person-month and should be based on numbers actually obtained by the developing organization. The choice of programming language and availability of a trained staff for this language will greatly affect the productivity rate.

There is always some cost associated with reusable software, even if it is a complete "lift," i.e., we don't have to modify a software component at all before we can use it. The associated costs include the time taken to understand the interfaces to the module and any documentation and retesting that must be performed. If we are transitioning software from one programming language to another, there is always a cost included with reprogramming algorithms and repackaging of modules. A way of estimating the total cost for a mixture of new, lifted, and transitioned software is to assign the latter two categories some percentage cost of what it would cost for new software to be developed. With new software at 100%, a lift may be estimated, for example, at 15–30%, and a transition from 35 to 65%. If the estimate for transitioned software exceeds 65%, it is probably better to redesign and reprogram the potentially reusable modules.

14.9 PARTS CATALOGUE

The components produced will be collected into a "parts" catalogue. Each part will contain the software component and associated documentation in the form of software requirements specification (SRS), design material, and PDL. It may seem a bit unnatural at first that a piece of the requirements specification should be directly linked to a software component. The rational for this approach is that we not only reuse software components, but the documentation as well. As shown in Figure 14.4, we take piecemeal software components and documentation and produce a tailored system and the required documentation for that system.

Component size and performance characteristics are also included for each part contained in the catalogue, along with any operational or platform dependent restrictions. Specific information to be available in the parts catalogue should include (at least) the following:

name of software module

associated requirements

restrictions for use

adaptation parameters

tailoring information (e.g., OS and platform)

size in SLOC

PDL file name

compilation dependencies

proposal and marketing information

configuration guide

timing and performance characteristics

Summary

Object-oriented reusable software components are created using a set of evaluation criteria for modularity and desirable coupling and cohesion. Ada generics facilitates the creation of reusable packages. One possible drawback with numerous generic packages is that a system that is subject to restarts may suffer long elaboration times each time the system is restarted.

The use of adaptation parameters is crucial in the creation of scalable systems.

A deliberate effort to produce sizing and timing estimates includes prototyping, modeling, and benchmarking. This information is vital in selecting suitable architectures for the various customer demands.

The production of a set of reusable software components represents a significant investment, and a careful analysis should be made of the various cost factors and cost reduction issues.

Reusable items are not limited to the software components. Associated software requirements specification and design material are extremely valuable in reducing the overall cost of producing tailored systems. The reusable products are placed in a parts catalogue for ease of access.

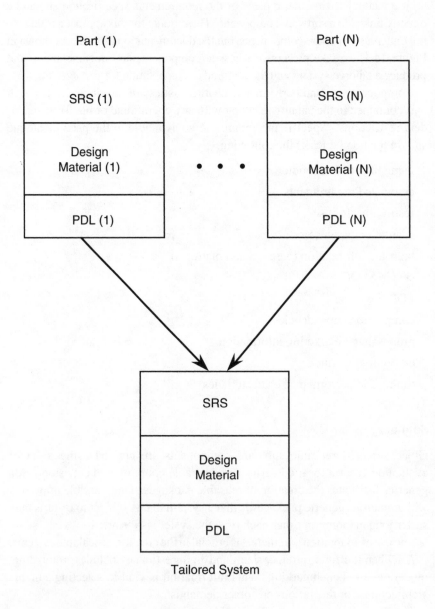

Figure 14.4 Building Systems from Parts

15

Library of Reusable Components

Up to this point we have only been concerned with the creation of reusable components from the point of view of the developers. For an organization to be successful in implementing a long term reuse program, careful considerations must be given to how the information is stored and maintained and how it can be retrieved. This chapter describes the storage and maintenance issues and suggests an approach to data retrieval. We assume that the potential users of the information stored are knowledgeable about the functionality in the problem domain and that they are familiar with the programming language used for the software components.

15.1 DATA ORGANIZATION

A parts catalogue and its content was mentioned briefly in the previous chapter. The main issue is how to organize the stored information for easy retrieval by the users. Since we are creating software components for a specific problem domain, most users will initially be interested in the functionality provided, and then the corresponding software components for the given functions.

The stored information can be organized in hierarchical layers with a functional description at the top. For an ATC system, for example, an alphabetized list of functional areas and subfunctions may include the following [FIE85, NOL90]:

1. **Adaptation**

   a. Off-line
   b. On-line

2. **Communication**

   a. AFTN (Aeronautical Fixed Telecommunication Network)
   b. CIDIN (Common ICAO Data Interchange Network)
   c. Interprocess Communication

3. **Configuration Management**

   a. Restart
   b. Sectorization
   c. Startup

4. **Controller Display Interface**

   a. Map Display
   b. Situation Display
   c. Tabular Display

5. **Flight Data Processing (FDP)**

   a. Airspace Management
   b. Flight Plan Activation
   c. Flight Plan Amendment
   d. Flight Progress Strips
   e. Flow Control
   f. Handover
   g. Repetitive Flight Plans
   h. Reporting and Billing
   i. Route Conversion
   j. Trajectory Estimation

6. **Radar Data Processing (RDP)**

   a. Conflict Alerts
   b. Coordinate Conversion

c. Minimum Safe Altitude Warning (MSAW)

d. Track Correlation

e. Track Initiation

f. Tracking

- Mosaic

- Multi radar

- Primary Surveillance Radar (PSR)

- Secondary Surveillance Radar (SSR)

g. Track to Flight Plan Pairing

h. Weather Data

7. **Radar Interfaces**

a. Radar X (make and model)

b. Radar Y (make and model)

The names of the functions and subfunctions must be sufficiently descriptive and unambiguous that a potential user, who is familiar with the problem domain, can immediately recognize the functionality.

The top level list of functions points to the documentation and the name of the software component that implements the function, as shown in Figure 15.1. The documentation consists of software requirements, top level and detailed design information, and a pointer to a software design folder. Data for the software component includes a directory path, specification, body, and subunits. We are assuming that Ada is the programming language here, but this scheme will work equally well for C and C++ components.

15.2 DOCUMENTATION

The documentation associated with a given subfunction must be presented in a uniform format. It is preferable that the format be based on a documentation standard that can be used for a wide range of systems. One such standard is DoD Military Standard 2167A [DOD88]. One problem with this standard is its comprehensive nature and the large number of different documents specified. All of these documents are not necessary for commercial implementations, and a tailoring can be performed by picking only those documents that make sense for the given problem domain. Further tailoring can be made by only including certain sections within each document. Tailoring is not unique for commercial projects, but concurrence is usually required by a military customer for our suggested tailoring.

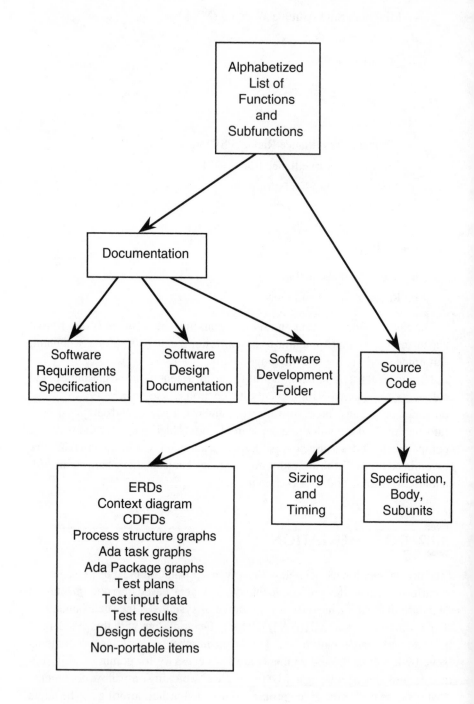

Figure 15.1 Information Hierarchy

The primary documents required for delivery of a system to a customer include a Software Requirements Specification (SRS), a Software Design Document (SDD), test plans and test results, and the code. The portions of this documentation that correspond to a software component that implements a functionality should be available for inclusion in the required documents for the systems built.

The SRS includes functional descriptions of customer requirements, and focuses on the "what" is to be performed by the system. An important part of this documentation is the listing of anticipated interfaces between the functions. For a message driven system this interface consists of a list of message names and their data elements. "Ownership" of these messages can be assigned to the subfunction/component that creates the message. The names of the messages and their data elements must be used consistently throughout the system, and similar names such as Connection Not Available and Connection Unavailable must not be allowed.

Design material includes data and control flow diagrams (CDFDs), process structure charts, Ada task graphs, Ada package graphs, English descriptions of design objects, and PDL. Some of this material will be collected in the SDD, and the remainder will be kept in a software development folder (SDF) for each component. Entity-relationship diagrams may be included in the requirements specification or developed as design material. The SDFs are usually kept in a file cabinet and stored by component name. Electronic SDFs have been created, but they do not include hand drawn charts, and this means having to look in two different places for the information. The SDFs should include any important design decisions that are made along the development path.

Source code for all the software components must be created uniformly using a Coding Standard. This standard should specify a prologue, indentation levels, naming conventions, and general coding guidelines. Since we are assuming Ada for the implementation language, the software components will include package specifications, package bodies, and associated subunits.

Test documentation should include test plans, test scripts, input data, and expected results. This information can be kept on electronic media or in the SDF. In most cases the plans, scripts, and input data will probably be on electronic media. The test results may be kept in the SDF if they were generated on a screen with the screen image printed. They would be on electronic media if an output file was created when the test was executed.

An important piece of documentation for a software component is any potential non-portable dependencies. This could include the use of task priorities, use of vendor-dependent pragmas, interrupt addressing, and use of executive service routines. Information regarding non-portable items should be included in the SDD or listed in the SDF. It should not be left to the user to dig this out of the code.

Each component should list the code size and timing details for critical modules. This data can be used for proposal and costing information, and for system performance evaluation. The data should be kept with the SRS sections, but accurate values cannot be obtained until after the component has been implemented and tested in the operational system.

15.3 SOURCE CODE LIBRARY

The source code for the software components should be kept in a protected library. This can be implemented either with a DBMS or a set of read-only files. Separate source files should be created for specifications, bodies, and subunits. Keeping the components as library units in an Ada library is not recommended because code will usually have to be recompiled for a new host and/or target.

For a project with limited resources, the simplest implementation of a source library is to create one or more controlled directories on a magnetic disk with backup on a tape. This does not require paying the (usually high!) license fee for a formal DBMS, and still provides controlled access. A source library administrator can modify the library, but users can only read and copy the components. A formal configuration management scheme is described in a later section in this chapter.

15.4 INFORMATION RETRIEVAL DISPLAY

The success of reusing software components for a given problem domain will be directly proportional to the ease with which the required information can be obtained by the users. If the components and documentation are kept informally without automated means, the time to locate and tailor the components for new systems will become inordinate, and the users are likely to look elsewhere.

An interactive information system can be implemented as shown in Figure 15.2. The users can select functions and subfunctions from menus. The example shown in the figure illustrates RDP as a major function with Minimum Safe Altitude Warning (MSAW) as the selected subfunction. Directory structures are displayed for the SRS and SDD sections for the MSAW component, along with the Ada file names for the package specification and body. This example shows no subunits for the MSAW component. The user has a choice of printing the information shown on the screen, returning to the main menu for a selection of another main function, or quitting.

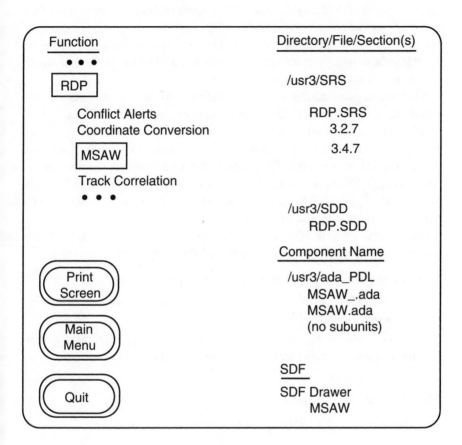

Figure 15.2 Information Retrieval Display

15.5 CONFIGURATION CONTROL

One of the fundamental assumptions throughout this book is that we are primarily concerned with the development of *large* real-time systems. This implies that several individuals and groups of developers need access to the same source files, and that source code is periodically updated. The different groups of developers must be working with a consistent set of source files when they build their program libraries, and this requires a certain control mechanism for maintaining this consistency.

A formal approach must be created for accepting documentation and software components into the library structure. The documentation must be reviewed for consistent format and accurate functionality. Software components must have been fully tested as individual units and when integrated with other components that it interfaces with. The code portions must be checked for conformance with the coding standards and design guidelines.

When the documentation and corresponding software components are submitted for inclusion into the library, a formal version control goes into effect. No changes are allowed to either documentation or software unless it goes through a formal configuration control (CC) process. This can be done with commercial off-the-shelf (COTS) products that are tailored for specific operating systems. Examples of COTS products for CC include DEC's Code Management System (CMS), and the Source Code Control System (sccs) which runs under the Unix operating system.

The general control of software components is referred to as *software configuration management* and can be divided into three separate activities:

- Change control — the maintenance of software changes.

- Version control — the recording and matching of a unique version number with a certain source file.

- Build control — the matching of a build number (representing a certain (partial) functionality) with a set of software components.

15.5.1 Change Control

Functions required of a CC program for change control include:

1. **Register.** Impounding a new source file.

2. **Check-out.** Checking out a source file that will be modified. A notification is made that a file is checked out, and it is expected that the file will be modified. No one else may check out the same file for modification until the file is checked back in.

3. **Check-in.** A modified file is checked back into the system.

4. **Extract.** A copy of a file that will be used for experimentation by a local user. An extracted file cannot be modified and checked back in.

5. **Difference.** Shows the differences between a file under CC and a local file.

6. **Checklist.** List of files checked out by a certain user.

7. **Make library.** Creates a new object library.

8. **Make object.** Compiles the given object.

9. **Link.** Compiles objects that the listed component depends on and links the current component.

The change control functions supported by a typical CC system are depicted in Figure 15.3. Note that an extracted file may be edited and compiled in a local user's workspace, but it cannot be checked back into the CC system. This can only be done with the check-out/check-in loop.

A high degree of change control formality can introduce a significant amount of overhead to the development process, including a Change Request Board (CRB). This means that before a programmer can modify a software component, a formal request form must be filled out and approval for the change must be made by the CRB. A less formal change control allows the developers to make changes via the check-in/check-out process until a specific configuration or build is tested.

15.5.2 Version Control

Version control can be affected by automated means without any specific action on the part of the developer. A software file is assigned a version number when it is first registered. The version number is automatically updated each time a file is updated and checked back in. This can be accomplished by including special characters as the first line in the source file. These characters are interpreted by the CC system which provides an update of the version number each time the file is checked in. An initial version number is established when the file is registered. The compiler simply ignores the first source line containing the special characters. As an example, the following format is used by sccs for version control:

```
# %W% Modified: %G% %U%
```

and the corresponding version 1.3 information appearing in the first source line of an Ada package with the file name ipc_services_.a could be

```
-- @(#)ipc_services_.a 1.3 Modified: 03/11/92 08:16:28
```

15.5.3 Build Control

Build control can be accomplished manually be creating a certain software configuration. Each configuration represents a given functionality that is executed by a set of software components with unique identifiers and associated version numbers. Early builds may support prototyping efforts to demonstrate operational concepts. Subsequent builds will contain significant portions of the functional requirements. A build strategy should be mapped out early in the project to ensure an efficient incremental development approach and adequate test plans.

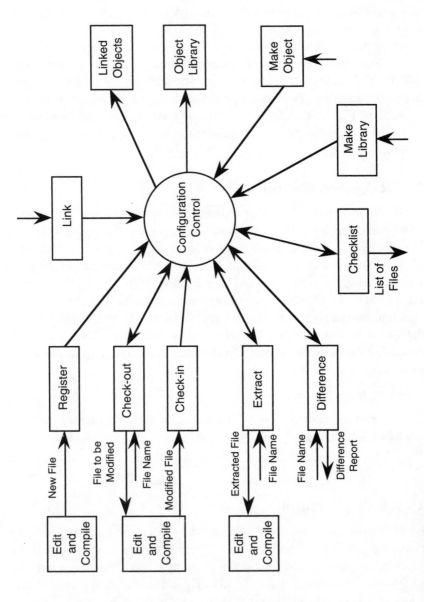

Figurre 15.3 Change Control Functions

One way to free the developers from having to worry about having an up-to-date version of the software being available, is to run an automated procedure (script) that recompiles all the source code checked in during the previous day. For a regular day-shift, this would, typically, be done after midnight such that the developers will have a fresh master library when they start work in the morning. A strict discipline must be impressed upon the developers to thoroughly test out a source file and make sure it compiles error free before it is checked in. If this is not adhered to, the new master library will not be ready for the morning staff, and the guilty programmers will probably suffer a certain amount of "ribbing" from their coworkers.

15.6 MAINTENANCE

When a component reuse capability is originally conceived, plans must be made for maintenance of the documentation and software components. The original effort will most likely be focused on building a set of core capabilities. A continuing effort will expand the core capabilities to include additional functionalities for the same problem domain. The core capabilities will be used to demonstrate a product line to potential customers. The follow-on effort will be based on specific system requirements demanded by the customers.

The maintenance effort will include tailoring small, medium, and large systems from the available software components, modifying some of the component interfaces, and building additional capabilities for expanded and new functionalities. It is extremely important that the automated mechanisms listed above for configuration control, and acceptance criteria for documentation and software, be implemented for the maintenance phase to be successful. Merely having a collection of software components will make it very difficult to promote the construction of tailorable systems.

Summary

A library of reusable components and associated documentation is essential for a successful implementation of tailoring small, medium, and large systems within a given problem domain.

The retrievable information can be organized as a hierarchy with the functional capabilities in the problem domain at the highest level.

Adequate documentation must be furnished for each software component. This includes a functional description of each capability, design information for the software component, source code, test plans and results, non-portable dependencies, and sizing and timing data.

The source code should be kept in a read-only library or protected by a DBMS.

Information retrieval should be made interactive and user-friendly.

All documentation and source code must be placed under configuration control with automated version updating.

A continuous maintenance effort will be required for (hopefully minimum) modification of module interfaces and implementation of expanded and new functionalities.

16

Development Approach Summary

The methodology developed in this book is a blend of modern object-oriented paradigms and proven structured techniques extended for real-time systems. We have not abandoned the methodologies that have been employed successfully by major software organizations over the last decade; rather, we are complementing these techniques with object-oriented paradigms. By building on known, available methodologies, the investment risk in using the newer paradigms is minimized.

In this chapter we provide a summary of the development approach. The approach is based on a software-first paradigm, and is eminently suited to distributed real-time systems. Special emphasis is placed on determining the concurrent objects of the real-time system, using process abstraction. The approach also supports the software engineering concepts of information hiding, data abstraction, and stepwise refinement. The steps of the methodology are complemented with heuristics to provide the necessary support for a practical implementation. Numerous graphical tools are used as aids to the design process, and provide important documentation of the final design. The top level design culminates with a set of application package objects encapsulating Ada tasks. These tasks are decomposed further during the detailed design emphasizing a parallel concern for functional decomposition (creating layered virtual machines) and for the generation of data managers (OOD).

The development approach is tailored to support the reusability of software components within a certain problem domain. Small, medium, and large distributed real-time systems can be designed from available component documentation and software modules.

16.1 APPROACH OVERVIEW

A summary of the complete development approach is illustrated in Figure 16.1. We will provide a short synopsis of each step, object-oriented issues, and the main points regarding reusability.

16.1.1 Domain Analysis

The first step in the development approach is to perform a domain analysis. This will identify the availability of in-house staff with systems and software expertise in the problem domain, and available documentation and software that can be reused and modified.

Objects and classes identified during this step are associated with main functional areas such as tracking, flight plan processing, robot control, and message translation. Attributes and operations (behavior) are identified for each object instance. Entity-relationship diagrams (ERDs) are used to get a better understanding of the major real-world objects and their relationships.

Reusability issues considered during this phase include the magnitude and quality of available software modules and related documentation, and plans for the creation of a library of reusable components. Additional decisions made in this step include functional areas suitable for prototyping and a demonstration project.

16.1.2 Requirements Analysis

This phase is used to model the system requirements. The context diagram illustrates the data flowing between the external interfaces and the system we are going to develop. Control and data flow diagrams (CDFDs) are used to model the processing flow through the system. The CDFDs are leveled until all areas containing concurrent processing have been uncovered. Major data areas are identified as potential objects to be implemented as data managers. ERDs can be used to decompose large objects and gain a better understanding of their relationships. State transition diagrams may be used to document functional areas with complex state changes.

16.1.3 Transitioning from Requirements Analysis to Design

This includes the process abstraction phase and represents the first major step in transitioning from analysis to design. The functions identified in the CDFDs are combined into abstract processes using the process selection rules. The product of this step is the process structure chart.

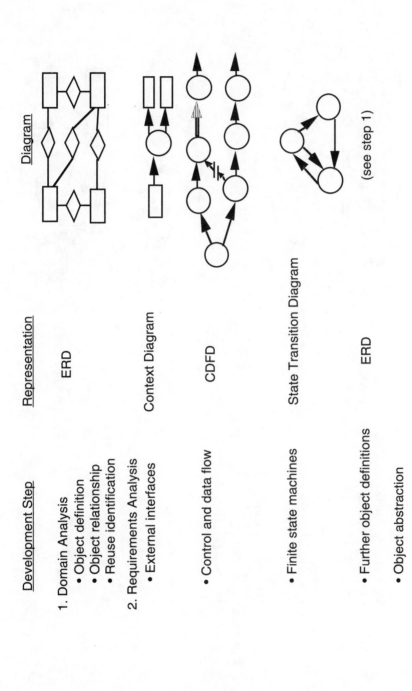

Figure 16.1 Development Approach Summary

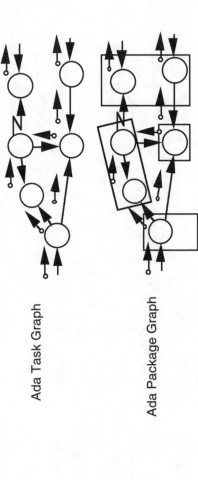

3. Transitioning from
Requirements Analysis to Design
   • Process selection   Process Id

   • Process abstraction   Process Structure Chart

   • Process transformation

4. Top Level Design

   • Task Structure   Ada Task Graph

   • Packaging   Ada Package Graph

Figure 16.1 Continued

4. Top Level Design (continued)

- Data Managers

OOD Diagram

- PDL

Ada PDL

5. Detailed Design

- Decomposition of large tasks
  LVM/OOD

Structure Chart
and OOD diagram

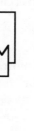

- Data Managers

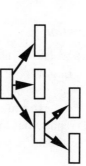

- PDL

Ada PDL

Figure 16.1 Continued

Process Interfaces

The processes identified during the process abstraction phase are analyzed for proper interfaces using the producer/consumer model. Each producer/consumer pair is evaluated with regard to a suitable coupling in terms of synchronous and asynchronous communication. Shared data areas are scrutinized for the required mutually exclusive data access. The product of this step is the process structure chart produced during the concurrency analysis with the specific coupling symbols added between each producer/consumer pair.

Process Transformation

During this step we translate the abstract processes into Ada tasks. Producer/ consumer pairs requiring a loose coupling may be implemented by adding intermediary tasks, e.g., for buffering of messages. The cost of adding intermediary tasks is the extra run-time overhead suffered during execution. The asymmetric Ada rendezvous requires a careful analysis of the caller/called relations between the tasks. A set of heuristics is furnished to support this analysis.

16.1.4 Top Level Design

The task structure developed during the transitioning step is illustrated in the Ada task graph. The tasks are not yet real design objects, since Ada tasks cannot be compilation units. This step includes the encapsulation of Ada tasks with packages, identifying additional data managers, and preparing Ada PDL.

Ada Packaging

A set of packaging rules is used to encapsulate the Ada tasks into the application packages described in the package taxonomy. These packages represent the major design objects of the problem domain and contain the primary functional requirements. The product of this step is the Ada package graph, which shows the encapsulation of the Ada tasks and the interfaces between the packages.

Creating Data Managers

The abstract objects that model the data managers are first identified during the analysis phase. The data structures that show up on the CDFDs are strong candidates for data managers. The objects identified are transformed into data managers in a bottom-up fashion just prior to the creation of the Ada PDL for the application packages. These data managers are formed by encapsulating types and operations in Ada packages.

Top Level PDL

The top level Ada PDL (application packages) is produced top-down after the data managers and generic units have been completed bottom-up. This is done to take advantage of Ada's interface and type checking capabilities. The product of this phase is compiled Ada PDL written in accordance with a set of Ada coding standards.

16.1.5 Detailed Design

Any task that contains more functionality than can reasonably be expressed within a single task body is decomposed into a set of subprograms and, possibly, data managers. The functional decomposition is accomplished with a set of layered virtual machines, and uses traditional structured design. Additionally, data managers are created using OOD in parallel with the functional decomposition. The products of this phase are structure charts showing the calling relations of the layered instructions and OOD diagrams for the data managers.

Detailed Design PDL

During this phase we furnish the details of the subunits that were deferred via the *separate* statement during top level design and the decomposition of the large tasks. The product of this phase is compiled Ada PDL written with the same Ada coding standards as the top level PDL.

16.2 REUSABLE PRODUCTS

Reusable products are not limited to software components. Here is a list of the products that can be reused from the various development phases:

1. **Domain analysis.** During this phase we determine sources of reusable software and documentation, and identify local problem domain expertise:

    a. *Reusable software.* Available software modules are associated with functions to be performed, programming language(s) used, module size, and an estimate of the effort required to transition the software to the programming language to be used.

    b. *Reusable documentation.* The quantity and quality of the documentation available for the potentially reusable software is identified in terms of SRS material providing functional descriptions, graphics tools such as ERDs, CDFDs, state transition diagrams, and design material such as process structure graphs, task graphs, structure charts, OOD diagrams, module or package graphs, and PDL listings. Additional material of interest includes coding standards and design guidelines.

c. *Local experts.* Systems and software engineers familiar with the functionality and software requirements of the problem domain should be identified. Some of these experts may have participated in a previous project that created software in a different programming language for the same problem domain. These individuals may become extremely valuable if a decision is made to transition software written in a different programming language. Other individuals to be identified early on are programming language consultants for a new language. This is particularly important for projects expecting to use Ada or C++. A significant educational investment may be required to establish a competent staff in either of these two languages.

2. **Requirements analysis.** If the SRS functional descriptions are tailored to a component view, the individual sections can be used to create the SRS that is required for each system that is composed from the components. Otherwise, the applicable functional areas will have to be written to fit the documentation required for the new system.

3. **Transitioning from analysis to design.** The reusable products of this phase include process structure charts and design decision used to determine the task structure.

4. **Top level and detailed design.** The primary product from these phases are Ada tasks graphs, Ada package graphs, structured charts, OOD diagrams, the compiled PDL, and the design documentation. Additional documents of interest include descriptions of how to use a particular debugger and how to construct and access software libraries.

The reusable products and descriptions for how to obtain them make up the components catalogue. Access to the various parts in the catalogue should be provided via an interactive interface that clearly shows component names, the files that contain the software components, and references to the associated documentation.

The overall development strategy presented in this book is a blend of OOA, structured analysis and design extended for real-time systems (SA/RTD) and OOD, with the emphasis on OOD. The primary elements of OOA is the determination of reusable objects during the domain analysis, and the object abstraction with identification of operations and attributes during the requirements analysis. ERDs are used as the primary graphical representation to illustrate real-world objects and their relationships.

We have complemented the newer OOA paradigms with the proven structured analysis and design paradigms to create object-oriented designs that support reusable components.

The domain analysis is the primary activity for the determination of a reuse strategy to be used for a large project. Elements to be reused should not be limited to software components, but should include SRS material and design documentation as well. If the SRS material is written in the traditional SA/RTD fashion, it should be used "as is." It makes little sense to retrofit this documentation with an OOA flavor if software components with a proper OOD architecture are available.

Designing and Implementing an IPC Mechanism

Most of the examples used throughout the text to illustrate the domain analysis and the requirements analysis steps of the development cycle were taken from an application domain of the hierarchy level. In this appendix we will demonstrate the development methodology with an example from the technology domain: an IPC mechanism that may be used for different real-time distributed applications. After applying our object-oriented principles to the top level design of a general IPC mechanism, we will focus the detailed design on an Ada RPC/XDR implementation for an Add function.

A.1 IPC FOR DISTRIBUTED REAL-TIME SYSTEMS

An IPC mechanism can be considered the glue that holds a distributed system together. By distributed real-time systems we mean multiple processes (or programs) that reside on different processors. These processes support a single application such as an air traffic control system or robot controller, and they have a need to communicate. There are, usually, no services available within a given programming language (e.g., Ada, C, or C++) nor as operating system (OS) services to provide interprocessor communication. Such a communication mechanism will have to be incorporated with the design of the application.

A general IPC mechanism should anticipate the need for reconfiguration of processes to support fault tolerance. This implies that processes originally distributed to different processors may be redistributed during reconfiguration and reside on the same processor. Processes should, thus, not be aware of where their neighboring processes reside. When we refer to "IPC," we mean *interprocess* rather than *interprocessor* to accommodate processes that may reside on the same processor.

The most important feature of an IPC implementation is efficiency. Every piece of data communicated between the processes in the real-time system will be funnelled through IPC. If the IPC mechanism is inefficient, it may create a major bottleneck to the flow of data, and performance requirements may not be satisfied.

Most of today's distributed real-time systems employ multiple processors with heterogeneous hardware architectures. This requires special data transformation services to accommodate different word lengths, different byte orderings, and memory references.

A.2 DOMAIN ANALYSIS

The development of an IPC approach belongs in the technology level of the domain hierarchy. The initial decision to be made is whether or not the IPC to be developed should span several related application domains (e.g., air traffic control and air defense) or should should only support a single application domain such as robotics. Reusability may be maximized with a multi-application IPC, but it may too ambitious and costly. We will only consider IPC for a single real-time application in this appendix.

A.2.1 Architecture Considerations

A view of the architecture used in a typical distributed real-time system is shown in Figure A.1. Interacting processes reside in the different processors which are connected via various forms of communication media. Processors 1, 2, and 3 are connected through a Local Area Network (LAN) and have access to shared memory. Processors 3 and 4 are connected via a bus and have local memory. Processor 2 also has local memory. Processors 1, 2, and 3 may have heterogeneous CPUs, whereas Processors 3 and 4 are likely to use homogeneous CPUs, or at least, CPUs within the same family (e.g., MC680X0 or Intel 80X86).

The processes shown in Figure A.1 contain software elements that represent the functional requirements of a given real-time application. These processes need to communicate, and our IPC mechanism must allow, for example, process P1.1 to communicate with P1.2 as well as with P4.1.

Specific architectural considerations for the IPC domain analysis include:

1. **Variations in the hardware architecture.** This includes the different processors that must be accommodated for systems in the application domain, e.g., Sun, VAX, and MC680X0.

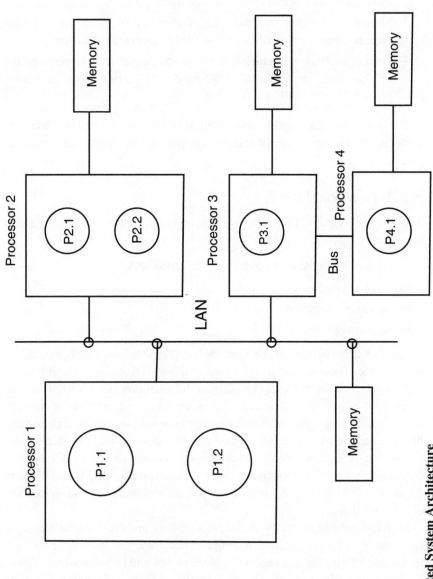

Figure A.1 Distributed System Architecture

2. **Communication media.** The type and capacity of the communication media to be used, e.g., a 10 Mbit/second Ethernet LAN, and/or a 20 Mbyte/second VMEbus must be identified.

3. **Memory.** The type and capacity of memory required, e.g., on-chip memory, memory boards, and disk space must be determined.

4. **Communication mechanism.** Data can be passed as a message with a unique identifier for each message, or via services such as remote procedure calls (RPCs).

These architectural considerations will form the basis for making decisions regarding the creation of reusable components to support the different architectures.

A.2.2 Functional Areas

The functions required for an IPC mechanism can be divided into the following major areas:

• interfaces to application programs (i.e., processes),

• storage management,

• message passing, and

• time management.

Interfacing to application programs include the establishment of connections between the processes and maintenance of a connection map. The interfaces will be required for processes residing in different processors or in the same processor. Functions must include the determination of whether or not data transformations are required between heterogeneous processors. The connection mechanism may be available as a part of a commercial communications protocol, e.g., Transmission Control Protocol/Internet Protocol (TCP/IP).

Storage management functions include allocation and deallocation of memory required to hold the data elements to be passed, and buffering and sequencing of message data.

Message passing functions include the sending and receiving of messages (with and without reply), handshaking and acknowledgements at the application level, prioritizing and sequences of messages, and transformation of data.

Time management functions include the maintenance of synchronized time between the various processors, as well as providing local time within each processor. Synchronized time may have to be available for multiple sessions, e.g., a live, operational session and a simulation session.

A.2.3 Reusable Functions

Reusable functions identified during the domain analysis include:

1. **Interfaces to application programs**

   • Create TCP/IP sockets and ports
   • Register application programs (processes)
   • Connect to application x
   • Accept all messages
   • Accept broadcast messages
   • Accept guaranteed messages
   • Close communications
   • Open broadcast channel
   • Open multicast channel

2. **Storage management**

   • Create buffer
   • Release buffer
   • Save buffer

3. **Message passing**

   • Send (with and without reply)
   • Send (with and without delay)
   • Send guaranteed message
   • Send broadcast message
   • Send multicast message
   • Receive (with and without delay)

4. **Time management**

   • Get synchronized time
   • Get local time
   • Register session

The functions identified here provide the kernel of reusable components to be obtained from previous projects, bought as commercial off-the-shelf (COTS) software, or developed with project funds.

A.2.4 Classes and Objects

We will predominantly identify objects rather than classes and objects. The reusable IPC functions identified within a given problem domain are low level entities and do not appear as instances of higher level entities. We will describe the functions identified above with the following objects:

1. **Application Program Interface**

   Attributes

   • Maximum number of connections
   • Application identifier
   • Channel number
   • Port number
   • Socket number

   Operations

   • Register application
   • Application available
   • Establish connection
   • Close connection
   • Report errors

2. **Storage Manager**

   Attributes

   • Maximum storage available
   • Storage type (permanent or temporary)

   Operations

   • Allocate storage
   • Deallocate storage
   • Report errors

3. **Message Passing Manager**

   Attributes

   • Message length
   • Message type (guaranteed/multicast/broadcast)

- Message header
- Maximum delay time

Operations

- Send (with and without reply)
- Send (with and without delay)
- Receive
- Transform data from local to external format
- Transform data from external to local format
- Report errors

4. **Time Manager**

Attributes

- Session identifier
- Time specifier (global or local)
- Time units (seconds, minutes, hours, etc.)

Operations

- Register session
- Get synchronized time
- Get local time
- Report errors

The objects identified here represent real-world objects in a technology domain. We can clearly see that they are at a lower level than objects identified at the application level. A Time Manager in an IPC mechanism is a lower level object compared to a Flight Data Manager in an ATC system.

A.3 REQUIREMENTS ANALYSIS

The primary purpose of an IPC mechanism is to provide a transparent interface between application programs residing in different processors. This mechanism must be efficient with regard to the number of messages that can be passed per unit time and the amount of storage required. Different levels of message delivery should include guaranteed (connection-oriented to single addressee), broadcast, and multicast (guaranteed to multiple addressees).

The IPC implementation must support a high degree of portability, and should shield the application functions from low level communications interfaces such as TCP/IP. These functions should also be shielded from interfaces to OS services. Applications should be easily rehosted to a multitude of different platforms with a variety of architectures.

Typical real-time distributed systems have a requirement for reconfiguration to support fault tolerance if software or hardware faults are detected. Even though IPC does not support the reconfiguration directly, it must interface to the application functions that provide the monitor and control services.

Time management is another requirement for real-time distributed systems. It is necessary that different parts of an application that reside in separate processors refer to time with the same base. The synchronization of time among the processors provide a global time reference. A local time reference is also required where an application is simply referring to a time interval. The time management function does not have to be assigned to IPC, but since IPC provides an interface between the processors, this is a logical place to allocate this function rather than to create a whole separate function for this purpose.

The functional requirements listed above can be implemented with the IPC client/server model shown in Figure A.2. To illustrate this model we have assumed two separate processors for the application programs and two display stations, with a total of four processors connected via a LAN. Each application program and display program has an associated IPC client. The interprocess (and interprocessor) functions are collected in the IPC server associated with each processor.

The context diagram for IPC is shown in Figure A.3. This diagram illustrates the IPC interfaces with external elements. An external time source (e.g., satellite time receiver) and the OS services provide external time (for synchronization) and CPU time, respectively. An adaptation program provides adaptation data for a given configuration. The application and display programs are considered external to IPC, since IPC provides message passing between them and the programs do not have any direct interfaces.

An entity-relationship diagram (ERD) is shown in Figure A.4 and illustrates the primary IPC entities and their relationships. The subentities Message Storage and Connection Directory have been added here. They were not identified as objects during the domain analysis phase.

A portion of the IPC processing is shown in the CDFD in Figure A.5. This figure is used as an aid in the transitioning process from analysis to design and provides the basis for the process abstraction analysis.

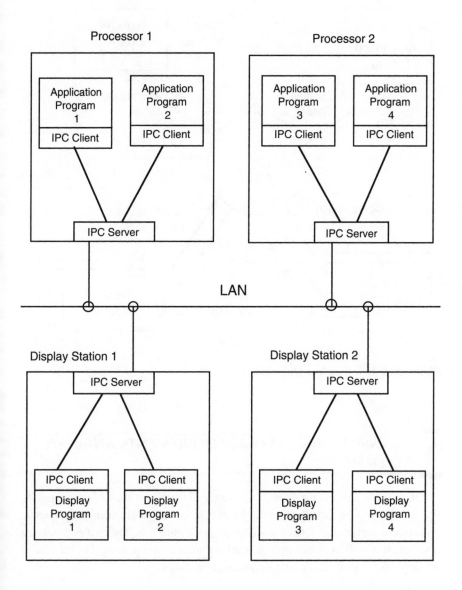

Figure A.2 IPC Client/Server Model

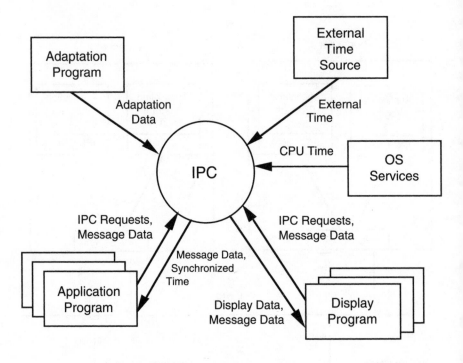

Figure A.3 IPC Context Diagram

A.4 TRANSITIONING FROM REQUIREMENTS ANALYSIS TO DESIGN

Combining the transforms shown in Figure A.5 (only a portion of the complete IPC functions is included) using the process selection rules given in Chapter 7, we arrive at the process abstraction depicted in Figure A.6. The circles represent abstract objects that can be implemented as concurrent elements. The interfaces are described using the notation presented in Chapter 7.

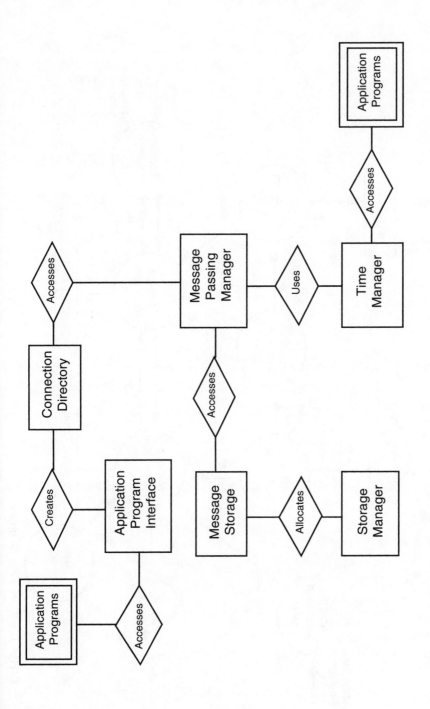

Figure A.4 IPC Entity-Relationship Diagram

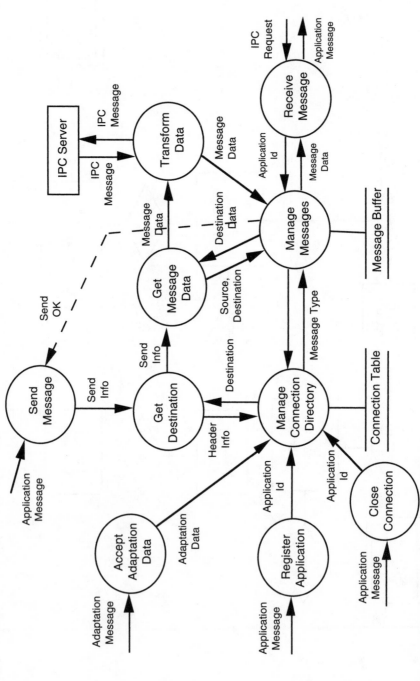

Figure A.5 Partial IPC Data Flow Diagram

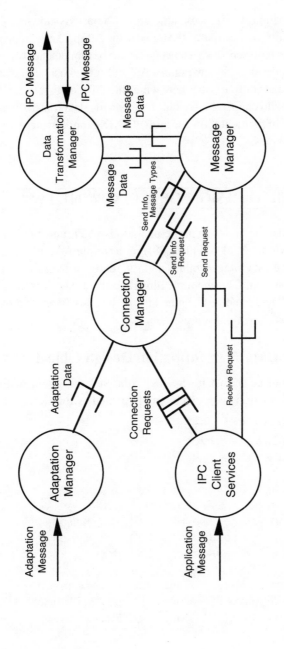

Figure A.6 IPC Process Structure Chart

A.5 TOP LEVEL DESIGN

The transformation of the process structure to Ada tasks is shown in Figure A.7, and the encapsulation of the tasks is illustrated in the Ada package graph in Figure A.8. The rectangles represent design objects that can be implemented directly with Ada PDL. The reader should view Figures A.7 and A.8 with a bit of caution. We are dealing with distributive issues here which are difficult to represent graphically. For the rest of this appendix we will focus on the data transformation manager and show an implementation for an RPC/XDR model where we do consider distributive issues.

A.6 DETAILED DESIGN OF RPC/XDR INTERFACE

This section demonstrates an implementation of RPC and XDR using commercial RPC services (AdaLAN [TEL88]) for a simple Add function that requires the addition of two integer values and the return of the result with a possible overflow condition. This example illustrates the use of the remote RPC client/ server model described in Chapter 11 and the associated data transformation mechanism as shown in Figure A.9.

A.6.1 The Data Transformation Design Object

The design object shown in the IPC Ada package graph in Figure A.8 as Data_Transformation_Mgr can be implemented as follows:

```
with AdaLAN_XDR_Memory;
with AdaLAN_RPC_Types;
with AdaLAN_Error_Handler;

package XDR_Conversions is
  -- Package Abbreviation : XCON
  package XM renames AdaLAN_XDR_Memory;
  package RT renames AdaLAN_RPC_Types;
  package EH renames AdaLAN_Error_Handler;

  Program_Number : constant RT.Prognums := 200_500;
  Version_Number : constant RT.Versnums := 1;
  Add_Proc_Num   : constant RT.Procnums := 1;
                              -- RPC proc number;

  type Add_In is   -- RPC data sent from client
    record
      First  : Integer;
```

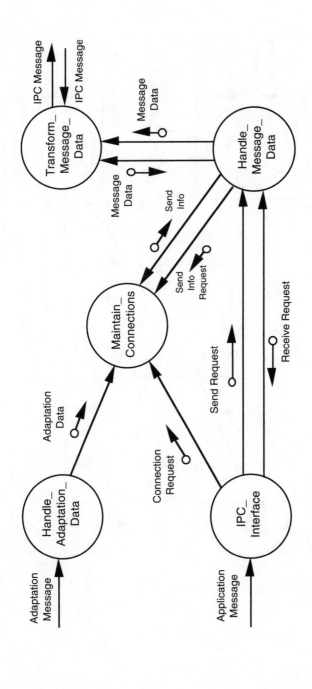

Figure A.7 IPC Ada Task Graph

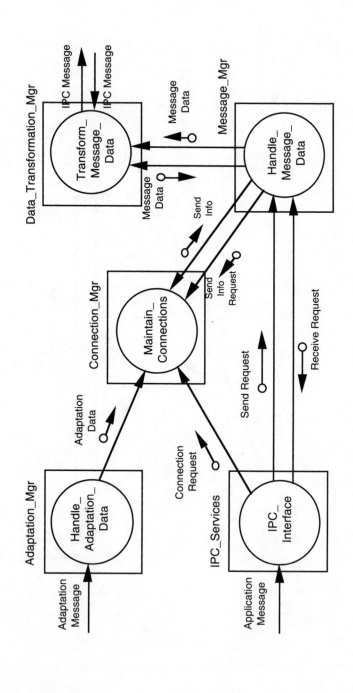

Figure A.8 IPC Ada Package Graph

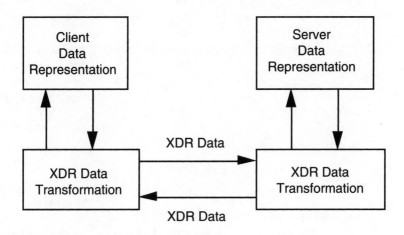

Figure A.9 Data Transformation with XDR

```
Second : Integer;
   end record;


-- XDR (RPC) in-data conversion routine
procedure XDR_Add_In (Error_Status : in     EH.Status;
                      XDR :          in out XM.Xdrs;
                      Data :         in out Add_In);

type Add_Out is  -- RPC data returned by server
   record
      Result   : Integer;
      Overflow : Boolean;
   end record;

-- XDR (RPC) out-data conversion routine
procedure XDR_Add_Out
              (Error_Status : in     EH.Status;
               XDR          : in out XM.Xdrs;
               Data         : in out Add_Out);
end XDR_Conversions;

package body XDR_Conversions is

   procedure XDR_Add_In
              (Error_Status :   in     EH.Status;
               XDR          :   in out XM.Xdrs;
               Data         :   in out Add_In) is
```

```
    procedure XDR_Integer is
               new XM.XDR_Integers(Integer);
    begin
      XDR_Integer (Error_Status, XDR, Data.First);
                                  -- first operand
      XDR_Integer (Error_Status, XDR, Data.Second);
                                  -- second operand
    end XDR_Add_In;

    procedure XDR_Add_Out

                     (Error_Status : in      EH.Status;
                      XDR          : in out XM.Xdrs;
                      Data         : in out Add_Out) is
      procedure XDR_Integer is
               new XM.XDR_Integers (Integer);
      procedure XDR_Boolean is
               new XM.XDR_Enumerations (Boolean);
    begin
      XDR_Integer (Error_Status, XDR, Data.Result);
      XDR_Boolean (Error_Status, Data.Overflow);
    end XDR_Add_Out;
  end XDR_Conversions;
```

The visible record types Add_In and Add_Out will be used to circumvent the problem in RPC of only passing one parameter and receiving a single reply. Each parameter type that is passed and returned may include a complex data structure that both the client and the server have visibility to. The design object to accomplish this is implemented as the data manager XDR_Conversions. The imported package AdaLAN_XDR_Memory is part of the Ada binding and provides memory management for the converted data. The binding layer is illustrated in Figure A.10.

A.6.2 Application Interface

The package specification and body is included on both the client and server machines. On the client machine, the procedure XDR_Add_In is used to convert the two input operands to be added from the representation on the client machine to the XDR standard format. XDR_Add_Out is used to convert results returned by the server from the XDR representation to the client representation. On the server machine, XDR_Add_In is used to convert from XDR format to the server representation, and XDR_Add_Out from server representation to XDR format. The flow of the data transformations is shown in Figures A.11 and A.12. Instantiations of generic procedures are made for the required types on the respective machines. This ensures the correct data representations in a heterogeneous, as well as a homogeneous environment.

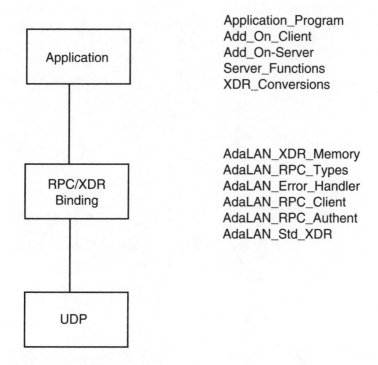

Figure A.10 RPC/XDR Ada Binding

The constants Program_Number and Version_Number (defined in the package specification) refer to the utility program on the server that the clients will access. The constant Add_Proc_Num defines a procedure number for the remote Add function. If other remote functions were included, such as, for example, Fast Fourier Transforms or other remote entry calls, they would be given different remote procedure numbers. The parameter XDR in XDR_Add_In and XDR_Add_Out refers to a buffer address and is used to locate the converted data elements.

A.6.3 Application Program

When a task or subprogram makes a call to another procedure or task, the location of the called module should be as transparent as possible to the caller to promote portable Ada code. The application program makes a call to the Add procedure specified in package Add_On_Client. The actual implementation of the Add function may be located on a remote machine, and this remoteness is transparent to the application:

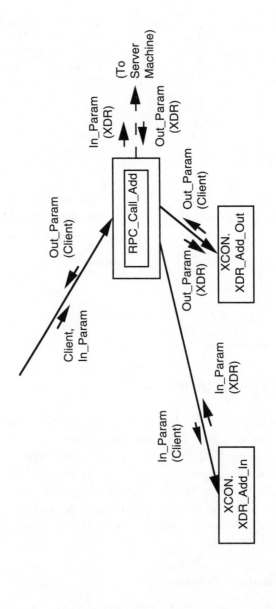

Figure A.11 Transformations on the Client Machine

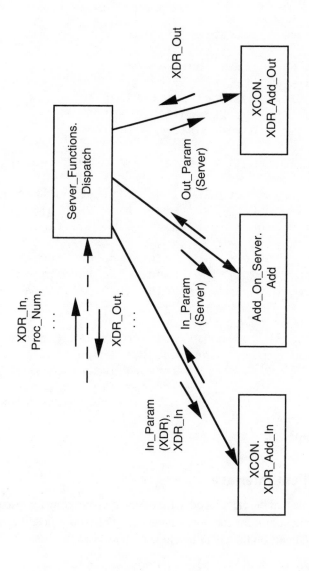

Figure A.12 Transformations on the Server Machine

```ada
with Add_On_Client;
with Text_IO;

procedure Application_Program is     -- main
   First       : Integer := 0;
   Second      : Integer := 0;
   Result      : Integer := 0;
   Overflow    : Boolean := False;
   Line        : String (1 .. 80);
   Line_Length : Natural;
begin
   Text_IO.Put_Line ("Test of Add_On_Client");
   loop
      Text_IO. Put_Line ("Enter first number");
      Text_IO.Get_Line (Line, Line_Length);
      First := Integer'Value (Line (1..Line_Length));

      Text_IO. Put_Line ("Enter second number");
      Text_IO.Get_Line (Line, Line_Length);
      Second := Integer'Value (Line (1..Line_Length));

      Add_On_Client.Add
                  (First, Second, Result, Overflow);
      Text_IO.Put_Line (Integer'Image (First) &
                  Integer'Image (Second) &
                  Integer'Image (Result) &
                  Boolean'Image (Overflow));
   end loop;
end Application_Program;
```

A.6.4 Client Interface

If we assume that the call to Add in the application program represents an RPC, one implementation of the environment for the Add procedure (in package Add_On_Client) on the client machine is as follows:

```ada
-- this package spec and body are placed on the client
-- machine

package Add_On_Client is
   procedure Add
         (First : in Integer; Second  : in  Integer;
          Result : out Integer; Overflow : out Boolean);
end Add_On_Client;
```

```
with AdaLAN_Error_Handler;
with AdaLAN_RPC_Client;
with XDR_Conversions;
with AdaLAN_RPC_Authent;
with AdaLAN_Std_XDR;

package body Add_On_Client is
  package EH   renames AdaLAN_Error_Handler;
  package RPC  renames AdaLAN_RPC_Client.UDP;
  package AU   renames AdaLAN_RPC_Authent;
  package SX   renames AdaLAN_Std_XDR;
  package XCON renames XDR_Conversions;

  Null_Gids     : AU.Unix_Grouparr := null;
  Local_Machine : SX.Access_String :=
                           new String'("clerc2");
  Retry_Delay   : constant Duration := 5.0;

  -- only one task at a time may use package
  -- Add_On_Client
  Client        : RPC.Clients;
  Error_Status : EH.Allocate_Status (1024);

  procedure Add
    (First  : in  Integer; Second   : in  Integer;
     Result : out Integer; Overflow : out Boolean)
                                      is separate;

begin
  RPC.Create (Error_Status,
              Client,
              XCON.Program_Number,
              XCON.Version_Number,
              Retry_Delay,    -- time between retries
              "clerc1");      -- server machine

  AU.Create_Unix (S       => Error_Status,
                  Auth    => Client.Auth,
                  Machine => Local_Machine,
                  Uid     => 1,
                  Gid     => 17,
                  Gids    => Null_Gids);
exception
  ...
end Add_On_Client;
```

A.6.5 Client/Server Linking

The package specification of Add_on_Client is the same regardless of whether the actual Add operation is performed on the client or server machine. The package body, however, will be tailored for a client and the server. The client implementation shown in the last paragraph includes local declarations used in the creation of UDP services. The call to RPC.Create attempts to allocate a buffer for the client, and checks if the conversion program is on the server. A call is made to the server machine (clerc1) and returns with a port number for access on the server. The client buffer is linked to the port number on the server. The call to AU.Create_Unix makes the client look like a Unix machine with a given user id and group id (the last parameter is not used).

A.6.6 Calling RPC on Client

The implementation of the Add procedure (subunit) on the client machine can be implemented as follows:

```
separate (Add_On_Client)
  procedure Add
      (First    : in  Integer;
       Second   : in  Integer;
       Result   : out Integer;
       Overflow : out Boolean) is

      package XCON renames XDR_Conversions;
      In_Param  : XCON.Add_In := (First, Second);
      Out_Param : XCON.Add_Out;

      procedure RPC_Call_Add is new RPC.Call
              (XCON.Add_Proc_Num,
               XCON.Add_In,
               XCON.Add_Out,
               XCON.XDR_Add_In,
               XCON.XDR_Add_Out);
  begin
    RPC_Call_Add
        (Error_Status, Client, In_Param, Out_Param);
    Result   := Out_Param.Result;
    Overflow := Out_Param.Overflow;
  exception
      ...
  end Add;
```

The generic RPC.Call is instantiated with the Add procedure number (= 1), types for *in* and *out* parameters, and the conversion routines for the *in* and *out* parameters. The parameters in the RPC_Call_Add include error status to be returned, the buffer address of the client, which is linked to the port address on the server, the input parameter, which will be converted to XDR format before the call, and the output parameter containing the result.

A.6.7 Server Interface

The modules to be loaded on the server machine include the same conversion functions as were loaded on the client machine, the various server functions, and the actual implementation of the Add procedure. The server functions shown below include the procedure Dispatch and an instantiation of the RPC.UDP services:

```
package Server_Functions is
end Server_Functions;


with AdaLAN_Error_Handler;
with AdaLAN_RPC_Types;
with AdaLAN_XDR_Memory;
with AdaLAN_RPC_Server;
with XDR_Conversions;

package body Server_Functions is
   package EH    renames AdaLAN_Error_Handler;
   package RT    renames AdaLAN_RPC_Types;
   package XM    renames AdaLAN_XDR_Memory;
   package RPC   renames AdaLAN_RPC_Server;
   package XCON  renames XDR_Conversions;

   Stack_Size : constant := 2048;

procedure Dispatch
      (Error_Status  : in EH.Status;
       Proc_Num      : in out RT.Procnums;
       XDR_In        : in out XM.Xdrs;
       XDR_Out       : in out XM.Xdrs;
       Accept_Status : in out RT.Accept_Status)
                                   is separate;

   package Example_RPC_Server is new RPC.UDP
      (XCON.Program_Number,
       XCON.Version_Number,
       RPC.Anyport,   -- system chooses port
       Stack_Size,
       Dispatch,
```

```
            RPC.Authenticate_Default);
    end Server_Functions;
```

The procedure Dispatch is called from a low level port server (not included here), and is used in converting input parameters from XDR standard format to the server format, and from server format to XDR representation for the output parameters for the given function, i.e., Add in our case. The instantiation of RPC.UDP creates a task that waits for client calls. After this task is started, it calls a port mapping function to inform it that the RPC program exists, and which port the task will wait on. Clients will find the server task via the RPC calls. The system will choose a port for the waiting server task (RPC.Anyport).

A.6.8 Data Transformation on Server

The implementation of the Dispatch procedure is as follows:

```
with Add_On_Server;
separate (Server_Functions)

    procedure Dispatch
         (Error_Status  : in      EH.Status;
          Proc_Num      : in out RT.Procnums;
          XDR_In        : in out XM.Xdrs;
          XDR_Out       : in out XM.Xdrs;
          Accept_Status : in out RT.Accept_Status) is
    begin
       case Proc_Num is
          when XCON.Add_Proc_Num =>
             declare
                In_Param  : XCON.Add_In;
                Out_Param : XCON.Add_Out;
             begin
                XCON.XDR_Add_In (Error_Status,
                                 XDR_In, In_Param);
                Add_On_Server.Add (In_Param.First,
                                 In_Param.Second,
                                 Out_Param.Result,
                                 Out_Param.Overflow);
                XCON.XDR_Add_Out (Error_Status,
                                 XDR_Out, Out_Param);
             end;
          when others =>
             Accept_Status := RT.Procedure_Unavailable;
       end case;
    exception
       . . .
```

```
end Dispatch;
```

The procedure Dispatch is called from the low level RPC services, and provides for the required data transformations for a given function. The only function included in the case statement is for a procedure number that corresponds to the Add function. The case statement can be expanded to include other functions by adding procedure numbers. Conversions from XDR format to server format are provided by calling XDR_Add_In. A call is made to the actual Add function, and results are returned in server formats. Parameters to be returned to the client are converted to XDR format before they are placed on the network. The implementation of the actual Add function is identical to the implementation on a uniprocessor system:

```
package Add_On_Server is
  procedure Add
    (First   : in  Integer; Second   : in  Integer;
     Result : out Integer; Overflow : out Boolean);
end Add_On_Server;

package body Add_On_Server is
  procedure Add
      (First    : in  Integer;
       Second   : in  Integer;
       Result   : out Integer;
       Overflow : out Boolean) is
  begin
    Overflow := False;
    Result   := First + Second;
  exception
    when Numeric_Error =>
      Overflow := True;
  end Add;
end Add_On_Server;
```

Summary

This appendix demonstrates the use of our object-oriented paradigms for an IPC application at the technology level of the problem hierarchy. The domain analysis identified the major IPC real-world objects to be Application Program Interface, Storage Manager, Message Passing Manager, and Time Manager.

An IPC client/server model was illustrated with the major design objects identified as Adaptation_Mgr, IPC_Services, Connection_Mgr, Message_Mgr, and Data_Transformation_Mgr.

A detailed design was implemented with an RPC/XDR model for an Add function. A reusable COTS Ada binding (AdaLAN packages) was used to create a layer between the application and the UDP protocol. A generic instantiation of the RPC call provided a reusable remote calling mechanism for the Add function.

Exercises

1. Analyze the trade-offs between an RPC mechanism and message passing (unique message id) with regard to

   • design

   • reusability

   • extendibility and maintenance

   • performance

2. List all the design decisions that will be affected if we replace the RPC mechanism with a remote entry call approach (i.e., extending Ada's rendezvous to include multi-program communication).

Object-Oriented Analysis and Design for an Air Traffic Control System

In this appendix we apply the methods outlined in the body of the book to an air traffic control system which fits in the application level of the problem hierarchy described in Chapter 8. This type of system satisfies the basic premises for which the methods are intended: real-time systems implemented with distributed architectures, and a distinct problem domain where reusability can be a significant cost factor for the creation of small, medium, and large systems from a set of software components.

The steps of the case study are performed in accordance with the recommended approach as summarized in Chapter 16. Excellent references that describe general ATC functions are [NOL90 and FIE85].

B.1 DOMAIN ANALYSIS

During this analysis we determine the major functions of the problem domain, and identify potential real-world classes and objects. We will only focus on the most important functions of an ATC system here. Many of the derived functions necessary to make an automated ATC system work will only be listed briefly.

B.1.1 System Overview

A general system view of an ATC system is shown in Figure B.1. Radars are positioned at certain locations along airway routes and near airports (sometimes referred to as aerodromes). The figure illustrates the use of primary surveillance radar (PSR) and secondary surveillance radar (SSR) for location and identification of aircraft. A separate weather radar may be used to detect weather conditions unfavorable to aircraft (heavy rain, snow, hail, and thunderstorms).

The exchange of (non-voice) messages between adjacent ATC centers and other flight related facilities is accomplished via a communications network. The types of data exchanged include meteorological (met) data, flight plan (FP) information, and handover messages as an aircraft is handed to another ATC center along the route or near a destination.

Operators can enter flight plan data, met data, and make changes to adaptation data through a visual display terminal (VDT). A magnetic disk with an appropriate backup media (this could be a tape drive) contains the major database items. These items will include repetitive flight plans (RPLs), data recorded during normal operations, and adaptation files.

A set of controller workstations (CWS) are used to display the current air situation for the airspace they are assigned to. The data displayed consist of situation displays and associated data blocks that give aircraft positions and indicated directions of flight, and various lists and alerts. Each CWS is associated with a *position* that signifies a certain functional responsibility, e.g., system control and monitoring, supervisor, trainee, and operational (controller) position.

B.1.2 Functional Areas

ATC systems can be broken down into the following major functional areas:

1. **Radar Data Processing (RDP).** This includes acceptance of radar data, creation and maintenance of *tracks* (e.g., aircraft in the air or on the ground, and fuel trucks on the ground), determination of potential conflicts (collision) between two aircraft, and determination of potential airspace penetration of restricted areas (e.g., military bombing ranges). It is the responsibility of RDP to create data to be displayed to a controller.

2. **Flight Data Processing (FDP).** This includes acceptance and maintenance of flight plan data and met data. Flight plans may be received individually or in bulk as RPLs (repetitive flight plans). Individual flight plans are used for general aviation and RPLs for scheduled airlines. Flight plans can be amended, activated, and cancelled. Other functions assigned to FDP include inter-facility and intra-facility distribution of flight plan data, calculation of estimated time over geographic fixes, and estimated time of arrival at a given airport. FDP also prepares data to be displayed to a controller.

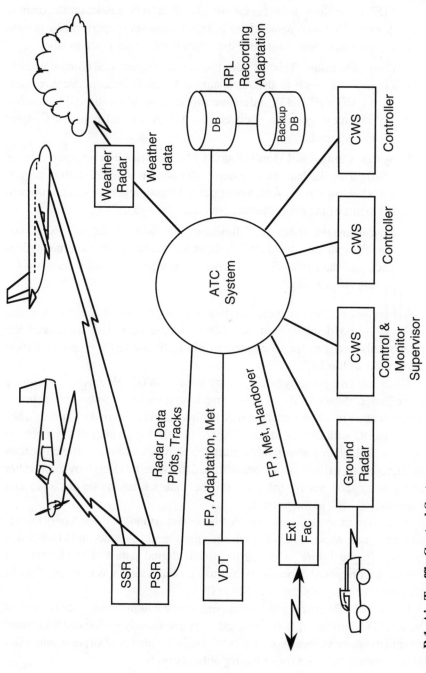

Figure B.1 Air Traffic Control System

3. **Human-Computer Interface (HCI).** This used to be called Man-Machine Interface (MMI) and creates the very important link between an operator and a VDT or CWS. HCI accepts data received from RDP and FDP and creates the necessary display data to be shown on the display device. HCI also responds to operator requests by performing certain commands or returning error messages if the requests are invalid.

4. **Communication.** This includes the handling of external communication via networks such as the Aeronautical Fixed Telecommunication Network (AFTN) [FIE85], and an interprocess communication (IPC) mechanism for message passing between the ATC functional areas (see Chapter 11 and Appendix A).

5. **System Control and Monitoring (SCM).** This function is responsible for configuring the hardware devices, allocating resources, startup, restart, and shutdown of the ATC system, and the assignment of workstations to segments of the controlled airspace (i.e., *sectors*).

6. **Miscellaneous.** Other ATC functions include recording of operational data for statistics, accident investigation, and billing of customers; playback and data reduction of recorded information; and simulation for testing and training.

Before we can start to list specific functions and real-world objects, we need to know some details about the different type of radars used, and the relationship between tracks created within RDP and flight plan calculation performed within FDP.

There are two basic types of radars used in ATC systems: (1) primary surveillance radars (PSR) for locating aircraft with a range and azimuth determination in a horizontal geometric plane; and (2) secondary surveillance radars (SSR) with the added capability of identifying an aircraft via a beacon code and calculating an aircraft's altitude. SSR is sometimes labeled beacon radar, referring to the beacon code assigned to a specific aircraft by a controller (e.g., octal 5264 set by the pilot on the transponder in the airplane) and "squawked" back to the ground.

Aircraft transponders are associated with certain modes: Mode A only reports a beacon code, Mode C reports both beacon code and altitude, and Mode S will be used in the future as an air-to-ground digital data link. The type of transponder required depends on the airspace the pilot wants to enter. For our purposes we will only consider Mode C.

PSRs and SSRs are not positioned everywhere within the airspace controlled by an ATC system. If both are used, they are usually co-located and rotate around the same vertical axis. PSRs tend to be located near airports, and SSRs along airways between major metropolitan airports.

The functional importance of the two radars is that the PSR is used for tracking, i.e., position location in range and azimuth, and the SSR is used to add the third dimension to the location (altitude) and for identifying the aircraft with the assigned beacon code. This implies another important function: when a new *track* of an aircraft is established, it is associated with the assigned beacon code listed in that aircraft's *flight plan*. This function is referred to as track to flight plan pairing, or simply *pairing*.

There is a considerable variation in the sophistication built into radar units and the kind of information supplied by different makes of radars. One radar may only return *plots*, i.e., position location information, whereas another may supply *track data*, including a track number, position information, and speed or how far the track has moved since the last report. There are also radars that return weather data in the form of vectors outlining an area and associated intensities for mapping of severe weather conditions.

The type of information listed in the last few paragraphs should make clear that the domain analysis must be made by personnel who are intimately familiar with functional details of the domain. This knowledge is used in decomposing general functional areas down to smaller areas that can form the basis for identifying reusable software modules.

B.1.3 Reusable Functions

The objective of this phase is to be able to identify well-defined functional areas with which we can associate personnel with the required expertise and potential sources of software already existing within the organization. To illustrate the process we will focus on some of the RDP and FDP functions outlined above.

The following subfunctions are all part of the general area of radar data processing:

1. **Radar interfaces.** Our system must anticipate accepting radar reports from a wide variety of radars with differing capabilities. Data coming from radars include plots, tracks, weather information, beacon codes, and altitudes.

2. **Tracking.** This is the capability of identifying and following tracks as they move through the assigned airspace. Subfunctions in this area include:

   a. *Altitude correction.* The altitude reported by the SSR is corrected using the regional QNH (barometric pressure) value received from the met data.

   b. *Correlation.* Association of new track data with existing tracks. This can be done at different levels of sophistication, e.g., by track number provided by a tracking radar, within a certain proximity, or same beacon code and flight plan identification.

c. *Filtering.* Acceptance of only relevant information for the assigned radar, area or volume.

d. *Coordinate conversion.* Incoming position data (e.g., range azimuth) is transformed to a different coordinate system (e.g., local x,y).

e. *Track initiation.* A track that does not correlate with any existing tracks may be assumed to be a new system track. A new track may also be initiated manually by an operator.

f. *Track number management.* There must be a unique method for assigning and reclaiming track numbers when a track is deleted.

g. *Track management.* Functions must be available to create, update, and delete tracks.

h. *Track monitoring.* This includes the calculation of estimated paths to determine potential conflicts (collisions), penetration of restricted airspace, and violation of minimum safe altitudes. Associated with this function is the creation of data for track displays and alerts.

Some of the subfunctions associated with the general area of flight data processing include:

1. **Flight plan management.** This is the general management of accepting, storing, amending, activating, and closing flight plans. The capability of handling repetitive (bulk) flight plans is included here.

2. **Airspace management.** This subfunction includes the assignment of portions of the airspace (sectors) to controller workstations. The partitioning is based on the particular airway structure and traffic flows in the area. All the aircraft located within a particular sector become the responsibility of the controller assigned to that CWS. An associated subfunction is the handover of an aircraft leaving one sector and entering the adjacent sector.

3. **Route conversion.** The original route entered in the flight plan is checked against known airways and associated fixes and junctions and converted to an acceptable route. The route conversion may include the use of Standard Instrument Departures (SIDs) and Standard Terminal Arrival Routes (STARs).

4. **Trajectory estimation.** The profile an aircraft is following is calculated using the converted route, flight plan data, and wind data. The wind data consists of wind speeds and directions at a number of flight levels (altitudes). The route data, the aircraft speed reported in the flight plan, and the wind data are used to estimate the ground speed and ground track

progress the aircraft is making. The estimates include time over certain fixes (known locations on or below the route) and the estimated time of arrival (ETA) at the destination.

5. **Pairing.** When a flight plan is activated, it is given a unique beacon code (4-digit octal code), which the pilot dials into the transponder in the aircraft. To positively identify an aircraft reported by radar returns, the code picked up by the radar is compared with the codes given to the various flight plans. A match of codes signifies a pairing, i.e., a positive identification of that aircraft. If there is no match, a new track may be started.

6. **Flight data distribution.** Before an aircraft is successfully handed over to a controller in another facility, the relevant flight data must be transferred. This consists of flight plan data submitted in the form of a *flight progress strip*, and current flight data in the form of post fixes. The latter includes estimated time of geographical fixes and estimated time of arrival at the destination.

B.1.4 Classes and Objects

Based on the functions specified above, we can now identify real-world objects and classes. One of these classes is Radars, with objects specified for a radar by a certain manufacturer such as Radar X or Radar Y. Some of the attributes associated with a radar include:

primary

secondary

plots

tracks

track number

position location

    range, azimuth

    x, y

    altitude

track speed

weather data

collimation (PSR/SSR alignment) error

Operations associated with radar objects include:

read adaptation data

read radar data

validate radar data

distribute radar data

set radar parameters

An object associated with the tracking function is a Track Store for the internal system tracks. If there is only one type of tracks there is no need to concoct a class. A class of Tracks could be pertinent if we had, for example, remote tracks and local tracks with different sets of attributes. Some of the attributes associated with a Track Store object include:

track id

flight plan id

state (controlled, uncontrolled)

position

   x, y

   altitude

speed

direction

Some of the operations to be performed on tracks include:

initiate a track

drop a track

update a track

read a track by track id

read tracks in a sector

extrapolate tracks

The primary object associated with FDP is a Flight Plan. There is no need to distinguish between RPLs and individual flight plans regarding the data, and a class is not necessary. The attributes of a flight plan include:

flight plan id

type (flying under visual or instrument rules)

aircraft id

aircraft type (and navigation equipment indicator)

true airspeed

departure point

departure time

cruising altitude

route of flight

destination

estimated time en-route

fuel on board

Some of the operations to be performed on a flight plan (FP) include:

activate

amend

cancel

suspend

add

delete

We have only outlined some of the classes and objects here that can be identified during the domain analysis. The conclusion of this phase is to identify each subfunction with existing software and relevant attributes, e.g., for the tracking function:

Type: alpha tracker

Programming language: C

Size: 15,000 SLOCs

Reuse: pragma Interface; may need to redesign for Ada

Problems: Unix low level calls

Subfunction Contact: A. Smith

Software Contact: P. Nelson

An ERD representing some of the ATC entities and their relationships is shown in Figure B.2.

B.2 REQUIREMENTS ANALYSIS

The analysis of a complete ATC system (ATCS) is impossible in the small space available here, and we will concentrate on a subset of the functions described above. The focus of our analysis will be restricted to RDP and a minimal set of FDP and HCI functions to demonstrate pairing and target display.

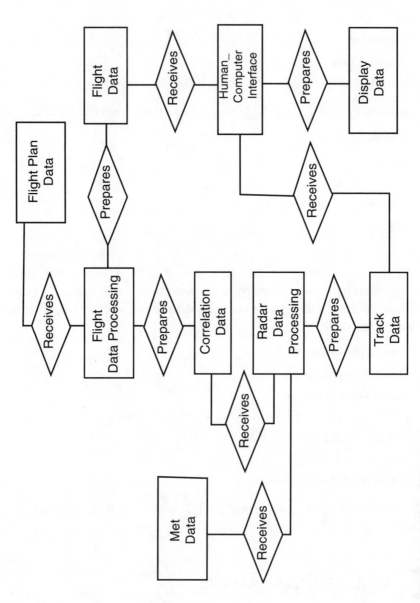

Figure B.2 ATC Entity-Relationship Diagram

B.2.1 System Description

A system overview is illustrated in the context diagram in Figure B.3. Radar data is accepted as plots, tracks, or weather data, depending on the type and capabilities of radars for a given system. Met data, Flight Plan (FP) data, and inter-facility messages are exchanged via the external communications interface. A recording device is used to record data for playback, billing, and reports. Operators can enter FP data, map requests, and new track data from one or more VDTs. Controllers can make requests for certain display data from a CWS, and target data, situation displays, maps, and tabular displays are shown to the controllers on the various positions associated with the CWSs.

B.2.2 External Interfaces

We must prepare software entities that can accept the data entering from the external interfaces shown in Figure B.3. We also must prepare the necessary messages that have destinations outside our local ATCS.

From an earlier discussion about the different types of radars used in ATC systems, the radar interfaces must be designed in a flexible manner to achieve reusability. In a world-wide market, we may have to interface to, for example, English, French, Russian, and American built radar units, and we must be able to accept the different message formats and protocols.

The external communications devices are also quite different, but some common systems have emerged. One of these is the Aeronautical Fixed Telecommunications Network (AFTN), with a message standard specified by the International Civil Aviation Organization (ICAO). Other networks, such as Common ICAO Data Interchange Network (CIDIN), will replace AFTN [NAR89) with the ICAO message standard intact or expanded. To design a set of reusable components, certain assumptions must be made about the external communications interfaces, and a reasonable prediction must be made about their expected longevity.

The recording devices are typically disks and tapes and are usually quite straightforward to interface with. Aside from specific data formats, the only other variables include status and error reporting.

Interfacing to VDTs does not usually present major problems, especially if the data exchange mechanism is via a command language and ASCII strings. Windows and pull-down menus are available with a large number of common VDTs, and should be relatively easy to interface with.

Preparing display data and interfacing with CWSs presents a major design problem. The various displays are extremely detailed, and the information must be updated at a rapid rate. The proper design of HCI for a high degree of reusability must be given high priority within the overall development effort.

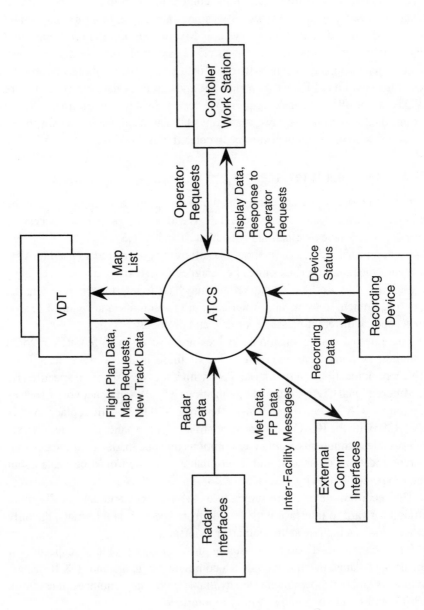

Figure B.3 ATCS Context Diagram

This area is a prime candidate for rapid prototyping and demonstration of ATC capabilities. An excellent treatment of HCI design issues can be found in [HAR89].

We will continue our analysis by focusing on a select number of ATC functions.

B.2.3 Control and Data Flow Analysis

A CDFD of ATCS is shown in Figure B.4. The names chosen for each bubble is in accordance with the traditional structured analysis approach using a transitive verb to describe some action to be performed by the function.

Potential object managers are noted in Figure B.4 by the stores illustrated with the two parallel bars. Access to these stores by multiple functions implies the possibility of shared data that must be implemented either with encapsulated data managers or shared data with mutual exclusion.

A leveled CDFD of Manage Track Data is shown in Figure B.5. It is important that major functional areas be decomposed until all possibilities of concurrent functions have been exposed. If this is not done, and further concurrency is detected later on during the development, the necessity for a redesign is very likely. Other functions that should be decomposed in a real project include Manage Flight Data, Determine Conflicts, Manage Console Data, Prepare Display Data, and Prepare Recording Data. All of these functions have the potential for harboring inherent concurrency that may affect the process abstraction. Prepare Weather Data and Manage Met Data are relatively simple functions that do not require further decomposition prior to the process abstraction phase.

B.2.4 Object Abstraction

An important part of the transitioning from analysis to design is to prepare a list of potential design objects. The determination of these objects is made with a triple view in mind: (1) encapsulated data managers; (2) concurrent elements with a balanced system view; and (3) components (modules) that anticipate a distributed architecture. The names chosen in this step reflect the object-oriented view, and are no longer strictly functional. It is important that all three concerns be treated in parallel. We are not simply looking for encapsulated data managers; the concurrency issue and the anticipation of a distributed architecture are extremely vital concerns for obtaining a highly reusable design.

As an illustration, here is a list of objects derived from Figures B.4 and B.5 with the three parallel concerns:

Radar Interfaces Module (reusable component)

External Interfaces Module (reusable component)

Weather Data Manager (reusable component and data manager)

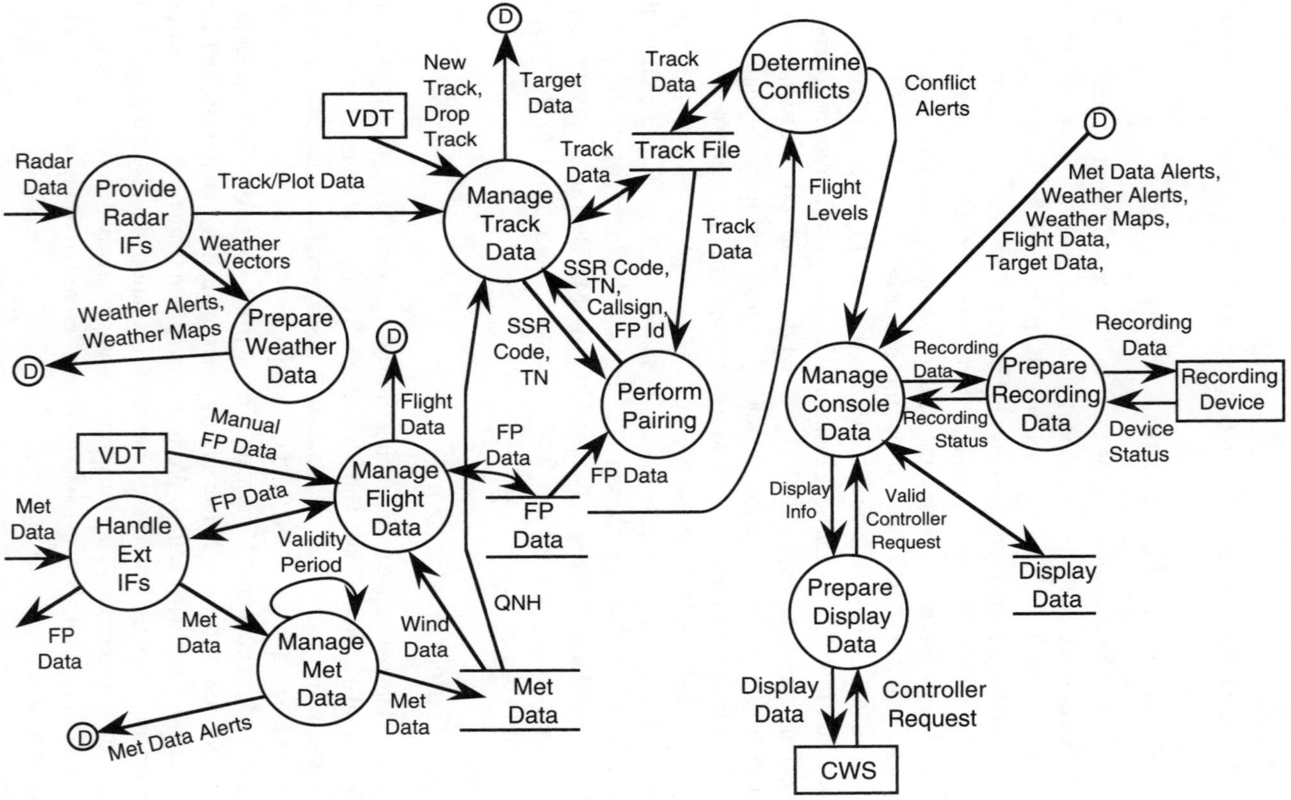

Figure B.4 ATCS CDFD

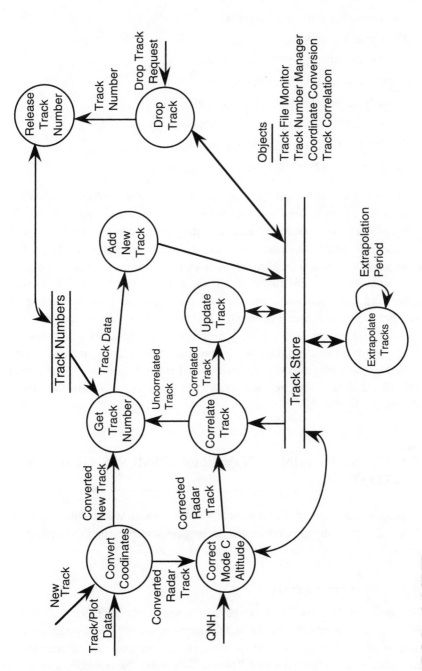

Figure B.5 Leveled CDFD

Flight Plan Manager (reusable component and data manager)

Flight Data Manager (data manager)

Met Data Manager (data manager)

Track File Monitor (concurrency)

Pairing Module (reusable component)

Conflicts Module (reusable component)

Track Number Manager (data manager)

Console Data Manager (reusable component and data manager)

Display Data Module (reusable component)

Recording Data Module (reusable component)

The data managers represent the normal encapsulated objects with a data type, a set of operations, and attributes. The modules represent reusable components that will be distributed according to the type of system to be built. The Pairing module, for example, may be considered part of the Flight Plan Manager function. For small systems, however, there may not be a significant flight plan management function, but the pairing function is still required. Separating this functionality out as a reusable (distributive) component allows a higher degree of reusability than if it had been combined with the flight plan management function. Some of the objects (e.g., Track File Monitor) are derived objects based on concurrency concerns. Simultaneous accesses into the track file must be protected and guaranteed mutual exclusion. The objects determined during this step are analyzed further as we create the process abstraction for our ATCS.

B.3 TRANSITIONING FROM REQUIREMENTS ANALYSIS TO DESIGN

The concurrent elements that represent the process abstraction of the system are determined by using the CDFDs and the process selection rules. The processes for ATCS and their interfaces are shown in Figure B.6.

B.3.1 Process Selection

The processes shown in Figure B.6 have been selected to satisfy the various rules that form a balanced concurrent system. Functions dealing with external devices, for example, should have separate processes to accommodate the different speeds and data periods of those devices. This is evidenced by the processes selected for Radar IFs (interfaces), External IFs, and Display Manager.

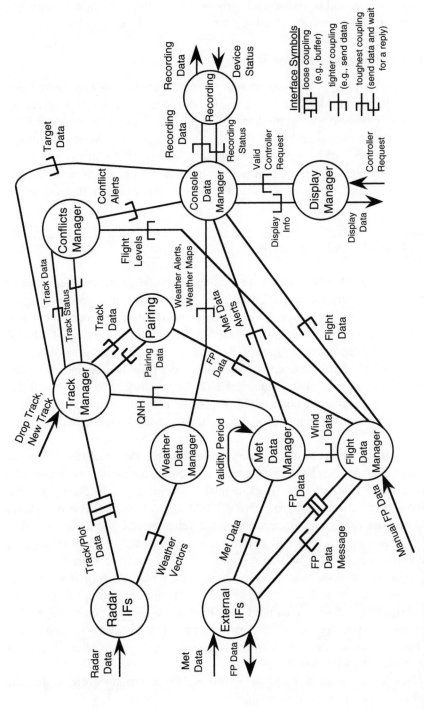

Figure B.6 ATCS Process Abstraction

Another rule used is that functions that may be distributed to different processors should be independent processes to facilitate the distribution. The complete list of process selection rules is presented in Section 7.1.

B.3.2 Process Interfaces

A loose coupling is required between the radar data accepted by Radar IFs to allow the Track Manager to process the data and Radar IFs to receive data without having to wait for the data to be processed. Most of the other interfaces shown represent simple data passing, for example, the wind data passed between Met Data Manager and Flight Data Manager. One instance of a very tight coupling between two processes is shown for the passing of recording data from Console Data Manager to Recording with the wait for a status reply.

B.4 TOP LEVEL DESIGN

The process structure shown in Figure B.6 is language independent and represents abstract objects that must be implemented in a certain program language. A transitioning to Ada tasks from the abstract process objects is shown in the Ada Task Graph in Figure B.7. The circles now represent Ada task objects and the directed graphs the direction of calls between the tasks (see Section 7.5). A decision must be made whether to use the Ada rendezvous for inter-task communication or a suitable IPC mechanism. We will assume that remote rendezvous are not available in distributed systems and that IPC will be required for the implementation of inter-task communication between processors.

The implementation of the loose coupling between the Radar IFs process and Track Manager has been implemented by introducing an intermediary buffer task (Track_Data_Buffer). Another intermediary task (Flight_Data_Buffer) is introduced between External_IFs and Flight_Data. Note that the names shown in the Ada Task Graph use underscores to reflect actual Ada tasks.

The annotated arrows with a circle at the end show the direction in which the data is passed. This will correspond to *in* and *out* parameters for an Ada rendezvous, and send and receive mechanisms for an IPC approach.

Since Ada tasks cannot be compilation units, they are encapsulated within Ada packages as shown in Figure B.8. Each of the polygons embodies an Ada application package as described earlier for the package taxonomy, and each of these packages represents a top level design object. The design objects are implemented with Ada PDL.

An example of a package specification and body follows for the Flight_Data_Manager design object:

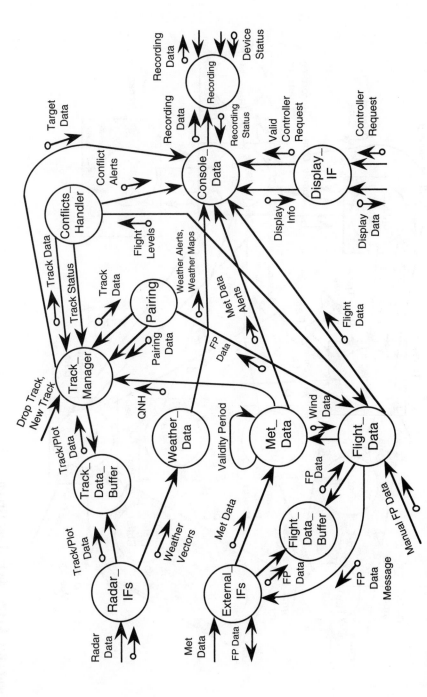

Figure B.7 ATCS Ada Task Graph

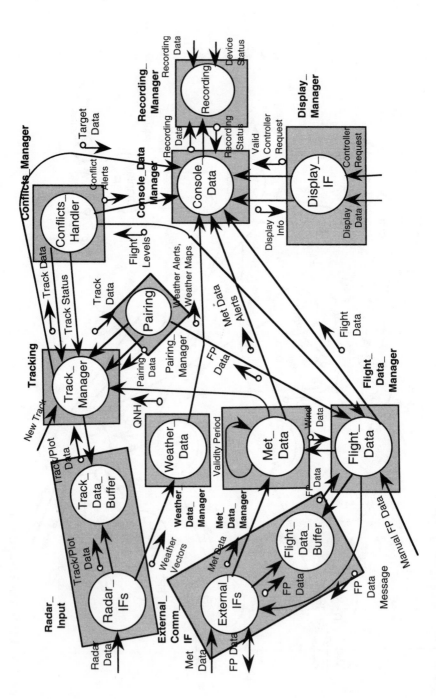

Figure B.8 ATCS Ada Package Graph

```
with Global_Types;   use Global_Types;
package Flight_Data_Manager is
   procedure Take_Manual_FP_Data (FP : in FP_Data);
   procedure Provide_FP_Data (FP : out FP_Data);
   provide Flight_Levels (Levels : out Flight_Levels);
end Flight_Data_Manager;

package body Flight_Data_Manager is
   task Flight_Data is
      entry Take_Manual_FP_Data
                             (FP      : in  FP_Data);
      entry Provide FP_Data
                             (FP      : out FP_Data);
      entry Flight_Levels
                        (Levels : out Flight_Levels);
   end Flight_Data;

   procedure Take_Manual_FP_Data (FP : in FP_Data) is
   begin
      Flight_Data.Take_Manual_FP_Data (FP);
   end Take_Manual_FP_Data;

   procedure Provide FP_Data (FP : out FP_Data) is
   begin
      Flight_Data.Provide FP_Data (FP);
   end Provide FP_Data;

  provide Flight_Levels (Levels : out Flight_Levels) is
   begin
      Flight_Data.Flight_Levels (Levels);
   end Flight_Levels;

   task body Flight_Data is separate;
 end Flight_Data_Manager;
```

The interface to the package is through the entrance procedures shown in the package specification. The specification and implementation of the task Flight_Data is hidden in the package body. We have assumed the use of the Ada rendezvous in this example, but the entrance procedures can just as well make calls to IPC services in distributed systems.

B.5   DETAILED DESIGN

All of the major algorithms and programming mechanisms deferred during top level design are supplied during the detailed design phase. An example is the task body Flight_Data specified inside the package body Flight_Data_Manager:

```
with Console_Data_Manager;
with External_Comm_IF;
with Met_Data_Manager;
separate (Flight_Data_Manager)
task body Flight_Data is
...
begin
  ..
  External_Comm_IF.Provide_FP_Data (Flight_Data);
  Met_Data_Manager.Provide_Wind_Data (Wind);
  ..
  Console_Data_Manager.Take_Flight_Data
                              (Flight_Data);
  ...
end Flight_Data;
```

Exactly how much detail should be provided for detailed design is subject to controversy, and there is sometimes a thin line between "detailed design" and "coding" when we use compilable Ada PDL. As a minimum, all primary and complex algorithms should be sketched out with skeleton Ada code (not necessarily pseudocode) with appropriate references to specific equations, e.g., coordinate conversion equations. The remaining details are then supplied during the coding phase.

Summary

This case study illustrates the combination of object-oriented paradigms with traditional structured analysis and design for a real-time system at the application level of the problem hierarchy. The domain analysis is used to determine the major functional areas, reusable functions, and abstract classes and objects. This analysis culminates by identifying existing software and relevant attributes, as illustrated for the tracking function.

The transitioning phase is used to determine concurrent elements and data managers for a selected number of ATC functions. A list of objects is derived from CDFDs based on object-orientation, concurrency concerns, and the potential for module distribution.

The top level design phase produces a set of application packages that contain the functions specified in the requirements document. These design objects are implemented in Ada PDL.

The detailed design phase produces the Ada PDL for the subunits deferred during top level design. Additional data managers are usually discovered during this phase.

Exercises

The following exercises are suggested for this case study:

1. Assume we have three separate processors hosting the FDP, RDP, and Display functions. Create a set of virtual nodes that include all the Ada packages shown in Figure B.8.

2. Create two separate Ada programs for FDP and RDP. Implement an IPC mechanism using RPC/XDR to pass data between the two programs.

3. Same as Exercise 2 except for the implementation of IPC with a message passing system rather than RPC/XDR.

Object-Oriented Analysis and Design for a Robot Control System

In this appendix we continue to apply the object-oriented paradigms to a problem in the application level of the domain hierarchy, this time to the control of robotics systems. This is another example of highly concurrent real-time systems implemented with distributed architectures, and a distinct problem domain where reusability can be a significant cost factor for the creation of different types of robot controllers from a set of software components.

The steps of the case study are performed in accordance with the recommended approach as summarized in Chapter 16. References describing general robotics control systems are [VUK89, MON91, and GRO86].

C.1 DOMAIN ANALYSIS

The use of robots in manipulation and sensing of physical objects has increased drastically in the last few years. Typical uses include assembly and disassembly of mechanical components, welding and spray painting, moving of objects from one location to another, handling toxic and nuclear materials, and space explorations. The primary advantages of using robots over humans is their accuracy and consistency in performing standard tasks, resistance to fatigue (except for occasional mechanical or electrical failures), and the ability to perform in hostile environments.

There is a wide variety of functional areas within the robotics domain. We will focus on the functions of robot control in this appendix, and explore the possibilities for reuse and the creation of classes and objects.

C.1.1 System Overview

A general system view of a robot control system (RCS) is shown in Figure C.1. An operator can prepare a set of programs, each consisting of a set of instructions that are converted into motion commands and sensor commands for setting sensor values. The robot control system interfaces with the robot via joint (axis) actuators and an internal servo feedback mechanism to monitor the joint movements in terms of position and velocity. Various external sensors are used to make sure the end-effector (gripper) does not damage the material the robot is acting on, or travel too far.

A specific control program is selected manually by the operator for execution by the control system. The program can be suspended, restarted, and terminated upon demand.

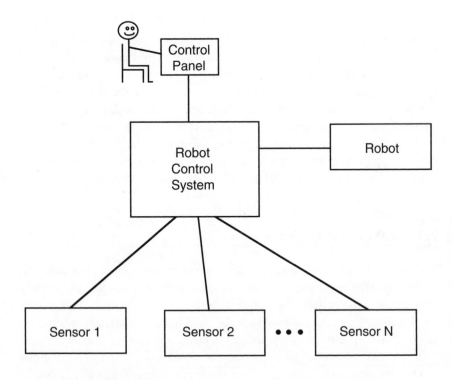

Figure C.1 Robot Control System

C.1.2 Functional Areas

A robot control system can be broken down into the following major functional areas [MON91]:

1. **Sensing.** Sensors used in robot control include vision, range, proximity, sound, force, torque, and touch. Any combination of these sensor types can be used in a given robot control system, depending upon the accuracy required and the particular features of the robot.

2. **Automated control.** This is the programmed sequences of instructions that are executed by one or more processors (CPUs). The processors are usually arranged in a distributed architecture.

3. **Intelligence.** This includes the acceptance and analysis of feedback and various sensor data to determine the proper movements of the various parts of the robot.

4. **Action.** This function activates and monitors the sensors, and controls the end-effector (gripper).

5. **Manual control.** This function allows a human operator to program a set of commands to be executed by the robot control system. The programs are stored in memory and the operator can select a specific program by specifying a program identifier. Manual selection can be made before the robot control is started and during normal operation of the robot. The operator can also stop the normal operations and move the robot manually.

C.1.3 Reusable Functions

The following subfunctions are all part of the general area of robot control:

1. **Coordinate transformation.** Various coordinate systems are used in robot control, and it is required to transform positional data and velocity vectors between the different coordinate systems. A coordinate system can be aligned with a control panel, the actual robot joints, a "world" system, and an internal system view. Specific transformations may include forward, inverse, reverse, rotation, and translation [GRO86, pp. 88–103].

2. **Trajectory calculations.** These calculations include matrix manipulations and the solution of kinematics equations with up to six degrees of freedom.

3. **Sensor interfaces.** There are a number of different types of external sensors used in robot control, and many of the interfaces can be implemented as reusable functions.

Reusable motion functions can be specified with respect to the kind of motion the robot is to follow, e.g., straight line or curved. The mathematical solutions can be grouped by degrees of freedom and specific coordinate systems.

The level of mathematics required for the solution of the motion equations is extremely complex, and an initial translation from another programming language, e.g., from Fortran to Ada or C should be considered. If the implementation language is Ada, the use of pragma Interface with direct use of existing modules is highly recommended. It would take a significant programming (and testing!) effort to establish this capability from scratch in a new programming language.

C.1.4 Classes and Objects

An example of a class for robot control is Sensors. Specific instances may include Vision, Range, Proximity, Sound, Force, Torque, and Touch. Some of the attributes associated with sensors include:

sensitivity

resolution

accuracy

response time

critical values

Operations associated with sensor objects include:

set default value

set critical value

read sensor input

A motion class can be specified with Direct Kinematic Motion and Inverse Kinematic Motion as objects of the class. Attributes of the motion objects may include

degrees of freedom

coordinate system

Operations associated with motion objects include:

calculate inverse

calculate transpose

calculate determinant

get velocity vectors

get coordinates

An ERD showing some of the robot control entities and their relationships is shown in Figure C.2.

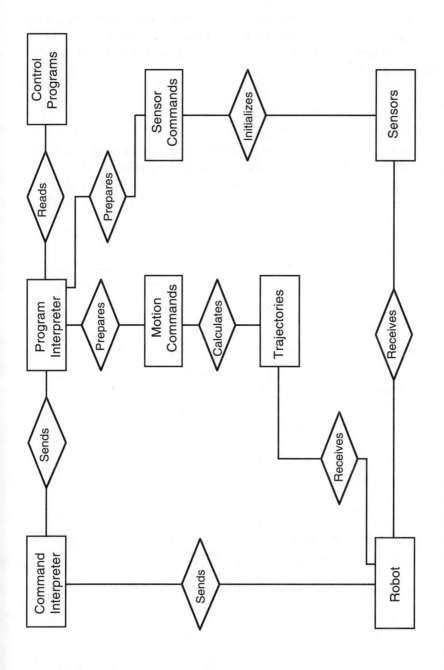

Figure C.2 RCS Entity-Relationship Diagram

C.2 REQUIREMENTS ANALYSIS

We will focus the requirements analysis on a robot control system that allows manual interactions via a control panel. The functionality used for this example is similar to what was published in [GOM84] with Ada solutions presented in [NIE88 and NIE90].

C.2.1 System Description

A system overview is illustrated in the context diagram in Figure C.3. RCS receives input from the control panel and returns error messages and status information to the panel. External sensors are used to monitor the robot motions.

Manual control with inputs from a control panel are considered part of this system, and affects the number of states and state transitions. A state transition diagram is shown in Figure C.4.

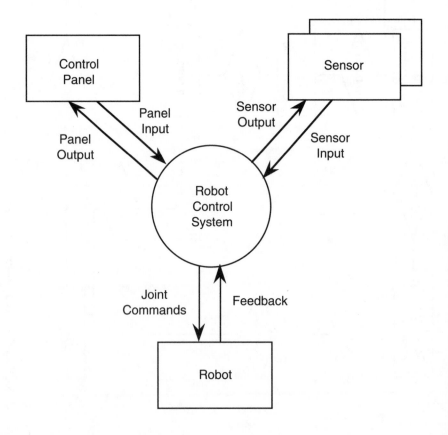

Figure C.3 RCS Context Diagram

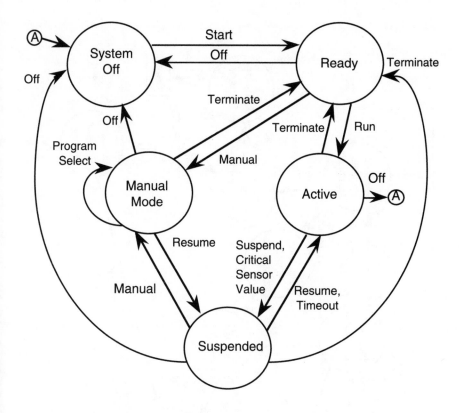

FIgure C.4 RCS State Transition Diagram

C.2.2 External Interfaces

The input from the control panel is received as commands (Suspend, Resume, Terminate) with regard to the status of the execution of a specific program. A program is started with a Program Id. Panel output is returned to the operator as error signals for invalid commands and an alert when a critical sensor value has been detected.

Initial sensor values are set when sensor commands are received as a program instruction, and sensor values are received when changes occur.

The robot is controlled via joint commands with adjustments made for motion position and speed based on the feedback received.

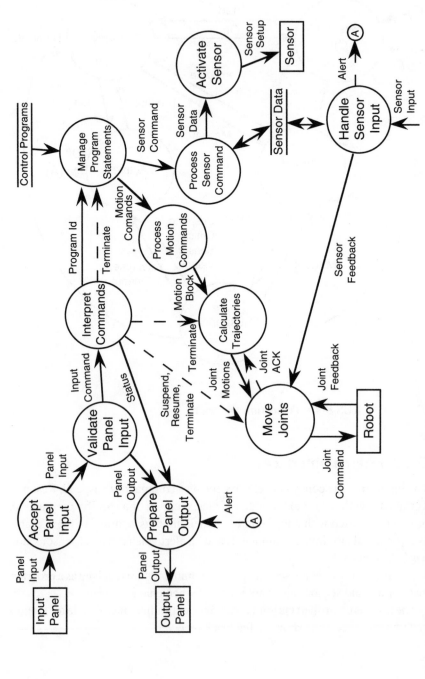

Figure C.5 RCS Control and Data Flow Diagram

C.2.3 Control and Data Flow Analysis

The data flow of the RCS is shown in Figure C.5. Potential object managers are noted for the Sensor Data and Control Program stores. Further decomposition of this CDFD is not shown here, and we are assuming that the concurrent elements can be determined from the transforms shown.

C.2.4 Object Abstraction

As was mentioned in the previous case study, objects are created from the triple view of encapsulated data managers, concurrent elements with a balanced system view, and the anticipation of a distributed architecture. Objects derived from Figure C.5 are as follows:

Panel Input Module (reusable component)

Panel Output Module (reusable component)

Trajectory Manager (reusable component and data manager)

Program Interpreter Module (reusable component)

Joints Manager (reusable component and data manager)

Motion Buffer Module (concurrency)

Sensor Monitor (concurrency)

Sensor Input Module (reusable component)

Sensor Activation Module (reusable component)

The most important objects that may be affected by a distributed system are the Joints Manager and the Trajectory Manager. The former will very likely be loaded on a processor that may reside with the actual robot, and the latter could be loaded on a special math processor.

The Motion Buffer Module will protect a queue of motion blocks, and the Sensor Monitor will protect the sensor data from simultaneous access.

C.3 TRANSITIONING FROM REQUIREMENTS ANALYSIS TO DESIGN

The concurrent elements that represent the process abstraction of the system are determined by using the CDFDs and the process selection rules. The processes for RCS and their interfaces are shown in Figure C.6.

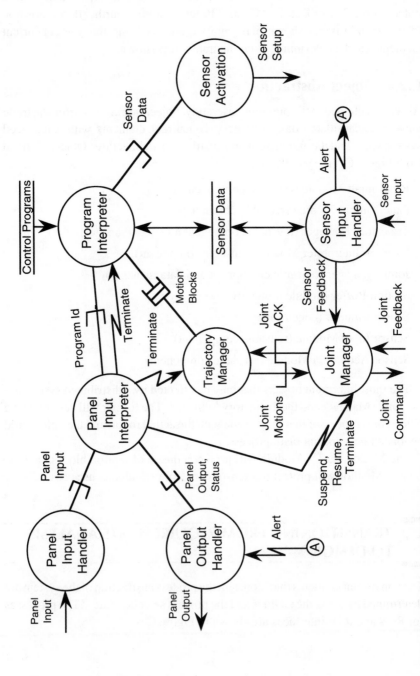

Figure C.6 RCS Process Structure Chart

C.3.1 Process Selection

The processes shown in Figure C.6 have been determined by combining the functions shown in the CDFD according to the process selection rules listed in Section 7.1. Functions interfacing with external devices are made independent processes as shown for Panel Input Handler, Panel Output Handler, Joints Manager, Sensor Input Handler, and Sensor Activation.

Even though the functions Move Joints and Calculate Trajectories are closely related functionally, there is a good chance that they will reside in different processors. They have therefore been made independent processes.

C.3.2 Process Interfaces

A loose coupling is desired between the processes Program Interpreter and Trajectory Manager to allow the latter to prepare trajectories without making Program Interpreter wait. We note that the data store Sensor Data is accessed via both reads and writes by two processes. This data store must be protected with mutually exclusive access to guarantee data integrity. One instance of a very tight coupling is shown between the Trajectory Manager and the Joints Manager. The Trajectory Manager only passes the next set of joint commands after it has received an acknowledgement for the last set provided.

C.4 TOP LEVEL DESIGN

The language independent processes shown in Figure C.6 are transformed to Ada tasks as shown in Figure C.7. The intermediary task Sensor_Monitor has been added to protect the integrity of the sensor data. An intermediary task (Motion_Buffer) is implementing the loose coupling between Program_Interpreter and Trajectory_Calculation.

The connection shown between Trajectory_Calculation and Joints_Manager can be interpreted either as an Ada rendezvous or a remote connection. If we think Joints_Manager may reside on a different processor than Trajectory_Calculation, the interface should be implemented via an IPC mechanism. The same holds true for the interface between Joint_Manager and Sensor_Input_Handler.

The encapsulation of the Ada tasks is illustrated in Figure C.8. Each polygon is an application package as described in the package taxonomy, and represents a design object that can be written in Ada PDL. An example of the package specification and body for Control_Panel is the following:

```
with Global_Types;  use Global_Types;
package Control_Panel is
   procedure Accept_Panel_Output
                    (Out : in Panel_Outputs);
```

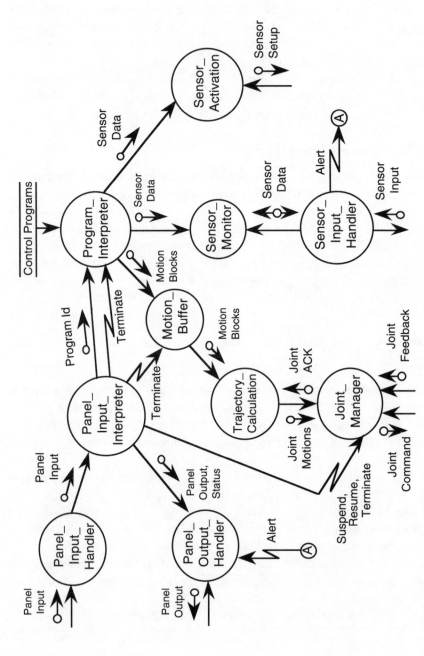

Figure C.7 RCS Ada Task Graph

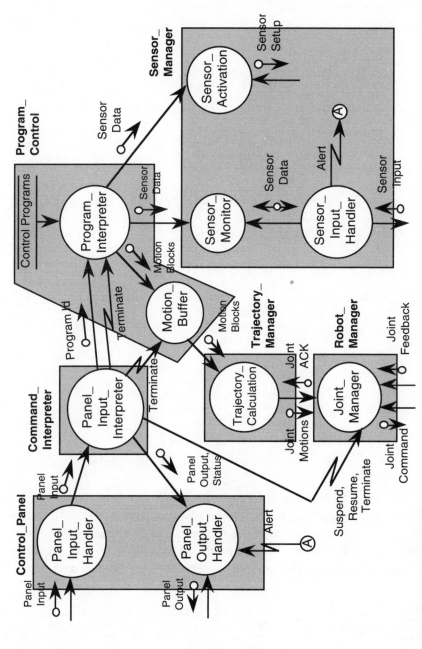

Figure C.8 RCS Ada Package Graph

```
    procedure Sensor_Alert;
  end Control_Panel;

with Robot_Hardware_Dependencies;
use Robot_Hardware_Dependencies;
package body Control_Panel is
  task Panel_Input_Handler is
    entry Panel_Input_Interrupt;
    for Panel_Input_Interrupt use at Input_Address;
  end Panel_Input_Handler;

  task Panel_Output_Handler is
    entry Panel_Output_Interrupt;
    for Panel_Output_Interrupt
                        use at Output_Address;
    entry Panel_Output (Out : in Panel_Outputs);
    entry Sensor_Alert;
  end Panel_Output_Handler;

  procedure Accept_Panel_Output
                    (Out : in Panel_Outputs) is
  begin
    Panel_Output_Handler.Panel_Output (Out);
  end Accept_Panel_Output;

  procedure Sensor_Alert is
  begin
    Panel_Output_Handler.Sensor_Alert;
  end Sensor_Alert;

  task body Panel_Input_Handler  is separate;
  task body Panel_Output_Handler is separate;
end Control_Panel;
```

We have linked the interrupt entries (Panel_Input_Interrupt and Panel_Output_Interrupt) to the actual hardware addresses via the "for use at" clause. The entrance procedures direct the calls to the operations visible in the package specification to the corresponding (hidden) task entries. This can be replaced by calls to an IPC mechanism for distributed systems.

C.5 DETAILED DESIGN

A skeleton subunit for the Panel_Output_Handler is the following:

```
separate (Control_Panel)
task body Panel_Output_Handler is
  ...
begin
  loop
    ...
    select
      accept Panel_Output
                        (Out : in Panel_Outputs) do
        ...
      end Panel_Output;
    or
      accept Panel_Input_Interrupt do
        ...
      end Panel_Input_Interrupt;
    or
      accept Sensor_Alert do
        ...
      end Sensor_Alert;
    or
      terminate;
      ...
    end select;
    ...
  end loop;
end Panel_Output_Handler;
```

The other subunits and data managers will be written in Ada PDL during this phase.

Summary

This case study illustrates another example of how we combine the object-oriented paradigms with the structured analysis and design techniques for real-time systems. Top level design objects are created with application packages (Control_Panel, Command_Interpreter, Program_Control, Trajectory_Manager, Robot_Manager, and Sensor_Manager), and detailed design objects are furnished as subunits in the form of task bodies and subprogram bodies (e.g., Panel_Output_Handler). Reusability is achieved by creating loosely coupled components that can be distributed to a number of processors. This is accomplished by restricting the use of the Ada rendezvous to tasks residing in the same package. Communication between tasks in different processors (and even processes) is made via an IPC mechanism.

Exercises

The following exercises are suggested for this case study:

1. Use the package taxonomy described in Chapter 4 and create Ada PDL for the detailed design.

2. Create a set of virtual nodes that include all the application packages and the additional data managers you created during detailed design.

3. Choose an IPC mechanism and implement the top four layers of the ISO/ OSI protocol.

Multiple Keyboard Input System (MKIS)

Almost all of the examples used to illustrate our development methodology have been in the application or technology level of the problem domain hierarchy. In this appendix we will utilize our methods in an example that straddles the application and execution levels of the hierarchy. Our object-oriented development strategy and reuse concepts will be illustrated here for low level system requirements dealing with device drivers and hardware buffers. The main points of this case study will be to demonstrate the use of unprotected shared memory, the creation of software layers, the use of objects, and reusability. The design model presented is very similar to the layering suggested by Dijkstra in [DIJ68].

One of the database issues discussed in Chapter 12 was the requirement to provide data integrity in a multiprocess environment. A data element that is updated with an atomic program statement does not have to be protected, since there can only be one process performing the update at any one time. For a program statement that translates to a series of machine instructions, interleaving of instructions may take place, and the instructions must be executed within a critical section. If we create a buffer that is accessed by exactly two tasks, one to perform the enqueue and the other to perform the dequeue, we can use a shared data structure without protection and still guarantee data integrity.

An example of the use of unprotected shared data is shown in this appendix, and demonstrates the handling of a number of inputs received from several keyboards. The input is multiplexed from the asynchronous keyboards, and an account is kept of any characters that may get lost. This case study has been adapted from material originally presented by Habermann and Perry [HAB83].

D.1 SOFTWARE REQUIREMENTS SPECIFICATION

The system presented here includes an arbitrary (user specified) number of keyboards that require servicing in an asynchronous manner. The maximum input rate for each keyboard is assumed to be 15 characters per second, and the maximum number of keyboards can be assumed to be 12 (default value).

The input characters from the keyboards are stored in a (circular) hardware buffer located at 00A0 (Hex). Each element in this buffer contains the incoming character and an identifier (integer) for the corresponding keyboard.

The "device" for which a handler is required is an Asynchronous Communications Interface (ACI), which puts the characters in the hardware buffer. This hardwired buffer consists of a head index (for removal), tail index (for insertion), and room for 64 elements (one character and the corresponding keyboard identifier).

If characters are filling up the buffer faster than they can be removed, characters may be lost. When (and if) this condition occurs, the most recent characters should be allowed to be overwritten rather than losing the whole buffer. Losing the entire buffer would occur if the handler were to adjust the buffer index such that the buffer state was changed from full to empty. For this exercise we simply keep a count of the number of characters lost.

A system diagram illustrating the multiple keyboard inputs is shown in Figure D.1. The portion on the left signifies the multiple keyboards and the multiplexing of the keyboard input to the Asynchronous Communications Interface (ACI). The characters are stored in the hardware buffer with their associated keyboard number. The middle portion of the figure shows the de-multiplexing of the keyboard input and the collection of characters into buffers corresponding to the individual keyboards. The middle part represents the layer of objects that isolate the user programs on the right side of the figure from the details of the keyboard interfaces.

The software required for the ACI handler and the User Interface handler must provide the following two functions:

1. Empty the hardware buffer as quickly as possible, (hopefully) without losing any of the input characters.

2. Provide the characters accumulated for a given keyboard to the requesting user programs.

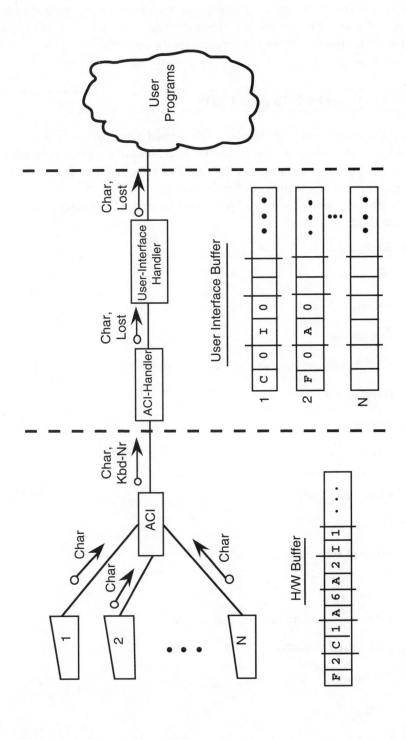

Figure D.1 MKIS System Diagrams

To illustrate a fully working Ada program, we will include additional requirements to provide stimulation of the software by emulating the keyboards using (software) character streams. The user programs will be replaced by an output device (printer) in the PDL created for the case study.

D.2 REQUIREMENTS ANALYSIS

The requirements for this problem are well defined with a narrow scope, and a complete domain analysis is not required. The creation of components could be important if we designed the system to handle a number of different keyboards, but we will not consider that any further here.

The following real-world objects emerge from the system view in Figure D.1:

1. **Keyboard**

   Attributes

   • Keyboard number

   Operations

   • Read keyboard number and character typed

2. **Hardware Buffer**

   Attributes

   • Size
   • Removal pointer
   • Insertion pointer

   Operations

   • Insert keyboard number and character typed
   • Buffer-empty
   • Buffer-full
   • Remove keyboard number and character typed

3. **User Interface Buffer**

   Attributes

   • Buffer id

- Buffer size
- Removal pointer
- Insertion pointer

Operations

- Insert character
- Remove character
- Maintain lost character count
- Read message data

4. **User Programs**

Attributes

- User id

Operations

- Receive keyboard message and lost count
- Print keyboard message and lost count

The single hardware buffer and multiple intermediate buffers have a similar structure, and we will be attempting to create reusable objects for these data structures.

A context diagram is shown in Figure D.2 with the keyboards sending characters to MKIS. The output device is not specified, and in our example it will be a printer.

The data flow diagram in Figure D.3 shows how the characters that are input to the hardware buffer are distributed to the intermediate (software) buffers. These buffers will contain messages that will be passed to the user programs (printed in our case).

D.3 TRANSITIONING FROM ANALYSIS TO DESIGN

The primary step in the transitioning is to determine the process abstraction that will model the concurrent elements. The ACI and the hardware buffer is treated as a single "device," and we are not concerned with the individual keyboards. We are, therefore, one step removed from having to handle the interrupts caused by the keyboards; i.e., we have abstracted away the details of the hardware interrupts.

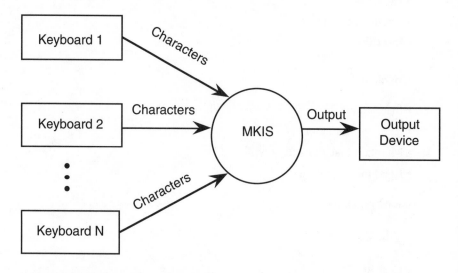

Figure D.2 MKIS Context Diagram

The process structure chart in Figure D.4 shows the processes necessary to perform the required functions. The producer/consumer pair Simulate Keyboards and ACI Handler are tightly coupled through the Asynchronous Communication Buffer. ACI Handler is tightly coupled to the Keyboard processes via the User Interface Buffers, and the characters and possible lost counts are passed to the User Program process.

D.4 TOP LEVEL DESIGN

The processes shown in Figure D.4 have been transformed into an Ada task structure as depicted in the Ada task graph in Figure D.5. Design decisions made for these tasks are as follows:

1. **ACI_Handler.** The emptying of the ACB_Buffer can be accomplished with a single high priority task. The only processes that could interfere with this task would be higher priority device and system processes, but that is of no concern here since we are only considering the Ada run-time features. ACI_Handler will remove characters form the ACB_Buffer for arbitrary keyboards and place them in their respective buffer. The ACI_Handler task will be implemented as an independent high priority (i.e., non-preemptive) task that has neither a server nor a caller function. It simply puts a character and a count (number of characters lost) into a user interface buffer for a given keyboard. These buffers are shared variables, and careful consideration must be given to the problem of mutual exclusion for their access.

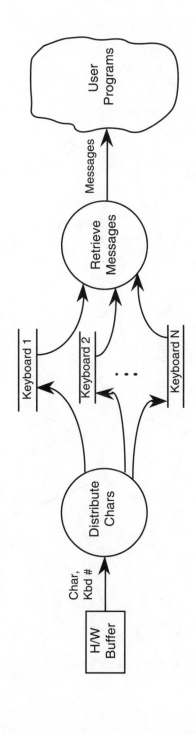

Figure D.3 MKIS Data Flow Diagram

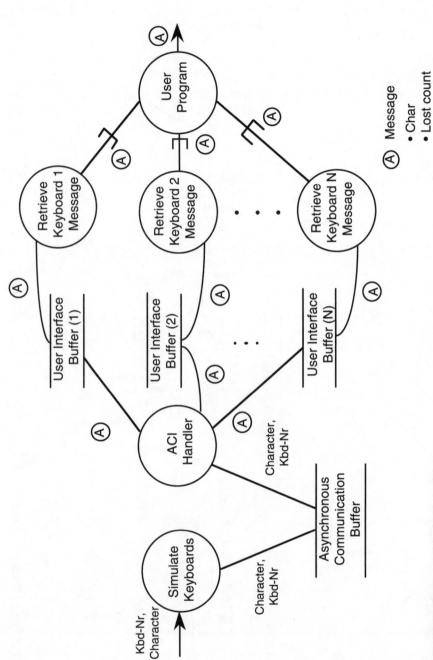

Figure D.4 MKIS Process Structure Chart

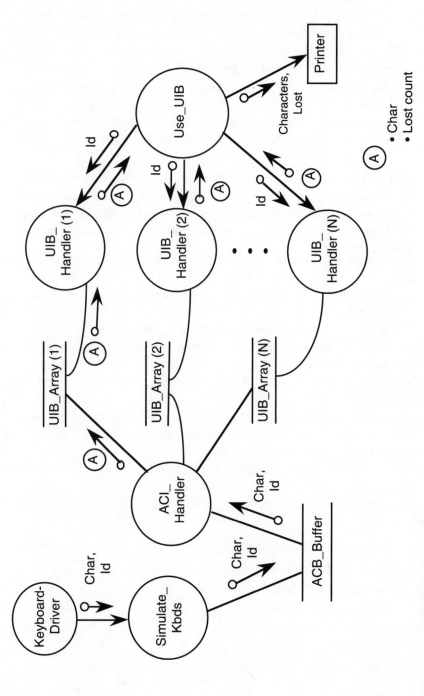

Figure D.5 MKIS Task Graph

2. **UIB_Handler.** A user interface handler is required to retrieve a character and a count from the buffer corresponding to a given keyboard and to return them to the requesting user program. This handler could be designed as a single task, but a more straightforward solution is to assign a user interface task to each keyboard buffer. This will be implemented by defining a task type and declaring an array of tasks of this type. An initialization is required to provide each task object with its identity.

3. **Simulate_Kbds.** This task simulates the insertion into the hardware buffer (ACB_Buffer) of the characters from the keyboards and their associated keyboard identifier. This task will receive its input from the main program, shown here as the task Keyboard_Driver (the "environment" task).

4. **Use_UIB.** This task simulates the user programs and requests a set of characters for a given keyboard from the UIB_Handler task that corresponds to the keyboard. A lost count is received with the set of characters. The character string and lost count are sent to an output device for display.

We have chosen to implement the interface between the intermediate buffers and the user programs with an Ada task (UIB_Handler (x)) for each buffer. This suggests a reuse possibility at the programming level: identical task objects with an identifier associated with a specific buffer.

The design objects for this problem are shown in the package graph in Figure D.6. The application packages for this design are represented by Kbd_Manager, ACI_Buffer, User_Interface, and User_Programs. ACI_Buffer and User_Interface create two levels of layering between the keyboards (Kbd_Manager) and the user programs (User_Programs). The ACB package is an instantiation of a generic data manager (Buffer_Module) for the ACB_Buffer (hardware buffer). The UIB package is an instantiation of the same generic data manager (Buffer_Module) with the intermediate buffers created as an array of buffers. The array index corresponds to a keyboard identifier, i.e., there will be one user interface buffer for each keyboard.

We note a direct mapping of the abstract real-world objects identified in section D.2:

1. Keyboard => Kbd_Manager
2. Hardware Buffer => ACI_Buffer
3. User Interface Buffer => User_Interface
4. User Programs => User_Programs

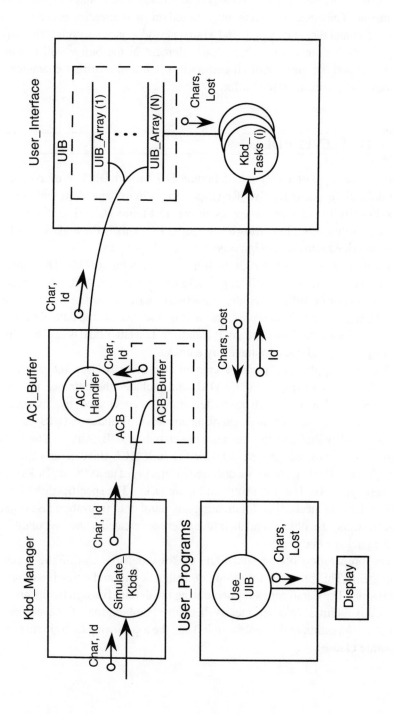

Figure D.6 MKIS Ada Package Graph

The intermediate buffers will be designed to have the same general structure as the hardware buffer: remove index, insert index, count, and some number of elements. The number of elements is based on an assumption about the input rate (15 characters per second) and a burst period, e.g., 2 seconds. This would require 30 elements per buffer. Each element in the buffer will contain a character and the number of characters lost before the current character was placed in the user interface buffer.

D.5 TOP LEVEL PDL

The Ada top level PDL is shown in Figures D.7 through D.13. We have created the definitions packages Sys_Rep_Spec for system dependent features, and Sys_Priority for task priorities, as shown in Figure D.7. The generic data manager (closed ADT) is shown in Figure D.8. This is the highest level of a parameterized reusable design object in an Ada program.

The application package ACI_Buffer is shown in Figure D.9. The hardware buffer is declared in the (visible) package specification as ACB_Buffer, and is an instantiation of Buffer_Module. The actual generic parameters are ACB_Index and ACB_Element. This represents the (unprotected) shared data between the two tasks Simulate_Kbds and ACI_Handler. The latter task is declared in the package body and does not have any entries.

The other application package created as a layer is User_Interface. The specification is shown in Figure D.10 and includes the entrance procedure Read_Kbd. The intermediate buffers have been created by instantiating Buffer_Module with the actual generic parameters UIB_Index and UIB_Element. An array of pointers to the buffers is declared as UIB_Array. The buffers provide (unprotected) shared data for the task ACI_Handler and the tasks Kbd_Tasks. The latter tasks are declared as an array of tasks (Kbd_Tasks) using the task type UIB_Handler shown in Figure D.11. The specification of a task type is the Ada mechanism for creating any number of (reusable) task objects. Note how the task objects and their identifiers are created in the executable part of the package body.

The preparation of the Ada PDL makes extensive use of the *separate* statement. This provides for hiding of design details and deferring of design decisions. The details are supplied during the detailed design by the creation of Ada subunits. We see clearly here the combination of the bottom-up approach (creation of the generic units) and the top-down paradigm (use of the separate clause).

```
-- System Representation Specification
--
package Sys_Rep_Spec is
  ACI_Location : constant := 16#00A0#; -- abs address
  ACI_Size     : constant := 64;
  UIB_Size     : constant := 30; -- 2 secs @ 15 chars/
sec
  Nr_Of_Kbds   : constant := 3;   -- Max # of kbds

  subtype Kbd_Index is Natural range 1 .. Nr_Of_Kbds;
end Sys_Rep_Spec;

-- Priority Specification

--
with System;
package Sys_Priority is
  ACI_Priority : constant System.Priority := 10;
                                  -- Hdw Handler
  UIB_Priority : constant System.Priority := 8;
                                  -- Interface task
end Sys_Priority;
```

Figure D.7 Definitions Package

```
-- Intermediate Buffer Specification

generic
  type Index_Type is range <>;
  type Element_Type is private;
package Buffer_Module is

  type Buffer is limited private;

    procedure Get   (B : in out Buffer; E : out
Element_Type);
    procedure Put   (B : in out Buffer; E : in
Element_Type);
  function  Empty (B : in Buffer) return Boolean;
  function  Full  (B : in Buffer) return Boolean;

  Underflow : exception;
  Overflow  : exception;
```

```
  private
    type Buf_Type is array(Index_Type) of Element_Type;
    type Buffer is
      record
        Head  : Index_Type := 1;   -- remove
        Tail  : Index_Type := 1;   -- insert
        Buf   : Buf_Type;          -- array of elements
      end record;
  end Buffer_Module;


  package body Buffer_Module is

    procedure Get (B : in out Buffer; E : out Element_Type)
                                                   is separate;
    procedure Put (B : in out Buffer; E : in Element_Type)
                                                   is separate;
    function Empty (B : in Buffer) return Boolean
                                                   is separate;
    function Full (B : in Buffer) return Boolean
                                                   is separate;
  end Buffer_Module;
```

Figure D.8   Closed Generic ADT

```
  with Sys_Rep_Spec;   use Sys_Rep_Spec;
  with Buffer_Module;

  package ACI_Buffer is

    -- ACI_Buffer contains param specs and
    -- instantiation of the hdw buffer handler.

    type ACB_Index is new Integer
                        range 1 .. ACI_Size + 1;

    type ACB_Element is
      record
        Char   : Character;
        Kbd_Nr : Kbd_Index;
      end record;

    package ACB is new Buffer_Module
                    (ACB_Index, ACB_Element);
```

```
    ACB_Buffer : ACB.Buffer; -- unprotected shared data

end ACI_Buffer;

package body ACI_Buffer is



    -- Task specifications for the ACI handler (for
    -- the hdw interface).  This task gets chars from
    -- the hdw buffer to the user interface buffers.

  ' task ACI_Handler is
    end ACI_Handler;

    task body ACI_Handler is separate;
end ACI_Buffer;
```

Figure D.9 Application Package ACI_Buffer

```
with Sys_Rep_Spec;   use Sys_Rep_Spec;
with Buffer_Module;

package User_Interface is

  procedure Read_Kbd
    (K : in Kbd_Index; C : out Character;
                              L : out Natural);
    -- A char is returned from a specific kbd to a user

    -- User_Interface contains the parameter
    -- specifications and instantiation of the user
    -- interface buffers.  User interface buffers are
    -- available to the user programs.
    -- These buffers contain the chars removed from the
    -- hdw buffer by ACI_Handler.

    type UIB_Index is new Integer
                              range 1 .. UIB_Size + 1;

    type UIB_Element is
      record
        Char : Character;
        Lost : Natural;  -- no. of chars lost (if any)
```

```
      end record;

   package UIB is new Buffer_Module
                  (Index_Type   => UIB_Index,
                   Element_Type => UIB_Element);

   type Buffer_Ptr is access UIB.Buffer;
   UIB_Array : array(Kbd_Index) of Buffer_Ptr;
          -- One intermediate buffer for each kbd
          -- Have pointers to the unprotected
          -- shared buffers
   end User_Interface;
```

Figure D.10 Application Package User_Interface (specification)

```
package body User_interface is
   task type  UIB_Handler is
      entry Init (ID : in Kbd_Index);
          -- Init required to identify the specific kbd
          -- the task is controlling
      entry Read (C : out Character; L: out Natural);
          -- Access the intermediate buffer for a
          -- specific kbd
   end UIB_Handler;

   Kbd_Tasks : array (Kbd_Index) of UIB_Handler;
          -- Handler for each intermediate buffer

   -- Procedure for reading a char from a specific
   -- kbd

   procedure Read_Kbd
   (K : in Kbd_Index; C : out Character;
                                   L : out Natural) is
   begin
      Kbd_Tasks(K).Read(C, L);
   end Read_Kbd;

   task body UIB_Handler is separate;

   -- Initialize kbd interface

begin
   for I in Kbd_Index loop
```

```
      UIB_Array (I) := new UIB.Buffer;
                                   -- shared buffers
   end loop;

   for I in Kbd_Index loop
     Kbd_Tasks(I).Init(I);
                   -- Init each task with its kbd id
   end loop;
end User_Interface;
```

Figure D.11 Application Package User_Interface (body)

```
with Sys_Rep_Spec;   use Sys_Rep_Spec;
package Kbd_Manager is
   procedure Take_Char
           (Id : in Kbd_Index; C : in Character);
end Kbd_Manager;

package body Kbd_Manager is
   task Simulate_Kbds is
     entry Take_Char
             (Id : in Kbd_Index; C : in Character);
   end Simulate_Kbds;

   task body Simulate_Kbds is separate;

   procedure Take_Char
           (Id : in Kbd_Index; C : in Character) is
   begin
     Simulate_Kbds.Take_Char (Id, C);
   end Take_Char;
end Kbd_Manager;
```

Figure D.12 Application Package Kbd_Manager

```
package User_Programs is
end User_Programs;

package body User_Programs is
   task Use_UIB is
   end Use_UIB;
```

```
task body Use_UIB is separate;
end User_Programs;
```

Figure D.13   Application Package User_Programs

D.6 DETAILED DESIGN

Before the detailed design can be completed, several design decisions must be considered and settled. Some of these considerations include:

1. **ACI_Handler.** There is a possibility that the ACI handler finds the hardware buffer empty. The handler can then be delayed (suspended) for an appropriate period of time before it interrogates the buffer again. A maximum rate of 15 characters per second for 12 keyboards corresponds to 180 characters per second (we are only using 3 keyboards for this case study). The actual rate is expected to be considerably less. If we choose too big a delay, characters may get lost, and too short a delay would result in more unnecessary "busy wait." A reasonable first try is a delay period of 100 milliseconds corresponding to a maximum input of 18 characters (fine tuning on a VAX 8600 resulted in a value of 10 msec for successful execution of this example).

2. **UIB_Handler.** To avoid a "busy wait" if the particular keyboard buffer is empty, the task can periodically check for data using a *delay* statement. A first approximation for this delay is 200 msec with subsequent fine tuning to balance the system with the ACI_Handler. Note how each task receives its individual identifier via the accept Init.

Any time we use shared data between tasks, we should expect to have to perform fine tuning to balance the tasks and their priorities. This is counteractive to the portability we are striving for, and unprotected shared data should only be used when it is necessary to satisfy certain run-time performance requirements. (See the exercises at the end of the appendix for further discussion on this topic.)

The Ada PDL for the detailed design and code is shown in Figures D.14 to D.23.

```
with Text_IO;  use Text_IO;
with User_Interface;
separate (ACI_Buffer)
```

```
-- Processing of the characters:
-- 1.  Remove from hdw buffer and put in interface
--     buffer;
-- 2.  Maintain 'lost count' for each intermediate
--     buffer when full;
-- 3.  Pass appropriate char to intermediate buffer
--     when possible;
-- 4.  Maintain max value when 'lost count'
--     overflows;

task body ACI_Handler is
  Lost : array (Kbd_Index) of Natural := (others => 0);
        -- Number of chars lost for each kbd

  procedure Process_Char is separate;

begin
  Put_Line ("Start of ACI_Handler");
  loop
    if ACB.Empty (ACB_Buffer) then
      delay 0.010;
                -- Wait 10 msec if hdw buffer empty
    else
      Process_Char;
                -- Get char & kbd-number; put them
                -- into interm. buffer
    end if;
  end loop;

exception
  when ACB.Overflow =>
    Put_Line ("Overflow handled in ACI_Handler");
  when others =>
    Put_Line ("Unknown exception in ACI_Handler");
end ACI_Handler;
```

Figure D.14 Task Body ACI_Handler (subunit)

```
separate (ACI_Buffer.ACI_Handler)
procedure Process_Char is
  Input : ACB_Element;
begin
  -- Get from H/W buffer
  ACB.Get (ACB_Buffer, Input);
```

```ada
   -- Place in user interface buffer (for specified kbd)
   User_Interface.UIB.Put
       (User_Interface.UIB_Array(Input.Kbd_Nr).all,
       (Input.Char, Lost(Input.Kbd_Nr)));
                                       -- Aggregate

   Lost(Input.Kbd_Nr) := 0;

exception
   when ACB.Underflow => null;        -- Hdw buffer empty
   when User_Interface.UIB.Overflow =>
                                  -- Intermediate buffer full
      begin
         Lost(Input.Kbd_Nr) := Lost(Input.Kbd_Nr) + 1;
         Put_Line ("Lost char in Process_Char");
         Put_Line ("  kbd_Nr =" & Natural'Image
                                    (Input.Kbd_Nr));

      exception
         when Numeric_Error =>
            Put_Line (" Numeric_Error in Process_Char");
            Put_Line ("   kbd_Nr =" & Natural'Image
                                       (Input.Kbd_Nr));
         Lost(Input.Kbd_Nr) := Natural'Last;
                 -- Maintain max count of lost chars
      end;
end Process_Char;
```

Figure D.15 Procedure Process_Char (subunit)

```ada
with Text_IO;   use Text_IO;
with Sys_Rep_Spec;  use Sys_Rep_Spec;
separate (User_Interface)

-- Task body for the UIB handler

task body UIB_Handler is
   My_Id     : Kbd_Index;
   UIB_Data : UIB_Element;

begin
   accept Init (Id : in Kbd_Index) do
     My_Id := Id;
```

```
     Put_Line ("Init of UIB_Handler. Id=" &
                            Kbd_Index'Image (My_Id));
  end Init;

  loop
    select
      when not UIB.Empty (UIB_Array(My_Id).all) =>
        accept Read (C : out Character;
                            L : out Natural) do
          UIB.Get (UIB_Array(My_Id).all, UIB_Data);
          C := UIB_Data.Char;
          L := UIB_Data.Lost;
        end Read;
    or
      delay 0.2; -- wait 200msec to check for data
                 -- in the (intermediate) buffer
    end select;
  end loop;
end UIB_Handler;
```

Figure D.16 Task Body UIB_Handler (subunit)

```
with Text_IO;  use Text_IO;
separate (Buffer_Module)

procedure Get
        (B : in out Buffer; E : out Element_Type) is
begin
  if not Empty(B) then
    E := B.Buf(B.Head);
    B.Head := (B.Head mod B.Buf'Last) + 1;
  else                        -- empty
    Put_Line ("Underflow in Get");
    raise Underflow;
  end if;
end Get;
```

Figure D.17 Procedure Get (subunit)

```
with Text_IO;   use Text_IO;
separate (Buffer_Module)

procedure Put
        (B : in out Buffer; E : in Element_Type) is
begin

   if not Full(B) then
     B.Buf(B.Tail) := E;
     B.Tail := (B.Tail mod B.Buf'Last) + 1;
   else                          -- buffer full
     Put_Line ("Overflow in Put: T="
                   & Index_Type'Image (B.Tail));
     raise Overflow;
   end if;
end Put;
```

Figure D.18 Procedure Put (subunit)

```
separate (Buffer_Module)

function Empty (B : in Buffer) return Boolean is
begin
   return (B.Head = B.Tail);
end Empty;
```

Figure D.19 Function Empty (subunit)

```
separate (Buffer_Module)

function Full (B : in Buffer) return Boolean is
begin
   return (((B.Tail mod B.Buf'Last) + 1) = B.Head);
end Full;
```

Figure D.20 Function Full (subunit)

```
with Text_IO; use Text_IO;
with ACI_Buffer;
separate (Kbd_Manager)
task body Simulate_Kbds is
begin
  Put_Line (" Start of Simulate_Kbds");
  loop
    select
      accept Take_Char
             (Id : in Kbd_Index; C : in Character) do
          ACI_Buffer.ACB.Put
                 (ACI_Buffer.ACB_Buffer, (C, Id));
      end Take_Char;
    or
      terminate;
    end select;
  end loop;

exception
  when ACI_Buffer.ACB.Overflow =>
    Put_Line ("H/W buffer full");
end Simulate_Kbds;
```

Figure D.21 Task Body Simulate_Kbds (subunit)

```
with Text_IO; use Text_IO;
with User_Interface;
separate (User_Programs)
task body Use_UIB is
  Char : Character;
  Lost : Natural;

begin
  Put_Line (" Start of Use_UIB");
  for J in Kbd_Index loop
    for K in Text'Range loop
      User_Interface.Read_Kbd (J, Char, Lost);
      Put (Char);
      if Lost > 0 then
        Put (Natural'Image(lost));   -- Chars lost
      end if;
    end loop;
    Put_Line ("  End Of Buffer");
```

```
      end loop;

   exception
      when others =>
         Put_Line ("Unknown exception in Use_UIB");
   end Use_UIB;
```

Figure D.22 Task Body Use_UIB (subunit)

```
   with Text_IO; use Text_IO;
   with Kbd_Manager;
   with User_Programs;
   procedure Kbd_Driver is

      Max_String : constant := 30;
      subtype Text is String (1 .. Max_String);

      Kbd_1 : Text := "Analog is used for FM Voice     ";
      Kbd_2 : Text := "Digital for Voice, Data & HIFI";
      Kbd_3 : Text := "TDMA is simpler with Digital    ";

   begin
      Put_Line ("Start of Kbd_Driver (Main)");
      for I in Text'Range loop
         Kbd_Manager.Take_Char (1, Kbd_1(I));
         Kbd_Manager.Take_Char (2, Kbd_2(I));
         Kbd_Manager.Take_Char (3, Kbd_3(I));
      end loop;
   end Kbd_Driver;
```

Figure D.23 Main Program Kbd_Driver

Summary

The primary emphasis of this case study has been to illustrate a database issue and the vertical layering described in Chapter 10. Object-oriented features and reusability are utilized in the software layering by placing modules between the hardware buffer and the user programs. Reusability is further demonstrated by the use of generics for different kinds of buffers, and the creation of an array of tasks that execute the same function. Data managers are created with Ada packages to provide the desired encapsulation and data hiding.

The simulated hardware buffer (ACB_Buffer) and the intermediate buffers (UIB_Array) were instantiated in the package specification of ACI_Handler and User_Interface, respectively. The buffers are globally visible to anyone who is *with*ing these packages, and normally this would create data integrity problems. A solution to this problem is to encapsulate the data structures with a single task that can provide the necessary mutual exclusion. Every time we introduce another task into our design, however, we have to suffer a run-time overhead associated with task scheduling, and dispatching, and context switching. Using shared data eliminates the use of encapsulating tasks and associated run-time overhead. The reason shared data can be used here is that only one task is setting the insert pointer and another task is setting the remove pointer. If other tasks were involved, this mechanism would not work.

Design objects have been created in the form of application packages, data managers, and definitions packages. Detailed Ada PDL was included to illustrate the combination of the top-down and bottom-up design paradigms.

Layers were crated to abstract away the details of the (simulated) keyboards, the hardware buffer, and the intermediate buffers. The only interface to the user programs is through the entrance procedures in the User_Interface package.

Reusability is demonstrated through the use of the generic buffer package. The same package was instantiated for buffers with different types of elements and sizes. A task array was used to create identical tasks for each one of the intermediate buffers. The layering also supports reusability since lower layers can be changed with only affecting the next higher layer (if the interface is changed).

Exercises

The following exercises are suggested for this case study:

1. Replace the buffer mechanism shown here with the semaphore approach illustrated in Chapter 12, section 12.8. What effect does this change have on the object-orientation of the solution suggested here? What about reusability?

2. A certain amount of fine tuning (using delay statements) may be required to keep from attempting to read a character from an empty hardware buffer or distributing a message from an intermediate buffer (see the task bodies for ACI_Handler and UIB_Handler). This implies non-portability issues in our solution. Suggest and implement design and code changes that will make the solution more portable. How does this affect system performance? What about object-orientation? List the trade-offs between a high degree of reusability and run-time performance.

References

ABB83   Abbott, R.J., Program Design by Informal English Description, *Communications of the ACM*, Volume 26, Number 11, November 1983.

AND90   Andrews, T. and Harris, C., Combining Language and Database Advances in an Object-Oriented Development Environment, in *Readings in Object-Oriented Database Systems*, S.B. Zdonik and D. Maier, eds., Morgan Kaufmann, San Mateo, CA, 1990.

ANS89a   Database Language – SQL with Integrity Enhancement, American National Standards Institute, X3.15-1989.

ANS89b   Database Language - Embedded SQL, American National Standards Institute, X3.168-1989.

ATK88   Atkinson, C et al. *Ada for Distributed Systems*, Cambridge University Press, Cambridge, England, 1988.

AUE89   Auer, K., Which Object-Oriented Language Should We Choose?, *Hotline on Object-Oriented Technology*, Volume 1, Number 1, November 1989.

BAI89   Bailin, S.C., An Object-Oriented Requirements Specification Method, *Communications of the ACM*, Volume 32, Number 5, May 1989.

BAR89   Barnes, J., *Programming in Ada*, 3rd ed., Addison-Wesley, Reading, MA, 1989.

BLA88   Blaha, M.R., et al., Relational Database Design Using an Object-Oriented Methodology, *Communications of the ACM*, Volume 31, Number 4, April 1988.

BOE88   Boehm, B.S., A Spiral Model of Software Development and Enhancement, *IEEE Computer*, May 1988.

BOO86   Booch, G., Object-Oriented Development, in *IEEE Transactions on Software Engineering*, Volume SE-12, Number 2, February 1986.

BOO87   Booch, G., *Software Engineering with Ada*, Second Edition, Benjamin/Cummings, Menlo Park, CA, 1987.

BOO87a   Booch, G., *Software Components with Ada: Structures, Tools, and Subsystems*, Benjamin/Cummings, Menlo Park, CA, 1987.

BOO91   Booch, G., *Object-Oriented Design with Applications*, Benjamin/Cummings, Menlo Park, CA, 1990.

BRA89   Brathwaite, K.S., *Systems Design in a Database Environment*, McGraw-Hill, New York, NY 1989.

BUL91   Bulman, D., Refining Candidate Objects, *Computer Language*, January 1991.

BUR85   Burns, A., *Concurrent Programming in Ada*, Cambridge University Press, Cambridge, England, 1985.

BUR90   Burns, A. and Wellings, A., *Real-Time Systems and Their Programming Languages*, Addison-Wesley, Workingham, England, 1990.

BUT91   Butterworth, P., ODBMS as Data Managers, *Journal of Object-Oriented Programming*, February 1991.

CHE76   Chen, P., The Entity-Relationship Model — Toward a Unified View of Data, *ACM Trans. on Database Systems*, Volume 1, Number 1, 1976.

COA91   Coad, P., and Yourdon, E., *Object-Oriented Analysis*, Second Edition, Yourdon Press, Englewood Cliffs, NJ, 1991.

COD69   Database Task Group of CODASYL Programming Language Committee, *Report*, October 1969.

COD70   Codd, E.F., A Relational Model of Data for Large Shared Data Banks, *Communications of the ACM*, Volume 13, Number 6, June 1970.

COD82   Codd, E.F., Relational Database: A Practical Foundation for Productivity, *Communications of the ACM*, Volume 25, Number 2, February 1982.

COR91   Corbin, J.R., *The Art of Distributed Applications*, Springer-Verlag, New York, 1991.

COU91   Coulouris, G.F., and Dollimore J., *Distributed Systems, Concepts and Design*, Addison-Wesley, Workingham, England, 1991.

DAH70   Dahl, O., et al., *Simula 67 Common Base Language*, S-22, Norwegian Computing Center, Oslo, Norway, 1970.

DAT81   Date, C., *An Introduction to Database Systems*, Vol. 1, Addison-Wesley, Reading, MA, 1981.

DIJ68   Dijkstra, E.W., The Structure of the "THE" - Multiprogramming System, *Communications of the ACM*, Volume 11, Number 5, May 1968.

DIJ72   Dijkstra, E.W., Notes on Structured Programming, in Structured Programming, by O.-J. Dahl et al., Academic Press, Inc., London, 1972.

DOD83   Reference Manual for the Ada Programming Language, ANSI/MIL-STD 1815A, U.S. Department of Defense, 17 February, 1983.

DOD88   Military Standard for Defense System Software Development, DOD-STD-2167A, U.S. Department of Defense, 29 February 1988.

DON87   Donaho, J.E.D. and Davis, G.K., Ada-Embedded SQL: The Options, *Ada Letters*, Volume VII, Number 3, May/June 1987.

EIL45   Eilenberg, S., and Maclane, S., General Theory of Natural Equivalences, in *Transactions American Mathematical Society*, Volume 58, 1945, pp. 231–294.

FIE85   Field, A., *International Air Traffic Control*, Pergamon Press, Oxford, England, 1985.

FIR90   Firesmith, D., Object-Oriented Requirements Analysis, in *TRI-Ada'90 Tutorial Proceedings*, Volume I, December 3-7 1990.

FIR91   Firesmith, D., Structured Analysis and Object-Oriented Development are not Compatible, *Ada Letters*, Volume XI, Number 9, November/December 1991.

GOL83   Goldberg, A., and Robson, D., *Smalltalk-80: The Language and Its Implementation*, Addison-Wesley, Reading, MA, 1983.

GOM84   Gomaa, H., A Software Design Method for Real-Time Systems, *Communications of the ACM*, Volume 27, Number 9, September, 1984.

GRO86   Groover, M.P., et al., *Industrial Robotics, Technology, Programming, and Applications*, McGraw-Hill, New York, 1986.

HAB83   Habermann, A.N., and Perry, D.E., *Ada for Experienced Programmers*, Addison-Wesley, Reading, MA, 1983.

HAM85   Hammons, C., and Dobbs, P., Coupling, Cohesion, and Package Unity in Ada, *Ada Letters*, Volume IV, Number 6, May/June 1985.

HAR89   Hartson, H.R., and Hix, D., Human-Computer Interface Development: Concepts and Systems, *ACM Computing Surveys*, Volume 21, Number 1, March 1989.

HEN91   Henderson-Sellers, B. and Constantine, L., Object-Oriented Development and Functional Decomposition, *Journal of Object-Oriented Programming*, Volume 3, Number 5, January 1991.

HOA74   Hoare, C.A.R., Monitors: An Operating System Structuring Concept, *Communications of the ACM*, Volume 17, Number 10, October, 1974.

ICH86   Ichbiah, J. et al., Rationale for the Design of the Ada Programming Language, Report Number AD-A187 106, 1986, DTIC.

LEC90   Lecluse, C., et al., O_2, an Object-Oriented Data Model, in *Readings in Object-Oriented Database Systems*, S.B. Zdonik and D. Maier, eds., Morgan Kaufmann, San Mateo, CA, 1990.

LIP89   Lipman, S.B., *C++ Primer*, Addison-Wesley, Reading, MA, 1989.

LIS86   Liskov, B., and Guttag, J., *Abstraction and Specification in Program Development*, The MIT Press, Cambridge, MA, 1986.

LIV90   Livingston, D., Here Come Object-Oriented Databases!, *Systems Integration*, July 1990.

MAI90   Maier, D., and Stein, J., Development and Implementation of an Object-Oriented DBMS, in *Readings in Object-Oriented Database Systems*, S.B. Zdonik and D. Maier, eds., Morgan Kaufmann, San Mateo, CA, 1990.

MCC90   McCoy, L. Scott, Bindings and Ada, *Ada Letters*, Volume X, Number 8, November/December 1990.

MEY88   Meyer, B., Object-oriented Software Construction, Prentice Hall, New York, 1988.

MON91   Mongi, A., et al., Autonomous Robotic Inspection and Manipulation Using Multisensor Feedback, *IEEE Computer*, April 1991.

NAE89   Naecker, P.A., What's Happening to Structured Query Language?, *DEC Professional*, May 1989.

NAR89   Narkus-Kramer, M.P., et al., A Technology Comparison of the Federal Republic of Germany's Air Traffic Control System with those of France, the United Kingdom, and the United States, MTR-89W00202, Mitre, September 1989.

NIE86   Nielsen, K.W., Task Coupling and Cohesion in Ada, *Ada Letters*, Volume VI, Number 4, July/August 1986.

NIE88   Nielsen, K.W., and Shumate, K., *Designing Large Real-Time Systems with Ada*, McGraw-Hill, New York, 1988.

NIE90   Nielsen, K. W., *Ada in Distributed Real-Time Systems*, McGraw-Hill, New York, 1990.

NOL90   Nolan, M.S., *Fundamentals of Air Traffic Control*, Wadsworth Publishing Company, Belmont, CA, 1990.

PAG80   Page-Jones, M., *The Practical Guide to Structured Systems Design*, Yourdon Press, New York, 1980.

PAR86   Parnas, D.L., and Clements, P.C., A Rational Design Process: How and Why to Fake It, *IEEE Transactions on Software Engineering*, Volume SE-12, Number 2, February 1986.

PRE90   Premerlani, W.J., et al., An Object-Oriented Relational Database, *Communications of the ACM*, Vol. 33, No. 11, November 1990.

PYL85   Pyle, I. C., *The Ada Programming Language*, 2d ed., Prentice-Hall International, London, England, 1985.

SCH88   Schlaer, S., and Mellor, S., *Object-Oriented Systems Analysis*, Prentice Hall, Englewood Cliffs, NJ, 1988.

SEI91   Rational for SQL Ada Module Description Language SAMeDL, Software Engineering Institute, Carnegie Mellon University, Pittsburgh, PA 15213, 1991.

SHU88a   Shumate, K., and Nielsen, K.W., A Taxonomy of Ada Packages, Ada Letters, Volume VIII, Number 1, March/April 1988.

SHU88b   Shumate, K., *Understanding Concurrency in Ada*, McGraw-Hill, New York, 1988.

SHU91   Shumate, K., Structured Analysis and Object-Oriented Design are Compatible, *Ada Letters*, Volume XI, Number 4, May/June 1991.

SHU92   Shumate, K., and Keller, M., *Software Specification and Design: A Disciplined Approach for Real-Time Systems*, John Wiley, New York, 1992.

STR87   Stroustrup, B., *The C++ Programming Language*, Addison-Wesley, Reading, MA, 1987.

SUN86   Remote Procedure Call Protocol Specification, Remote Procedure Call Programming Guide, and External Data Representation Protocol Specification, Sun Micro Systems, Mountain View, CA, 1986

TEL88   TeleAda-LAN User Manual, TeleLogic AB, Sweden, 1988

TSI76   Tsichritzis, D.C. and Lochovsky, F.H., Hierarchical Database Management Systems, *ACM Computing Surveys*, Vol. 8, No. 1, 1976.

VUK89   Vukobratovic, M., and Stokic, D., *Applied Control of Manipulation Robots*, Springer-Verlag, Berlin, Germany, 1989.

WAR85   Ward, P.T., and Mellor S.J., *Structured Development for Real-Time Systems*, Volumes 1-3, Yourdon Press, New York, 1985.

WAR89   Ward, P.T., How to Integrate Object Orientation with Structured Analysis and Design, *IEEE Software*, March 1989.

WEG87   Wegner, P., The Object-Oriented Classification Paradigm, in *Research Directions in Object-Oriented Programming*, MIT Press, Cambridge, MA, 1987.

WHI10   Whitehead, A.N., and Russell, B, *Principia Mathematica*, Volume I, Cambridge University Press, Cambridge, England, 1910, p. 37.

ZDO90   Zdonik, S. B., and Maier, D., *Readings in Object-Oriented Database Systems*, Morgan Kaufmann, San Mateo, CA, 1990.

Index